WORKBOOK
TO ACCOMPANY

SEVENTH EDITION

MICROECONOMIC THEORY

**BASIC
PRINCIPLES
AND
EXTENSIONS**

WALTER NICHOLSON
Amherst College

Prepared by **DAVID C. STAPLETON**
Lewin-VHI

The Dryden Press
Harcourt Brace College Publishers

Fort Worth   Philadelphia   San Diego   New York   Orlando   Austin   San Antonio
Toronto   Montreal   London   Sydney   Tokyo

ISBN: 0-03-024697-0

Address for Orders
Harcourt Brace & Company, 6277 Sea Harbor Drive, Orlando, FL 32887-6777
1-800-782-4479

Address for Editorial Correspondence
Harcourt Brace & Company, 301 Commerce Street, Suite 3700, Fort Worth, TX 76102

Web Site Address
http://www.hbcollege.com

THE DRYDEN PRESS, DRYDEN, and the DP LOGO are registered trademarks of Harcourt
Brace & Company.

Printed in the United States of America

8 9 0 1 2 3 4 5 6   023   9 8 7 6 5 4 3 2

The Dryden Press
Harcourt Brace College Publishers

CONTENTS

Harcourt Brace & Company

PART VI MODELS OF IMPERFECT COMPETITION

PART VII PRICING IN INPUT MARKETS

PART VIII LIMITS OF THE MARKET

ANSWER KEY

Harcourt Brace & Company

PREFACE

WHY THIS WORKBOOK?

It has been my experience that many students become frustrated in attempting to solve the problems at the end of each chapter in *Microeconomic Theory*. The primary reason for this is that they are struggling to understand the mathematics and therefore find it difficult to see the connection between mathematical expressions and economic ideas. The frustration does not generally stem from the content of the problems, but rather from the necessarily concise ways in which they are written.

The content of the problems in this workbook is quite similar to the content of those in the text, but the presentation is quite different. Students are led through most problems step-by-step, in a way that clarifies the connection between the mathematics and the economic ideas. Graphs play an important role in this process. Students often fail to draw graphs carefully when asked to do so from scratch because it is tedious to do so. Inclusion of partially complete graphs makes this task substantially less onerous.

HOW TO USE THIS WORKBOOK

Each chapter begins with a section entitled "Key Concepts." This is a list of terms and equations that are defined and developed in the text. You should begin each chapter by looking over these concepts to be certain that you have at least some familiarity with each. If a term or equation appears completely new or incomprehensible, you should find and review the relevant part of the chapter in the text. The Key Concepts also serve as a handy reference to be used while working on the problems in the second section of the chapter.

Do your best to work through each problem on your own. Once you are finished (or if you get completely stuck), compare what you have done to the answer in the back of the workbook. At all times resist the temptation to simply read the problem and look at the answer. If you do this, you will not learn very much—a fact that will surely be reflected on your exams! If you managed to get the right answer, but think you need more practice, try doing a parallel problem from the text. Related text problems are indicated in brackets at the beginning of most workbook problems.

For many problems you will need a calculator and a ruler. You will find that drawing graphs carefully pays off when it comes to obtaining numerical solutions. Sometimes you are required to draw curves. Often the easiest way to do this is to first find the coordinates of three or four

Harcourt Brace & Company

points on the curve—enough to give you an idea of the curve's shape—then draw a curve, passing through all of the points. If you have access to personal computers and graphics software, you may enjoy using them to draw the graphs, rather than drawing them by hand. The graphs in the workbook were drawn on a Macintosh using Cricket Graph and MacDraw.

ACKNOWLEDGEMENTS

I would like to thank Walter Nicholson for his encouragement, his assistance in developing the style of the problems, and his specific comments on a number of them. I would also like to thank my son Michael, who assisted me in the preparation of this edition.

CHAPTER 1

ECONOMIC MODELS

Marshallian supply-demand synthesis

economic model:
    assumptions
    verification

ceteris paribus

optimization

normative vs. positive

value:
    in use
    in exchange
    labor theory
    marginalism

equilibrium:
    partial
    general

comparative statics

production possibility frontier

opportunity cost

t.i.n.s.t.a.a.f.l. (popular abbreviation
    for "there is no such thing as a
    free lunch")

KEY CONCEPTS

PROBLEMS

(Numbers in brackets at the beginning of problems below refer to related examples and problems in the text.)

1.1. [Related to text example 1.1.] Consider the following supply and demand curves:

$$Q_D = 300 - 20P \qquad Q_S = -100 + 20P$$

a. In graphs of supply and demand curves, it is conventional to put price on the vertical axis and quantity on the horizontal axis. In mathematics it is conventional to put the variable from the left-hand side of an equation on the vertical axis of a graph. Since you are accustomed to the latter convention, it will be easier for you to draw graphs of supply and demand curves if you first invert them; that is, solve for P as a function of Q. For the demand curve above, subtract 300 from both sides then divide both sides by –20 to get:

$$P_D = 15 - Q/20$$

Note that the subscript D is now attached to P, rather than Q. It is not necessary to make this switch, but it is consistent

1

Harcourt Brace & Company

with the interpretation of the inverse demand function to do so. The inverse function tells us the highest price that consumers are willing to pay (demand price) for quantity Q. What is the vertical intercept of the line that is described by this equation? (1)_____ What is the slope of this line? (2)_____ How is the slope of the line related to the coefficient of P in the original equation? (3)_____ Draw the line on the diagram below and label it D.

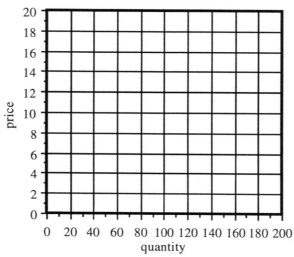

Now, find the inverse of the supply function.

P_S = (4)_____

What is the interpretation of the inverse supply function? (5)_____

_____

What is the vertical intercept of the line that is described by this function? (6)_____ What is the slope of this line? (7)_____ How is the slope of the line related to the coefficient of P in the original equation? (8)_____ Add this line to the diagram above and label it S.

b. Now, find equilibrium Q and P in three different ways:

(i) *Graphically.* Label the equilibrium values on the graph with Q* and P*.

(ii) *Using the supply and demand equations.* First, equate Q_D to Q_S and solve for P*.

Now substitute the value you obtained for P* into the demand equation and solve for Q*.

Check your solution by substituting the value you obtained for P* into the supply equation and confirming that you get the same value for Q*.

(iii) *Using the inverse supply and demand equations.* Determine Q* first by equating P_D to P_S, then determine P by substituting Q* into the inverse demand equation, and finally check your solution by substituting Q* into the inverse supply equation.

Be sure that you understand why all of these methods yield the same solution. You will have numerous occasions to use them in this workbook and the text. Often one method will be much simpler than the other two.

c. Suppose that the demand curve shifts to $Q_D = 380 - 20P$. At any value of P, this new demand curve is (1)_____ units to the right of the old curve. Add the new curve to the graph, label it D', and determine the new equilibrium values for P and Q by any method you wish. (Try all three if you had any trouble with **b.**)

$Q^* = (2)$_____ $P^* = (3)$_____

d. Suppose that the supply curve shifts to $Q_S = -180 + 20P$. At any value of P, this new supply curve is (1)_____ units to the right of the old curve. Add the new curve to the graph, and label it S'. Using the original demand curve, determine the new equilibrium values for P and Q by any method you wish.

$Q^* = (2)$_____ $P^* = (3)$_____

e. If you observed a price increase in a market, how would you know whether it was due to a shift in demand or a shift in supply?_____

_____

1.2. [Related to text example 1.2.] A production possibility frontier (PPF) for goods X and Y is depicted in the diagram below.

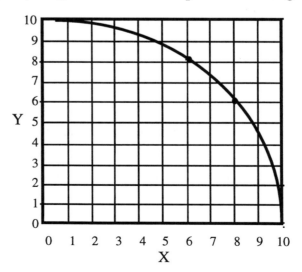

Harcourt Brace & Company

The equation for the PPF is $Y = (100 - X^2)^{.5}$.

a. If $X = 6$, what is the most Y that can be produced?

(1)_____ What is the opportunity cost of X in terms of Y? [There are two ways to find it. One way uses the line that is tangent to the PPF at $X = 6$. The second way uses the derivative of Y with respect to X. If your derivatives are rusty, you may want to come back to this after completing Chapter 2.]

(2)_____

b. Repeat **a** for $X = 8$. (1)_____ (2)_____

CHAPTER 2

THE MATHEMATICS OF OPTIMIZATION

derivative rules:

1. If b is a constant, then

$$\frac{db}{dx} = 0$$

2. If a and b are constants and $b \neq 0$,

$$\frac{d(ax^b)}{dx} = bax^{b-1}$$

3. [Natural Log Rule] Define $\ln(x)$ to be the natural logarithm of x. [An alternative notation for natural logarithms that is used in some texts is $\log_e(x)$.] Then:

$$\frac{d[\ln(x)]}{dx} = \frac{1}{x}$$

4. [Power Rule] If a is any constant, then

$$\frac{d(a^x)}{dx} = a^x \ln(a)$$

5. [Sum Rule] For the sum of two functions, $f(x)$ and $g(x)$,

$$\frac{d[f(x) + g(x)]}{dx} = f'(x) + g'(x)$$

6. [Product Rule] For the product of two functions, $f(x)$ and $g(x)$,

$$\frac{d[f(x)g(x)]}{dx} = f(x)g'(x) + f'(x)g(x)$$

7. [Quotient Rule] For the quotient of two functions, $f(x)$ and $g(x) \neq 0$,

$$\frac{d[f(x)/g(x)]}{dx} = \frac{f'(x)\,g(x) - f(x)g'(x)}{[g(x)]^2}$$

8. [Chain Rule] If $y = f(z)$ and $z = g(x)$ and both $f'(z)$ and $g'(x)$ exist, then

$$\frac{dy}{dx} = \frac{dy}{dz}\frac{dz}{dx} = f'[g(x)]g'(x)$$

Harcourt Brace & Company

second derivative:

$$\frac{d^2f}{dx^2} = f'' = \frac{d(f')}{dx}$$

partial derivatives:

$$\frac{\partial f}{\partial x_1} = f_1 = \frac{df}{dx_1}\bigg|_{\bar{x}_2, \bar{x}_3, \ldots, \bar{x}_n}$$

total differential:

$$dy = f_1 dx_1 + f_2 dx_2 + \ldots + f_n dx_n$$

implicit function:

$$f(x, y) = 0$$

implicit function theorem:

$$dy/dx = -f_x/f_y$$

unconstrained maximization of $f(x_1, x_2, \ldots, x_n)$:

first order conditions: $f_i = 0$ for $i = 1, \ldots, n$

second order conditions for $n = 1$: $f'' < 0$ at $x*$

envelope theorem:

$$dy*/da = \partial y/\partial a\{x = x*(a)\}$$

duality

maximization of $f(x_1, x_2, \ldots, x_n)$ subject to the constraint $g(x_1, x_2, \ldots, x_n) = 0$:

Lagrangian: $\pounds = f(x_1, x_2, \ldots, x_n) + \lambda g(x_1, x_2, \ldots, x_n)$

First order conditions: $g(x_1, x_2, \ldots, x_n) = 0$

$$\frac{f_1}{-g_1} = \frac{f_2}{-g_2} = \ldots = \frac{f_n}{-g_n} = -\lambda$$

PROBLEMS

(Numbers in brackets at the beginning of problems below refer to related examples and problems in the text.)

2.1. For each of the following functions, calculate the derivative with respect to x.

a. $f(x) = 2 + 4x^3$

b. $f(x) = \dfrac{3}{\sqrt{x}}$ [Hint: rewrite this in the form ax^b]

Harcourt Brace & Company

c. $f(x) = \ln(4x^3)$ [Hint: use rules 2, 3, and 8; let $z = 4x^3$]

d. $f(x) = e^x$ [Hint: $e = 2.71828$ is the base of natural logarithms. This is an important special case of rule 4. What is $\ln(e)$?]

e. $f(x) = 2e^{5x}$ [Hint: use rule 8 and your result in **d.**]

f. $f(x) = a - bx + cx^2 - dx^3$, where a, b, c, and d are constants.

g. $f(x) = e^x x^2$

h. $f(x) = \dfrac{x^2}{e^x}$

i. $f(x) = \dfrac{e^{2x}(x^3 - 3x + 1)}{\ln(x)}$

2.2. Compute f_x and f_y for each of the following functions.

a. $f(x, y) = x^{.7}y^{.3}$

b. $f(x, y) = x^a y^b$, where a and b are constants.

c. $f(x, y) = e^{(x^2 + y^2 + 2xy)}$.

[Hint: use the chain rule. Let $z = g(x, y) = (x^2 + y^2 + 2xy)$ and let $w = e^z$. What are dw/dz, g_x and g_y ? Be sure to leave your answers in terms of x and y.]

d. $f(x, y) = a + bx^2 + cy^2 + dxy$, where a, b, c, and d are constants.

e. $f(x, y) = (ax^2 + by^2)^{.5}$, where a and b are constants.

Harcourt Brace & Company

f. $f(x, y) = \ln(x^2 y^3)$ [Hint: first apply the rule $\ln(x^a y^b) = a \ln(x) + b \ln(y)$, where a and b are constants.]

g. $f(x, y) = 1/\ln(x^a y^b)$, where a and b are constants.

2.3. [Related to text example 2.1 and problem 2.1.] For each of the following functions, find all critical points and identify their type (i.e., maximum, minimum, or point of inflection).

a. (Illustration) $f(x) = 3x^2 - 2x + 1$

Answer: First, $f'(x) = 6x - 2$ and $f''(x) = 6$. Since $f''(x) > 0$, any critical point will be a minimum. The critical points must satisfy the "first order condition": $f'(x^*) = 6x^* - 2 = 0$. This condition is satisfied only for $x^* = 1/3$. The value of the function at this point is $3(1/3)^2 - 2(1/3) + 1 = 2/3$. This is the function's smallest possible value. A graph of the function appears below.

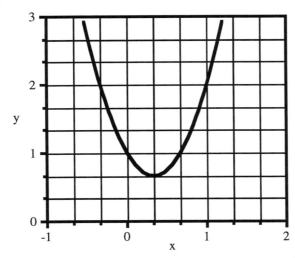

Harcourt Brace & Company

b. $f(x) = 4 - 2x^2 + 3x$

c. $f(x) = ax^2 + bx + c$, where a, b, and c are constants. The type depends on the sign of a. How?

2.4. [Related to text example 2.4.] This question illustrates the envelope theorem. In **2.3c**, you should have found:

$$x^* = -b/2a.$$

a. Substitute this result into the function, $y = f(x) = ax^2 + bx + c$, to find the function that describes the maximum value of y as a function of the parameters a, b, and c.

b. Find the partial derivative of the function you obtained with respect to a.

c. Now, find the partial derivative of the original function with respect to a.

Harcourt Brace & Company

The result you obtained should be a function of x. Replace it with the critical value of x, namely –b/2a.

Compare your result to your answer in **b**. What do you find?

d. Repeat **b** and **c,** this time with respect to the parameter b.

2.5. [Related to text example 2.5 and problem 2.6.] Many constrained maximization problems in economics can be understood by thinking of them in terms of the problem of finding the highest point on a hill among those points that satisfy the constraint. In this problem your task will be to solve an explicit "hill climbing" problem. As you encounter economic maximization problems in later chapters, you may find the hill climbing analogy useful.

The Patagonian Hemisphere Ant makes a very regular ant hill. The height of the hill at its center is always exactly 100 millimeters (mm). At a point that is Nmm to the North of the center and Emm to the East of the center, the height is given by:

$$H = 100 - N^2 - E^2$$

a. All points on the hill that have a height of 91mm satisfy the equation $91 = 100 - N^2 - E^2$. Carefully plot this equation on the graph on the next page. A compass will help. [Hint: the equation for a circle centered at point (a,b) with a radius of r is $(X - a)^2 + (Y - b)^2 = r^2$. Let each square on the graph represent one unit.] The line you have drawn is a "contour" line for the hill; it is the locus of points that have a height of 91mm. Draw a second line representing the locus of points that have a height of 84mm and a third line for points having a height of 64mm. Label each of the three lines with the corresponding values of H. What you have drawn is called a topographical ("topo") map of the top of the ant hill.

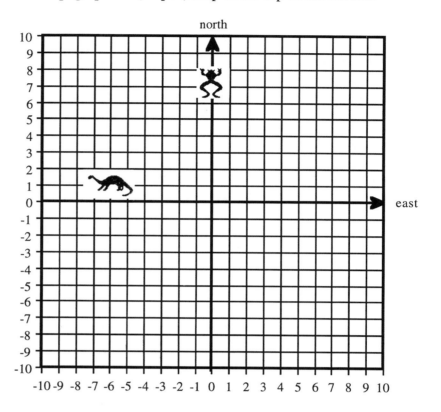

b. A Patagonian Beeline Frog is on the hill at the point defined by the coordinates (0, 6) looking for her lunch. On her last leap she spied a lizard sunning himself at (–6, 0). She knows that she can reach the lizard in one more leap provided that she doesn't have to leap higher than 25mm above her current height. Your job is to determine whether or not she can make it. You are to solve this problem in three different ways in order to demonstrate that they all lead to the same answer and to help you better understand the connections between them.

(i) *The graphical way.* Carefully draw a straight line between these two points. This is the frog's line of flight. What is the equation for this line? N =

(1)_____ What is the highest contour line that the line of flight touches? Read the coordinates of the point where the path touches this line.

They are (2) (____,____). What is the height on this

contour line? H = (3)_____. What is the

height where the frog is now? H = (4)_____.

Can she make it? (5)_____.

(ii) *The three equations, three unknowns way.* You need to
find particular values for E, N, and H—the three
unknowns. In this approach you will set up three
equations that are functions of these unknowns and that
are all satisfied at the point we are looking for. You will
then solve these equations for the values of E, N and H
that satisfy them all simultaneously. In fact, it is a little
simpler than that: the first two equations will depend on
E and N only, so they can be solved for E and N. The
solutions for E and N can then be plugged into the third
equation to get H.

The first equation is just the equation for the line of
flight. Rewrite it for answer (I) near the middle of the
next page. The second equation is derived from noting
that the line of flight is just tangent to the highest contour
line it touches. In fact, this is the only place it is tangent
to a contour line. Another way of saying this is that the
derivative of the contour line equals the derivative of the
line of flight:

$$\frac{dN}{dE}\bigg|_{H\,=\,constant} = \frac{dN}{dE}\bigg|_{on\ the\ line\ of\ flight}$$

This is the source of the second equation. You need to
replace the expressions on both sides of the equation with
functions of E and N. An easy way to find an expression
for the left-hand side is to first totally differentiate the
equation for H:

$$dH = H_N\,dN + H_E\,dE$$

where H_N and H_E are the partial derivatives of the height
function with respect to N and E. This tells us how H
changes when we move dN to the North and dE to the

East. For movements along a contour line, dH = 0. Hence for such movements you can equate the right-hand side of the differential to zero and then solve for the derivative you are looking for:

$$\frac{dN}{dE}\bigg|_{H = \text{constant}} = -\frac{H_E}{H_N}$$

Now, find H_E and H_N: H_E = (6)_____, H_N = (7)_____. Next, write minus their ratio before the equals sign after the (II) below. Now, find

$$\frac{dN}{dE}\bigg|_{\text{on the line of flight}}$$

—it is just the derivative of the equation for the frog's path and very simple. Write your result after the equals sign in (II).

(I) N = (8)_____.

(II) (9)_____ = (10)_____

Now you have your two equations in N and E. Call the values that satisfy both of these equations N* and E*. What are they?

N* = (11)_____, E* = (12)_____.
If you have done this correctly, you should have obtained the same coordinates that you found by the graphical method. Hence, you will get the same height as you obtained the graphical way.

(iii) (The Lagrangian way.) One way of looking at the problem is that we are trying to choose N and E to maximize $100 - N^2 - E^2$, subject to the restriction that we stay on the line of flight. Write the equation for the line of flight in the form $N - a - bE = 0$; the left-hand side will appear in the Lagrangian:

Harcourt Brace & Company

$$\pounds = (13)\underline{\hspace{3cm}} + \lambda (\underline{\hspace{3cm}})$$

$$\underset{\text{function to be maximized}}{} \qquad \underset{\text{constraint}}{}$$

Now, find the partial derivatives of $\pounds$ with respect to E, N, and λ, and equate them to zero to get your first order conditions—three equations in E, N, and λ.

$\pounds_E$: (14)\underline{\hspace{6cm}} $= 0$

$\pounds_N$: (15)\underline{\hspace{6cm}} $= 0$

$\pounds_\lambda$: (16)\underline{\hspace{6cm}} $= 0$

This is a system of three equations which can be solved for N*, E*, and λ*. To simplify, first reduce the system to a system of two equations in two unknowns, N and E, as follows: Solve both the first and second of the equations for λ as functions of N and E:

(from first equation): $\lambda = $ (17)\underline{\hspace{4cm}}

(from second equation): $\lambda = $ (18)\underline{\hspace{4cm}}

Now, equate the right-hand sides of these latter two equations to get a single equation in which λ has been eliminated:

(19)\underline{\hspace{3cm}} $=$ \underline{\hspace{4cm}}

This equation and the third first-order condition (from $\pounds_\lambda$) together are the system of two equations in N and E, which can be solved for E* and N*. But before doing that, compare them to equations (I) and (II) from method **ii**, above. If you have done this correctly, they should be identical. Hence you will get the same result! Thus, the Lagrangian method led you to set up the same system of equations that you set up on the basis of examining the graph in method **ii**.

2.6. [Related to text example 2.6 and problems 2.7.] The Dump'em and Forget'em Nursery School wants to build a fenced play area for its two year olds. The area will be rectangular in shape and one side will be a side of the school building, which is very long. The school has enough money to buy 100 feet of fence. It wishes to maximize the play area, subject to the constraint that the total length of the three fenced sides not exceed 100 feet.

a. How long should the fence parallel to the school be? How long should the two sides that are perpendicular to the school be? [Hint: call the length of the parallel fence L and the length of each perpendicular fence W. What is the equation for the area? What is the equation for the constraint? Set up a Lagrangian.]

b. Could a larger area be obtained if a trapezoidal shape was used, with the school's wall as the long side of the trapezoid?

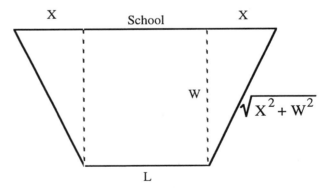

Begin by writing both the area of the trapezoid and the length of the fence as functions of X, L, and W. Then set up the Lagrangian and choose X, L, and W to maximize the area. The first order conditions will look complicated, but judicious manipulation of them will yield a solution.

c. This part of the problem illustrates duality. In **a**, you should have maximized the area of the playground, A = WL, subject to the constraint that 2W + L ≤ 100. Here you are to minimize the amount of fence used, 2W + L, subject to the constraint that the area must be at least 1250 sq. ft., i.e., WL ≥ 1250.

Compare your answers to your answers in **a**. What do you find?_____

_____

_____

CHAPTER 3

PREFERENCES AND UTILITY

axioms of rational choice:

    completeness

    transitivity

    continuity

utility and preferences:

    cardinal vs. ordinal

    direct and indirect utility functions

indifference curve

marginal utility:

$$MU_X = \partial U / \partial X$$

marginal rate of substitution:

$$MRS_{XY} = -\left.\frac{dY}{dX}\right|_{U=constant} = \frac{MU_X}{MU_Y}$$

    diminishing MRS and concavity to the origin

utility function examples:

Cobb-Douglas:	Utility $= X^\alpha Y^\beta$
perfect substitutes:	Utility $= \alpha X + \beta Y$
perfect complements:	Utility $= \min(\alpha X, \beta Y)$
CES:	Utility $= \alpha \dfrac{x^\delta}{\delta} + \beta \dfrac{Y^\delta}{\delta}$

PROBLEMS

(Numbers in brackets at the beginning of problems below refer to related examples and problems in the text.)

  3.1. [Related to text examples 3.1 and 3.2, and to problems 3.1 through 3.5.] For each of the following utility functions, (i) graph a typical indifference curve, (ii) find MU_X and MU_Y and determine whether they are positive for positive values of X and Y, and (iii) find MRS_{XY} and determine whether it diminishes as

X increases (i.e., determine whether the indifference curves are convex).

a. (Illustration) $U = X^{.5}Y^{.5}$

Answer: By definition, utility is constant along an indifference curve. It will be convenient to graph the curve for which $U = 1$. Square both sides to get $1 = XY$, which can be rewritten as $Y = 1/X$. Now, choose some values for X, find the corresponding values for Y, and graph the points:

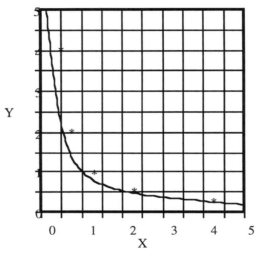

X: 1/4 1/2 1 2 4

Y: 4   2   1 1/2 1/4

Note that as $X \to \infty$, $Y \to 0$, and vice-versa; that is, the X and Y axes are asymptotes for the indifference curve.

$$MU_X \equiv \frac{\partial U}{\partial Y} = .5X^{-.5}Y^{.5} \text{ and } MU_Y \equiv \frac{\partial U}{\partial Y} = .5X^{.5}Y^{-.5} \text{ ,}$$

which are both positive for X and Y.

$$MRS_{XY} \equiv -\frac{dY}{dX}\bigg|_{U=cons\tan t} = \frac{MU_X}{MU_Y} = \frac{.5X^{-.5}Y^{.5}}{.5X^{.5}Y^{-.5}} = \frac{Y}{X}.$$

[To confirm that this is minus the slope of the indifference curve, find the derivative of $Y = 1/X = X^{-1}$ with respect to X: $dY/dX = (-1)X^{-2} = -X^{-1}X^{-1} = -(Y/X) = -MRS_{XY}$.] MRS_{XY} does diminish with X. To see this, note that as we move along the

Harcourt Brace & Company

indifference curve toward the right (increasing X), Y falls. Therefore the ratio Y/X diminishes. This confirms what can be seen graphically: the indifference curve is convex.

b. $U = X + Y$

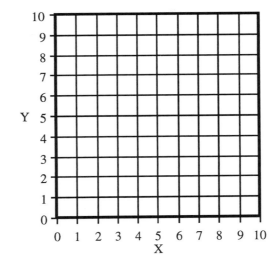

c. $U = 2X + Y$

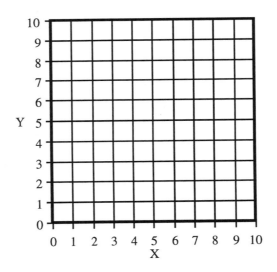

d. $U = \alpha X + \beta Y$, where α and β are positive constants. (Since α and β are not given particular values, you will not be able to graph this one.)

Harcourt Brace & Company

e. $U = X^{.75}Y^{.25}$

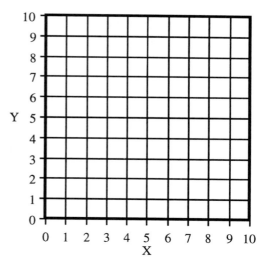

f. $U = \sqrt{X^2 + Y^2}$ (Hints: use U = 1 for the graph. Use the chain rule to get MU_X and MU_Y.)

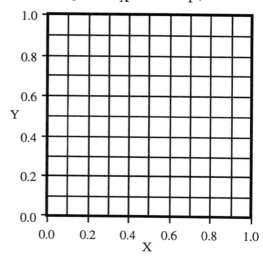

g. $U = \sqrt{X^2 - Y^2}$

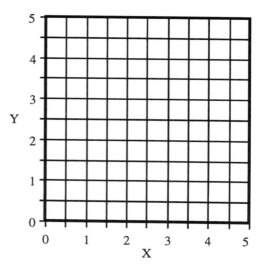

Harcourt Brace & Company

3.2. [Related to text problem 3.2.] Find and compare MRS_{XY} for the following people:

a. Mr. Level: $U_L = X^\alpha Y^{1-\alpha}$ where $0 < \alpha < 1$.

b. Ms. Square: $U_S = (X^\alpha Y^{1-\alpha})^2$ where $0 < \alpha < 1$.

c. Mr. Root: $U_R = (X^\alpha Y^{1-\alpha})^{.5}$ where $0 < \alpha < 1$.

d. Ms. Natural Log: $U_{NL} = \alpha \ln(X) + (1-\alpha) \ln(Y)$ where
$$0 < \alpha < 1.$$

e. Mr. Half Log: $U_{HL} = .5[\alpha \ln(X) + (1-\alpha) \ln(Y)]$ where
$$0 < \alpha < 1.$$

f. Mr. Twice Log: $U_{TL} = 2[\alpha \ln(X) + (1-\alpha) \ln(Y)]$ where
$$0 < \alpha < 1.$$

Now fill in the blanks: "It turns out that MRS_{XY} is
(1)_____ for all of these people.
This can be explained by the fact that they all have the same
preferences, but they use different scales for measuring utility.
For instance, Ms. Square's utils are just the square of Mr. Level's
utils, i.e., $U_S = U_L^2$. Similarly, (2) $U_R = $ _____ ,
(3) $U_{NL} = $ _____ ,
(4) $U_{HL} = $ _____ , and
(5) $U_{TL} = $ _____ . This illustrates the
general rule that rescaling utility does not affect MRS_{XY}. In fact,
the entire indifference map is unchanged except that the value
attached to each indifference curve changes.

Thus, to draw an indifference map we only need a(n)
(6) (ordinal/cardinal) ranking of bundles of goods. Rescaling
can often be useful in simplifying the task of finding MRS_{XY}.
For instance, consider Mr. Bee Cee's utility function: $U_{BC} = X^\beta Y^\gamma$, with $0 < \beta < 1$ and $0 < \gamma < 1$. His function can be

Harcourt Brace & Company

rewritten as $U_{BC} = (X^{\alpha}Y^{1-\alpha})\beta+\gamma$ if we define $\alpha = (7)$_____.

Now we see that his preferences are the same as Mr. Level's, just measured on a different scale: (8) $U_{BC} =$

_____ .

Therefore, his MRS_{XY} is (9) _____

_____. [Note: as a final step in (9), be sure to replace "α" wherever it appears by its definition from answer (7).]

3.3. [Related to text problems 3.3 and 3.4.] Match each of the following people to a utility function and sketch their indifference maps.

   a. Miss Muffet likes Curds (X) and Whey (Y) and is always willing to give up a cup of Curds for ten fluid ounces of Whey.

   b. Jack Sprat can eat no fat (X), but he can always give it to his wife. She gives him lean (Y), which he can never get enough of. In fact, no matter how much he gets, each additional pound gives him the same additional satisfaction.

   c. King Kole smokes a pipe, but is very particular about the blend of tobacco he uses. The only blend he will smoke has 10 parts Havana Gold (X) to 1 part Virginia Splendor (Y).

   d. Jack Horner likes plum pie. Actually, he just likes the plums (X). He hates the crust (Y), but his mother won't give him any pie unless he eats the crust too. He prefers one pie (which has 10 plums and one crust) to none at all, is indifferent between none and two, and would never eat three.

a. $U = \min(10X, Y)$ 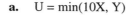   **b.** $U = 10X +Y$

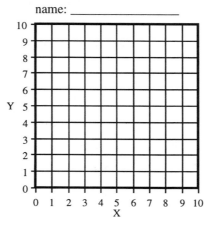

name: _____

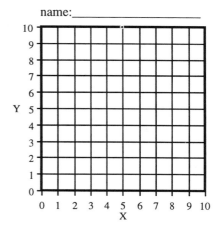

name:_____

Harcourt Brace & Company

c. $U = 2X - 10Y^2$

name: _____

d. $U = 10Y$

name: _____

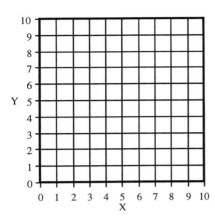

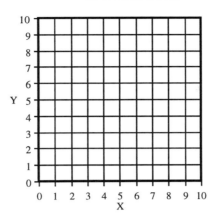

3.4. [Related to text problem 3.8] Ms. E. Senshal can't live without butter (B) and marmalade (M) on her toast. The utility she gets from a piece of toast is:

$$U = .4 \ln (B - 1) + .6 \ln (M - 2)$$

MU_B = (1)_____

MU_M = (2)_____

MRS_{BM} = (3)_____

What is the minimum amount of butter that she has to have on each piece of toast? (4)_____ The minimum amount of marmalade? (5) _____ If B = 2 and M = 3, how many units of M would she be willing to give up for another unit of B? (6)_____

[Hint: what is MRS_{BM} at this point?] How many units of B would she be willing to give up for another unit of M?

(7)_____

3.5. [Related to text problem 3.10.] The CES utility function is given by the following equation when $\delta \neq 0$.

$$U(X, Y) = \alpha \frac{X^\delta}{\delta} + \beta \frac{Y^\delta}{\delta}$$

a. Find MU_X and MU_Y for this function.

b. Use the results from **a** to find MRS_{XY}.

c. Is the CES function homothetic? Explain.

_____

_____

_____

_____

_____

d. What does your expression for MRS_{XY} reduce to if $\delta = 0$? Compare this result to MRS_{XY} for the Cobb-Douglas utility funtion.

_____

_____

_____

_____

_____

e. What does your expression for MRS_{XY} reduce to if $\delta = 1$? What would an indifference curve look like in this case? What is this case called?

_____

_____

_____

_____

_____

f. Find the derivative of MRS_{XY} with respect to the ratio X/Y. [Hint: replace X/Y in the MRS_{XY} equation with Z, find the derivative with respect to Z, then replace Z in the derivative with X/Y.]

g. The expression you found in **f** describes how MRS_{XY} changes when moving along an indifference curve as the ratio X/Y increases (i.e., as X is substituted for Y). Hence, it describes the curvature of the indifference curve, as a function of δ.

Describe the curvature when $\delta = 1$. (1)_____

_____

What happens to the curvature as δ becomes smaller than 1? (2)_____

Approaches $-\infty$? (3)_____

Becomes greater than 1? (4)_____

_____ What property

of utility functions is violated in the last case? (5)_____

_____

CHAPTER 4

UTILITY MAXIMIZATION AND CHOICE

KEY CONCEPTS

budget constraint:

$$P_1X_1 + P_2X_2 + \ldots + P_nX_n \leq I$$

first order conditions for maximization of utility, subject to the budget constraint:

$$MRS_{X_iX_j} = \frac{P_i}{P_j} \quad \text{for any two goods, } X_i \text{ and } X_j$$

$$P_1X_1 + P_2X_2 + \ldots + P_nX_n = I$$

second order conditions and the importance of diminishing MRS_{XY}

corner solutions

interpretation of Lagrange multiplier in utility maximization:

$$\lambda = \frac{MU_{X_1}}{P_1} = \frac{MU_{X_2}}{P_2} = \ldots = \frac{MU_{X_n}}{P_n}$$

Cobb-Douglas demand function:

$$X^* = \frac{dI}{P_X}$$

indirect utility function:

$$U\left(X_1^*, X_2^*, \cdots, X_n^*\right) = U[X_1(P_1, P_2, \cdots, P_n, I),$$

$$\cdots, X_n(P_1, P_2, \cdots, P_n, I)] = V(P_1, P_2, \cdots, P_n, I)$$

expenditure minimization (the dual to utility maximization)

expenditure function:

$$\text{minimal expenditure} = E(P_1, P_2, \ldots, P_n, U)$$

lump-sum principle

(Numbers in brackets at the beginning of problems below refer to related examples and problems in the text.)

PROBLEMS

4.1 [Related to text examples 4.1 and 4.2, and problems 4.1 and 4.2.] Fussy Eater likes only two kinds of vegetables: peas (P) and carrots (C). He gets utility from these vegetables according to the following function:

$$U = P^{1/4}C^{3/4}$$

a. His MRS of peas for carrots is _____
[Hint: see Problem 2.2.]

b. Each week he spends $4.00 on vegetables. Early in the summer the price of peas (P_P) is $.50 per pound, while the price of carrots (P_C) is $1.00 per pound. His weekly budget constraint is (1)_____. Draw this constraint in the graph below, putting P on the horizontal axis and C on the vertical axis. Shade in his budget set. The slope of the boundary of his budget set is (2)_____.
The maximum quantity of C he could buy is (3) _____. Label the corresponding point in the budget set with C_{max}. The maximum quantity of P he can buy is (4)_____. Label the corresponding point in the budget set with P_{max}.

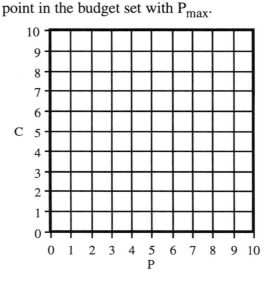

c. In order to maximize his utility, he must find the values of P and C that equate his "willingness to trade" P for C (i.e., MRS_{CP}) with the market's "terms of trade" between P and C (P_C/P_P). Find these values algebraically, plot the corresponding point on the graph, and draw in the indifference curve that passes through this point.

C* = (1)_____. P* = (2)_____.
He spends (3) $_____ on carrots. As a percentage of
his expenditures on vegetables, this is (4)
_____%.

d. Toward the end of the summer, the price of carrots falls to
$.50 per pound and the price of peas increases to $1.00 a
pound. Repeat **c** using these new prices.

C* = (1)_____. P* = (2)_____.
He spends (3) $_____ on carrots. As a percentage of
his expenditures on vegetables, this is (4)
_____%.

e. On one of his shopping trips toward the end of the summer,
Fussy finds a dollar bill as he is entering the store. Repeat **d**,
assuming that he spends all of his windfall plus his original
$4.00 on vegetables.

C* = (1)_____. P* = (2)_____.
He spends (3) $_____ on carrots. As a percentage of
his expenditures on vegetables, this is (4)
_____%.

f. Compare the percentages that he spends on carrots in parts **c**
through **e**. What do you find? _____

_____

How is your finding related to the exponents in his utility function?_____

_____

_____

_____

_____

4.2. [Related to text examples 4.4 and 4.5, and problem 4.5.] Mead N. Taters likes only steak (S) and potatoes (P), and gets utility from them according to:

$$U = S^{2/5}P^{3/5}$$

a. No matter how much Mead has to spend on groceries and no matter what the prices of steak and potatoes are, he always spends (1)_____% on steak and (2)_____% on potatoes. Thus, if Mead has $20.00 to spend on groceries, he will spend (3)$_____ on steak and (4) $_____ on potatoes. If the price of steak is $2.00 per pound and the price of potatoes is $.50 per pound, he will buy (5)_____ pounds of steak and (6)_____ pounds of potatoes. If the amount he has to spend on groceries, the price of steak, and the price of potatoes all double, he will then buy (7) _____ pounds of steak and (8)_____ pounds of potatoes. Would answers (7) and (8) change if Mead had any alternative "well-behaved" utility function? (9)_____. Why or why not? (10)_____

_____

_____

_____

b. Let I represent the amount of income that Mead budgets for food. In words, what is the interpretation of $P_S S/I$?

(1)_____

Harcourt Brace & Company

No matter what P_S and I are, Mead always chooses S so that

$P_S S/I$ = (2)_____. Now turn this relationship around

and write S as a function of P_S and I: S =

(3)_____. The analogous equation for P

is P = (4)_____.

c. Use your results from **b** to obtain Mead's indirect utility function. That is, substitute your functions for S and P into Mead's utility function so that U is written as a function of P_S, P_P and I.

d. Now, find Mead's expenditure function. That is, turn your indirect utility function around so that I is a function of P_S, P_M, and U. Viewed in this way, the function tells you how much Mead has to spend in order to achieve utility level U at prices P_S and P_M.

4.3. Remember Fussy Eater from 4.1? Towards the end of the summer Fussy notices that his skin has a peculiar orange palor. He is told by his doctor that he has been eating too many carrots. The doctor tells him that if he only eats carrots, he should never eat more than 5 pounds. In addition, if he eats peas he needs to eat even fewer carrots because the peas and carrots interact to make the problem worse. For every pound of peas he eats, he needs to reduce his carrot consumption by one half of a pound. The doctor also warns him that he will turn green if he eats more than 10 pounds of peas, regardless of how many pounds of carrots he eats.

a. Draw the "doctor's orders" constraint on the graph below.

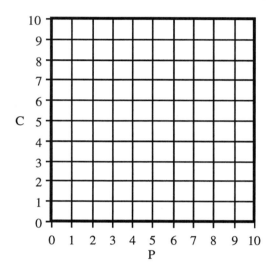

b. If Fussy has unlimited money to spend on vegetables, how many pounds of peas and carrots should he consume per week to maximize utility? [Hint: mathematically, this is just like maximizing utility subject to an income constraint. What is the equation for the doctor's orders constraint that you drew in **a**? Write the equation in the form aP + bC = c, where a, b, and c stand for specific numbers. Think of this constraint as a budget constraint. That is, a and b are the "medical prices" of P and C and c is his "medical income." What share of his medical income will he spend on peas? Carrots? How much of each can he "buy" with these shares?]

c. Of course, Fussy usually only has $4.00 to spend on vegetables. Suppose that $P_P = \$1.00$ and $P_C = \$.50$. Draw Fussy's budget constraint in the graph above and indicate the point he would choose if he ignored the doctor's orders (see part **d** of Problem 4.1). Shade in the part of his budget set that also satisfies the doctor's orders. If he obeys the doctor's orders, how many pounds of peas and carrots will he buy?

4.4. [Related to text example 4.3 and problem 4.4.] Al K. Haulich and his brother, Chuck A., have the same preferences for wine (W) and chocolate bars (C):

$$U = W^2 + C^2$$

a. Determine their MRS of C for W. Are the indifference curves convex?

b. Al lives in France, where the price of a bottle of wine is actually less than the price of a bar of chocolate. Describe Al's behavior and compare it to the behavior of brother Chuck; Chuck lives in Switzerland where a bottle of wine costs twice as much as a chocolate bar. It may help to sketch a typical indifference curve and budget constraints for each brother. Be sure that the constraints reflect the relative prices in the two countries.

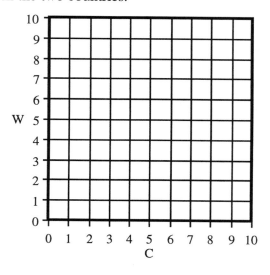

_____

_____

_____

_____

_____

_____

_____

4.5. Happy Goluki likes to go to the movies (M) and play video games (G) at an arcade. Her utility function is:

$$U = .4 \ln(G) + .6 \ln(M)$$

Happy has $10.00 to spend on entertainment. If P_G = $.25 and P_M = $4.00, how many movies will she go to and how many games will she play—taking into account that she can't buy a fraction of a game or a fraction of a movie. [Hint: first figure out what G* and M* would be if G and M were divisible. Given

indivisibility, are they feasible? Calculate her utility at feasible
points in her budget set that are near this point.]

4.6. Remember Miss Muffet from Problem 3.3? Her utility function
is $U = 10X + Y$, where X is Curds (in cups) and Y is Whey (in
ounces).

   a. If Curds are $1.00 per cup and Whey is $.11 per ounce, what
share of her expenditures on these items will go to Curds?
Whey?

   b. How will these shares change if the price of Whey drops to
$.09 per ounce?

   c. Can you tell what the shares will be if the price of Whey is
$.10? Why or why not?

4.7. [Related to text problem 4.5.] Remember Old King Kole from
Problem 3.3? Like all kings, he pays for his tobacco in gold. In
the good old days, he could buy one pound (16 ounces) of either
Havana Gold (X) or Virginia Splendor (Y) for an ounce of gold.
Recall that his utility function is:

$$U = \min(10X, Y)$$

   a. For each ounce of gold he spent on tobacco, how much of
each did he buy? [Hint: first write the budget constraint,

letting $P_X = P_Y = 1$ lb./oz. and I = 1. How much of X will he buy for each ounce of Y? Substitute this relationship into the budget constraint.]

b. The good old days ended with the Cuban Revolution. While King Kole publicly supports the trade embargo against Cuban tobacco, he still insists on the same blend for his pipe tobacco. Because of his political position, he goes to great lengths to avoid being caught purchasing Havana Gold. The cost of maintaining secrecy is so high that, to him, Havana Gold is literally worth its weight in real gold. That is, including the cost of secrecy, he must pay one ounce of gold for each ounce of Havana Gold. Assuming that the price of Virginia Splendor is unchanged, how much of each tobacco will he now buy for each ounce of gold he spends on tobacco?

c. Does the price change affect the proportions of X and Y that he uses? Why or why not?

_____

_____

_____

_____

_____

Harcourt Brace & Company

4.8. [Related to text problems 4.7 and 4.8.] Consider a single mother choosing between consumption of children's clothing (C) and other goods (Y). Assume that the units of C and Y are such that, initially, $P_C = P_Y = \$1.00$ and that the mother has $100 to spend.

a. Draw a diagram that depicts her utility maximization problem.

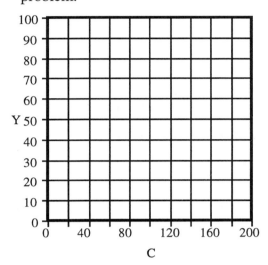

Assume that the mother's utility function is

$$U = CY$$

What point does she choose on her budget constraint? $C^* =$ (1) _____ $Y^* =$ (2) _____

Indicate the point on the graph with an **a**.

b. The government decides to subsidize her purchases of children's clothing by paying for one-half of all C that she buys. From the mother's viewpoint, how does this affect P_C?

$P_C =$ (1)$_____. Draw in a new budget constraint, reflecting this change, and indicate the mother's new choice with **b**. It is $C^{**} =$ (2)_____, $Y^{**} =$ (3)_____. The mother's new utility level is (4)_____. The government's expenditure on the subsidy is (5) _____.

c. Now suppose that, instead of subsidizing C, the government decides to give the mother a lump sum payment. How much will the government have to give her so that she can attain the same level of utility that she was able to attain under the subsidy in **b**? [Hint: find the mother's expenditure function, then plug in the prices and the new utility level.]

(1) $_____. Is this amount more or less than the government's subsidy in **b**? (2)_____Why?

(3)_____

_____

_____

_____

_____ How much C will she buy if the government gives her this amount? (4) _____ Is this more or less than under the subsidy in **b**? (5)_____

Why? (6)_____

_____

_____

_____How much would the lump sum have to be in order to induce the mother to purchase the same amount of C as in **b**? (7)_____

d. If the objective of the government is to increase the mother's utility, which is more efficient, subsidy or lump sum?

(1)_____ Why?_____

_____

_____

Does your answer change if the government's objective is

to increase her expenditure on C? (2)_____

Why?_____

_____

_____

_____

4.9. [Related to text problem 4.10.] Remember Ms. E. Senshal from Problem 3.4? Her utility function is

$$U = .4 \ln (B - 1) + .6 \ln (M - 2)$$

Suppose that $P_B = P_M = \$.01$ and for each piece of toast she eats she spends I dollars on butter and marmalade. We wish to determine how much B and M she uses for each piece of toast, as a function of I. There are several ways to do this. The objective of this problem is to help you learn an easy way.

a. First, write the budget constraint:

(1) _____

Now, define B* = B - 1 and M* = M - 2. Note that B* and M* are "discretionary" purchases of B and M — total purchases minus the minimums she must purchase in order to get positive utility from a piece of toast. Also define I* = I − .03. Note that .03 is the minimum amount she must spend on butter and marmalade in order to get utility from eating toast. I* is her "discretionary income"—the amount she can choose to spend on B or M after spending the required minimum on each. These definitions can be turned around: B = B* + 1, M = M* + 2, and I* = I + .03. Substitute these turned-around definitions for B and M in both the utility function and the budget constraint:

Utility Function: (2) _____

Budget Constraint: (3) _____

Maximizing this transformed utility function with respect to this transformed budget constraint should look like a familiar problem. If not, you have probably made an error. Correct it before proceeding. What share of her discretionary income will she spend on discretionary B (i.e., on B*)?

(4)_____ Write her choice for B* as a function of

I*: (5) B* = _____. Now, substitute the definitions of B* and I* into this equation to get the desired relationship between B and I: (6) B = _____. The corresponding relationship between M and I is (7) M = _____.

b. Can you generalize the functions you obtained in (6) and (7)? That is, suppose

$$U = a \ln(B - b) + (1 - a) \ln(M - m)$$

where b and m are the essential amounts of B and M. Also, let P_M and P_B stand for the prices of M and B, respectively. Write B and M as functions of P_B, P_M and I. [Hint: The easiest way to get the general result is to repeat each of the steps in part **a**, replacing the numbers with a, b, c, P_B, or P_M as is appropriate.]

As a last step, multiply both sides of the equation for B by P_B and both sides of the equation for M by P_M:

$P_B B = $ _____

$P_M M = $ _____

These two equations are known as the "linear expenditure system." In words, expenditure on the two goods is a linear function of discretionary income $(I - P_B b - P_M m)$. The intercepts of the linear functions are the essential expenditures on the respective goods and the slopes are the multiplicative factors for the respective goods in the utility function. What utility function would yield a linear expenditure system for three goods? _____

Harcourt Brace & Company

4.10. To get an orange, Suzy Scurvy would be willing to give up $.50 worth of other food. However, if she already had an orange she would only be willing to give up $.25 worth of other food to get a second. Her willingness to pay for a third orange diminishes to $.10. On a recent trip to the supermarket she found that oranges were $.35 each, or 2 for $.55. Since the price of one orange was less than her willingness to give up food for one orange, but the average price of two oranges ($.275) exceeded her willingness to give up other food for a second orange, she decided to buy one orange. Fortunately for her, she runs into you at the store. Explain to Suzy why her decision does not make her as well off as possible and tell her how many oranges she should buy in order to improve her well-being! A sketch of her budget constraint and two indifference curves might aid your explanation. Assume that she has $10.00 to spend on food. Also, draw the indifference curves that pass through the points (1, $9.65) and (2, $9.45).

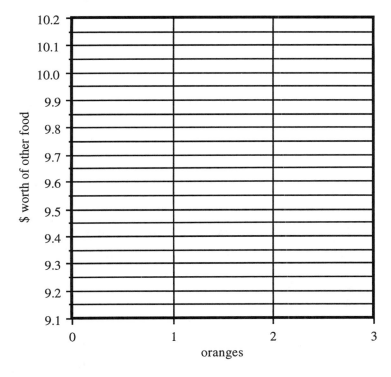

_____

_____

_____

_____

4.11 [Related to text problem 4.9.] The CES utility function is given by the following equation when $\delta \neq 0$.

$$U(X, Y) = \alpha \frac{X^\delta}{\delta} + \beta \frac{Y^\delta}{\delta}$$

In Problem 3.5 you found that the marginal rate of substitution for this function is:

$$MRS_{XY} = \frac{\alpha}{\beta} \left(\frac{X}{Y} \right)^{\delta - 1}$$

a. Write the first-order conditions for utility maximization of the CES function.

Now solve this equation for the ratio X/Y as a function of the price ratio, P_X / P_Y.

X/Y =

b. The shares of income spent on X and Y are defined as $S_X = P_X X / I$ and $S_Y = P_Y Y / I$. Use your result in **a** to write the utility maximizing share spent on X relative to the share spent on Y as a function of the price ratio, P_X / P_Y.

$$\frac{S_X}{S_Y} = \frac{P_X X}{P_Y Y} =$$

c. Find the derivative of your result from **b** with respect to the price ratio P_X / P_Y. [Hint: replace P_X / P_Y in the expression with Z, find the derivative with respect to Z, then replace Z in the derivative with P_X / P_Y.]

d. Describe, in words, how the relative shares change as P_X/P_Y increases. The answer depends on δ.

_____

_____

_____

_____

_____

e. Provide an intuitive explanation. [Hint: recall the relationship between δ and the curvature of the indifference curves. See problem 3.5.]

_____

_____

_____

_____

_____

CHAPTER 5

INCOME AND SUBSTITUTION EFFECTS

"ordinary" or Marshallian demand functions:

$$X_i = d_i(P_1, P_2, \cdots, P_n, I)$$

homogeneity of demand functions:

$$X_i^* = d_i(P_1, P_2, \ldots, P_n, I) = d_i(tP_1, tP_2, \ldots, tP_n, tI) \text{ for any } t > 0$$

effect of an income change on demand:

Engel curves and Engel's Law

normal and inferior goods

effect of a change in the good's price on quantity demanded:

Slutsky equation:

$$\frac{\partial d_X}{\partial P_X} = \left.\frac{\partial X}{\partial P_X}\right|_{U = \text{constant}} - X\frac{\partial X}{\partial I}$$

substitution and income effects

Giffen's paradox

compensated demand function:

$$X^* = h_X(P_X, P_Y, U) = d_X[P_X, P_Y, E(P_X, P_Y, U)]$$

Shephard's Lemma:

$$\partial E(P_X, P_Y, U)/\partial P_X = X^* = h_X(P_X, P_Y, U)$$

strong axiom of revealed preference

consumer surplus:

$$CS = \int_{P_X^0}^{P_X^1} h(P_X, P_Y, U)dP_X$$

Harcourt Brace & Company

PROBLEMS

(Numbers in brackets at the beginning of problems below refer to related examples and problems in the text.)

5.1. [Related to text examples 5.1 through 5.4, and problems 5.7 and 5.8.] Remember Mead N. Taters from Problem 4.2? To refresh your memory, his utility function for steak (S) and potatoes (P) is

$$U = S^{2/5}P^{3/5}$$

You should have found that he always spends 40% of his income, I, on S and 60% on P, no matter what his income is and no matter what the prices of S and P are. This fact should have led you to the conclusion that his utility maximizing choices of S and P are always determined by the following functions of I, P_S and P_P.

$$S = \frac{.4\,I}{P_S}$$

$$P = \frac{.6\,I}{P_P}$$

You should now recognize that these functions are his demand functions for steak and potatoes. In addition you found Mead's indirect utility function:

$$U = \frac{.51\,I}{P_S^{2/5}P_P^{3/5}}$$

and his expenditure function:

$$E = \frac{P_S^{2/5}P_P^{3/5}U}{.51}$$

a. Suppose that P_S = \$2.00 per pound, P_P = \$.50 per pound, and I = \$20. His utility maximizing choice of S will be (1)_____ and of P will be (2) _____. If the price of steak increases to \$3.00 per pound, his choices will then be S = (3) _____ and P = (4)_____. Draw the two budget constraints in the diagram below and indicate the points that are chosen.

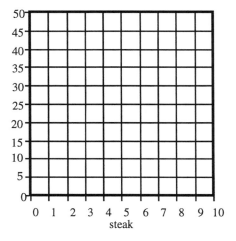

steak

Harcourt Brace & Company

b. When steak is only $2.00 per pound, Mead's utility is
(1)_____. [Hint: you can either plug his
maximizing values of S and P into his direct utility function
or plug the prices and I into the indirect utility function.]
When the price increases to $3.00 per pound, his utility falls
to (2)_____. At the new price, his
income would have to increase to (3) $_____
in order for him to attain his previous level of utility. [Hint:
remember that his expenditure function tells you the
minimum income he must have in order to attain a particular
utility level at the prevailing prices.] That is, the
compensation he would need in order to offset his loss in
utility is (4) $_____. On the graph above, draw
what his budget constraint would be if his income did
increase to this level, given the new higher price for steak.
Under this constraint, his utility maximizing consumption
levels would be S = (5)_____ and P = (6)_____.
Indicate this point on the budget constraint. Also draw in the
indifference curve that passes through both this point and the
choice he made before the price increase. Be sure that it is
tangent to both of the relevant budget constraints. Based on
your analysis, what are the income, substitution, and total
effects of the $1.00 increase in price of steak on the quantity
of steak Mead demands?

substitution effect   (7)_____

+ income effect   (8)_____

= total effect   (9)_____.

c. Of course, you could have used the demand function for S to get the three effects. That is, for a small change in P_S, ΔP_S, the Slutsky equation tells us that

$$\Delta S = \frac{\partial S}{\partial P_S}\Delta P_S = \left.\frac{\partial S}{\partial P_S}\right|_{U = \text{constant}}\Delta P_S - S\frac{\partial S}{\partial I}\Delta P_S$$

total effect $=$ substitution effect + income effect

For this problem:

$$\frac{\partial S}{\partial P_S} = (1)\underline{\hspace{2cm}}, \quad \frac{\partial S}{\partial I} = (2)\underline{\hspace{2cm}},$$

and $\left.\dfrac{\partial S}{\partial P_S}\right|_{U = \text{constant}} = \dfrac{\partial S}{\partial P_S} + S\dfrac{\partial S}{\partial I} = (3)\underline{\hspace{3cm}}.$

Now compute the values of the derivatives. To do this, you will need to choose values for I, P_S, and S. The obvious choice for I = $20.00. For P_S, try the midpoint between the original and new values. Do the same for S.

$$\left.\frac{\partial S}{\partial P_S}\right|_{U \text{ constant}}\Delta P_S \quad (4)\underline{\hspace{3cm}}$$

$$+ \qquad\qquad -S\frac{\partial S}{\partial I}\Delta P_S \quad (5)\underline{\hspace{3cm}}$$

$$= \qquad\qquad \frac{\partial S}{\partial P_S}\Delta P_S \quad (6)\underline{\hspace{3cm}}$$

Compare these results to the substitution, income, and total effects you found in part **b**. Are they the same? Why or why not? \underline{\hspace{5cm}}

\underline{\hspace{8cm}}

\underline{\hspace{8cm}}

\underline{\hspace{8cm}}

d. Graph the Engel curve for S when P_S = $2.00 and P_B = $.50 in the diagram below. [Hint: substitute the two prices into the demand function for S. The result is the function you want to graph.] Is steak a normal good for Mead?

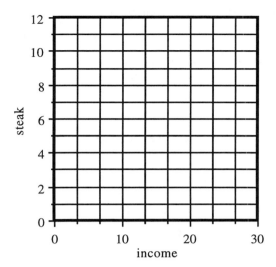

What happens to the Engel curve when the price of steak increases? Illustrate your answer by drawing an Engel curve with $P_S = \$3.00$. What happens to the Engel curve when the price of potatoes increases to 1.00? Graph a third Engel curve to illustrate.

e. Draw Mead's demand curve for steak when $P_P = \$.50$ and $I = \$20.00$ on the graph below.

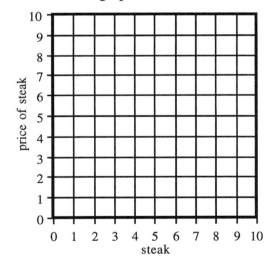

What happens to the demand function when I increases? Illustrate by drawing a second demand function for $I = \$30.00$. What happens to the demand function when P_P increases? _____

_____

f. Shephard's Lemma says that Mead's compensated demand function for S is the derivative of his expenditure function with respect to P_S. That is,

$$S* = \frac{\partial E}{\partial P_S} = (1) \underline{\hspace{6cm}}$$

The compensated demand curve for P is P* =

(2)_____. Repeat your drawing of Mead's ordinary (i.e., not compensated) demand curve for S and indicate his original position on this curve on the graph below. Next, draw the compensated demand function that passes through this point. To do this, find his utility level at this point (see **b,** above) and substitute this value for U in your compensated demand curve for S. Also, plug in P_P = $.50. The result is the equation you need to graph:

S* = (3)_____.

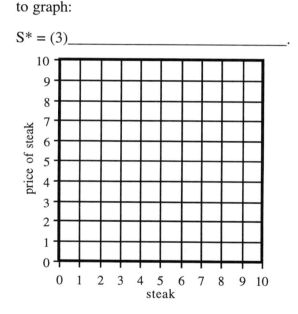

Which is steeper, the ordinary demand curve or the compensated demand curve? Why? (4) _____

_____

_____

_____Along which curve is I constant? (5)_____ Along which curve is U constant? (6)_____ Now return to the general form of S*. Find its partial derivative with respect to P_S and compare your result to answer (3) in

Harcourt Brace & Company

part **c.** Before you make the comparison, you need to get rid of the U that appears in the derivative. Substitute the indirect utility function for U. What do you find? Why? (7)

_____

_____

_____

_____

_____

5.2. Remember Fussy Eater from Problem 4.1? Recall that he gets utility from peas (P) and carrots (C) according to

$$U = P^{1/4}C^{3/4}$$

a. We neglected to mention that Fussy is a gardener. One week in July he harvests the last of his pea crop, 3 pounds, and the first of his carrots, 2 pounds. Draw Fussy's budget constraint, assuming that he cannot buy or sell peas and carrots, and indicate his utility maximizing choice with an **a**. [Note: throughout this problem, assume that Fussy ignores the "doctor's orders" of Chapter 4.]

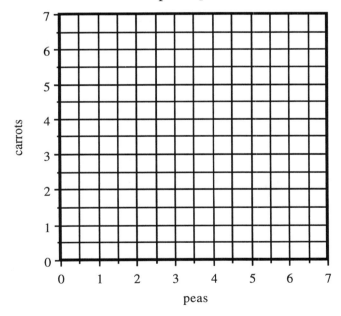

b. Now suppose that he can buy or sell peas at the local farmers' market for $.50 per pound, and that he can buy or sell carrots for $1.00 per pound. Graph his new budget constraint above and write the equation for the constraint below. Assume that he spends any money he earns from selling one vegetable on the other and that he has no other money to spend.

(1)_____= 0

What quantities of peas and carrots will he bring home from the market? Indicate his choice on the graph with a **b**. [Hint: you could set up a Lagrangian and crank out an answer, but there is an easier and more instructive way. Reduce this problem to one you already know how to solve: If he sold all of his peas and carrots, how much money would he get? How many peas and carrots would he buy if he went to the market with this amount of money to spend and no peas and carrots to sell?]

quantity of peas = (2)_____ quantity of carrots = (3)_____ Does the existence of the market make him better off? Explain. (4)_____

_____

_____

_____

_____

c. What happens to Fussy's budget constraint when the price of peas rises to $1.00 per pound? Draw in the new budget constraint, and indicate his new choice with a **c**. Also illustrate the income and substitution effects on the demand for peas in your diagram, as follows: Sketch the budget constraint that, under the new prices, would leave him just as well off as under the original constraint. To do this, you will first need to sketch Fussy's original indifference curve. While it is not necessary to sketch the indifference curve exactly, it should be drawn in a way that is consistent with the fact that both peas and carrots are normal goods for Fussy. Indicate the substitution and income effects on the graph. Is the income effect positive or negative? (1)_____.

Is the substitution effect positive or negative? (2)_____.

Is Fussy better off or worse off? Why? (3)_____

_____

_____

Without actually working it out, do you think the income
effect of an increase in the price of carrots on the demand for
carrots would be positive or negative? Explain.

(4)_____

_____

Will Fussy be better or worse off if the price of carrots rises?

Why? (5)_____

_____

_____

_____ Compare answers (1) through (5) to
the answers you would get if Fussy was not a gardener and
just took cash to the market. (6)_____

_____

_____

_____

_____

_____

_____

_____

d. The Slutsky equation in the text does not apply to Fussy
because he has an endowment of peas and carrots. When the
price of peas goes up, his implicit income—the amount he
would earn if he sold all his peas and carrots—goes up too.
In this part of the problem you will derive a more general
Slutsky equation that applies to the general case of two
goods, X and Y, for which the consumer originally has
endowments X* and Y*. For prices P_X and P_Y, the
consumer's implicit income, called I*, is: I* =
(1)_____, and the consumer's
budget constraint can be written as:
(2)_____ $\leq$ I*. If I* didn't change
when P_X increased, the Slutsky equation for X would be the

usual one, with I replaced by I*:

$$\frac{\partial X}{\partial P_X} = (3) \underline{\hspace{8cm}}$$

But I* does change, by $\frac{\partial I}{\partial P_X} = (4) \underline{\hspace{3cm}}$

We need to multiply this change by the effect of a change in I* on demand for X, dX/dI*, and add it to the old Slutsky equation to get the new one. The result reduces to:

$$\frac{\partial X}{\partial P_X} = (5)\underbrace{\underline{\hspace{3cm}}}_{\text{(substitution effect)}} - (6)\underbrace{\left(\underline{\hspace{4cm}}\right)}_{\text{(new income effect)}} \frac{\partial X}{\partial I^*}$$

How does the sign of the new income effect depend on whether the consumer is originally a net buyer or seller of X?

(7)_____

_____

_____

Relate your answer to your answer in part **c**.

(8)_____

_____

_____

_____

_____

_____

_____

_____

Now, suppose that the consumer has a fixed income, I, as well as her endowment. How will this affect the new Slutsky equation, if at all?

(9)_____

_____

_____

_____

_____

5.3. [Related to text problem 5.5.] An Income Expansion Path for X and Y is depicted in the following diagram.

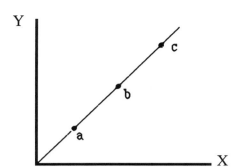

Consider the points labelled **a, b,** and **c**. What must be true of MRS_{XY} at these points? (1)_____

_____Of

course this particular expansion path was drawn for a particular price ratio. Suppose the price of Y increased relative to X. Would the new expansion path lie above or below the old one? (2)_____ Explain why the two expansion paths could not cross. (3)_____

_____

_____

_____ Is this new expansion path necessarily a straight line? (4)_____ If it is a straight line, what must be true of MRS_{XY} at all points on it? (5)_____

_____

_____ If the expansion paths for all price ratios are linear (i.e., straight lines), the consumers preferences are said to be "homothetic." One way to check for homotheticity is to determine whether MRS_{XY} depends on just the ratio Y/X, and not the levels of X and Y. Since this ratio is constant along a ray from the origin (the ratio is the slope of the line), if MRS_{XY} only depends on the ratio Y/X, it must be constant along any ray from the origin. Is the utility function $U = X^a Y^{1-a}$ homothetic? (6)_____

_____

5.4. Annie O'Brand lives in a town with two gas stations—Mobil and Gulf. She always buys her gas at the station with the lowest price.

a. Graph Annie's utility maximization problem below, depicting a situation where she has $10.00 to spend on gas, the price of Gulf is $2.00 per gallon, and the price of Mobil is just $1.00

per gallon. Show both her budget constraint and the indifference curve that touches it.

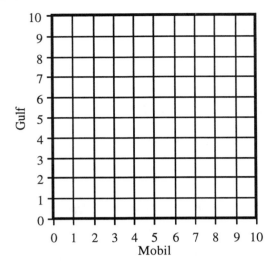

b. Trace out the change in Annie's choice as the price of Mobil increases toward and then beyond $2.00 per gallon; that is, draw in her Price Expansion Path. Then sketch her demand curve for Mobil on the graph below.

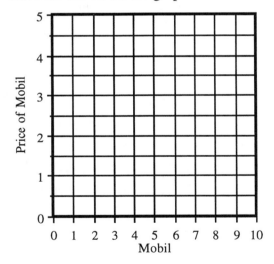

c. How much Mobil would Annie purchase if the $P_{Mobil} = \$1.50$ and she is compensated just enough so that she can get the same utility from gasoline consumption as when the price was $1.00 and she spent $10.00 on gasoline? Assume that she does not change her consumption of goods other than gasoline.

_____ Draw the compensated demand curve that passes through her ordinary demand curve at $P_{Mobil} = \$1.00$.

d. Describe the compensated demand curve that goes through the point on Annie's ordinary demand function where P_{Mobil} = $2.00. _____

_____

_____

5.5. [Related to text problem 5.2.] When Hafta Match buys a new pair of shoes (S), she always buys a new handbag (H) of the same color.

a. Sketch Hafta's utility maximization on the diagram below, assuming that she has $100 to spend on shoes and handbags, P_S = $30, and P_H = $20.

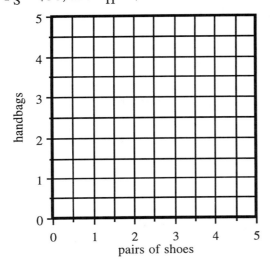

b. On the diagram above, trace out her choice of S and H as P_S increases if she continues to spend $100 on these two items. Assume that these items are divisible. Draw her demand curve for shoes in the diagram below.

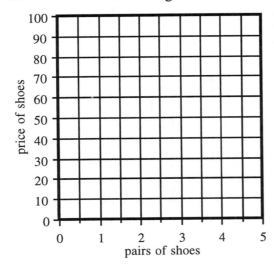

c. If P_S increases to \$40 but Hafta is compensated so that she can attain the same utility level as in **a**, how many pairs of shoes will she purchase? Assume that she does not change her consumption of goods other than shoes and handbags.

_____ Add the compensated demand curve that goes through the ordinary demand curve at $P_S =$ \$40 to the graph in **b**.

5.6. Noah Fect has the following utility function for beer (B) and soft drinks (S).

$$U = S + \ln(B)$$

a. Find Noah's MRS_{BS}.

b. Find Noah's demand function for beer.

c. Suppose that Noah has \$6.00 to spend on beer and soft drinks, $P_B =$ \$1.00 and $P_S =$ \$2.00. How much of each will he buy? B = (1)_____ S = (2)_____ Draw his utility maximization on the diagram below. Include his budget constraint and the indifference curve that passes through the point at which he maximizes utility.

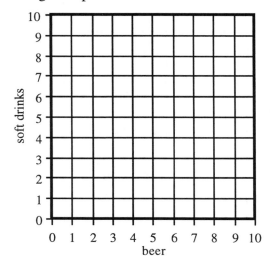

d. Now suppose that Noah has $8.00 to spend on beer and soft drinks. How much of each will he buy? B = (1)_____ S = (2)_____ Add his new utility maximization to the diagram in **c**.

e. Draw Noah's demand curve for beer in the diagram below, assuming that P_S = $2.00 and that he spends $5.00 on these two items.

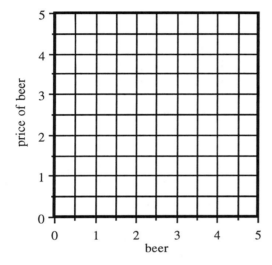

f. Will the demand curve when P_S = $2.00 and he spends $8.00 on these two items be above or below the curve you just drew? Explain.

_____

_____

_____

_____

_____

_____

g. Which is steeper, Noah's ordinary demand curve for beer that you drew in **e**, or the compensated demand curve that passes through his ordinary demand curve at P_B = $1.00? Explain.

_____

_____

_____

_____

_____

_____

5.7. When walnuts are $.20 per ounce and cashews are $.40 per ounce, Hilary Hazelnut buys 30 ounces of walnuts and 20 ounces of cashews, along with many other goods. Sketch her utility maximization problem below.

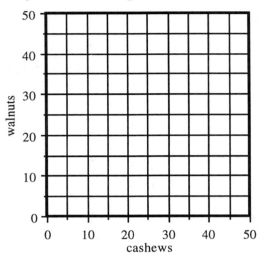

If the price of walnuts increases to $.30 per ounce and the price of cashews falls to $.25 per ounce, while all other prices and Hilary's income remain constant, will Hilary still **be able** to buy the same quantities of walnuts and cashews? (1)_____.
Draw her new budget constraint and indicate the section of the new constraint on which you would expect to find her new choice. Will she still **choose** to buy the same quantities? (2)_____
If not, will she increase or decrease the quantity of walnuts she buys? (3)_____ The quantity of cashews?
(4)_____ Will she be better off or worse off?
(5)_____

5.8. [Refers to text example 5.8.] Recall that Mead N. Taters' expenditure function (Problem 5.1) is

$$E = \frac{P_S^{2/5} P_P^{3/5} U}{.51}$$

Also, recall that if I = $20, P_S = $2.00, and P_P = $.50 he buys 4 pounds of steak, 24 pounds of potatoes and achieves U = 11.72!

a. The government proposes a farm subsidy program that would reduce the price of steak to $1.00 per pound. It also proposes an increase in income tax to pay for the program. Mead carefully examines the new tax schedule and determines that the program will cost him $5.00. Will Mead be willing to give up this amount in order to secure the lower steak price?

[Hint: use his expenditure function to determine how much income he would need to maintain his current utility level at the new price. Compare the difference between this amount and his current expenditure ($20.00) to the tax ($5.00).]
(1)_____ What is the largest tax that Mead would be willing to pay? (2)_____.

b. Sections of Mead's compensated and ordinary demand curves for steak are drawn below. You may recognize the diagram as a blow-up of a graph you drew in part **f** of Problem 5.1. Recall that both curves are drawn with $P_P = \$.50$, that $I = \$20.00$ along the ordinary demand curve, and that $U = 11.72$ along the compensated demand curve.

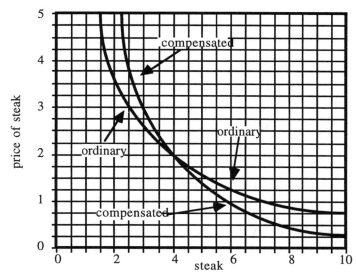

Outline the area in the graph that represents the consumer surplus Mead will gain if the price of steak is reduced from $2.00 to $1.00. Count the squares in this area. (1)_____.
Eight squares have an area of (2)$_____. Hence, the consumer surplus is (3)$_____. Compare this to

answer (2) in part **a.** What do you find? Why?

(4)_____

_____

_____

_____

_____

_____

_____ If

Mead had used his ordinary demand curve to compute his consumer surplus, would he have made the same decision about the farm subsidy program? Why or why not?

(5)_____

_____

_____

_____

_____

_____

c.   Now imagine a different scenario. As before $P_P = \$.50$ and I = $20.00. However, the original price of steak is $1.00 per pound. In order to provide income tax relief, the government proposes a $1.00 per pound tax on steak. Assuming that the full price of steak to Mead will become $2.00, by how much would Mead's income tax have to fall if he is to favor the new tax? [Hint: you may use the expenditure function to get your answer, but beware that his original utility level is different than in the previous scenario.] (1) $_____

The following graph is a repetition of the previous graph. Indicate on this graph the area that represents his loss in consumer surplus. Before you can do so, you will have to sketch a new compensated demand curve. You do not need to draw it exactly, but it should be consistent with the fact that S is a normal good for Mead. How does this measure of consumer surplus compare to what you would get if you used the original compensated demand curve? (2)_____

_____ The ordinary

demand curve? (3)_____

_____

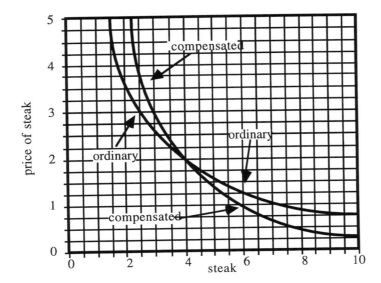

CHAPTER 6

DEMAND RELATIONSHIPS AMONG GOODS

effects on demand of a change in the price of another good (cross-price effects):

$$\frac{\partial X}{\partial P_Y} = \frac{\partial X}{\partial P_Y}\bigg|_{U=constant} - Y\frac{\partial X}{\partial I}$$

substitution and income effects

classification of pairs of goods:

	substitutes	complements
gross	$\frac{\partial X_i}{\partial P_j} > 0$	$\frac{\partial X_i}{\partial P_j} < 0$
net	$\frac{\partial X_i}{\partial P_j}\bigg|_{U=constant} > 0$	$\frac{\partial X_i}{\partial P_j}\bigg|_{U=constant} < 0$

symmetry of cross-price substitution effects

composite commodity theorem

implicit prices of attributes

(Numbers in brackets at the beginning of problems below refer to related examples and problems in the text.)

6.1. [Related to text example 6.1 and problem 6.1.] Recall Mead N. Taters' demand functions for steak and potatoes:

$$S = \frac{.4\,I}{P_S} \quad and \quad P = \frac{.6\,I}{P_P}$$

a. Is steak a **gross** complement or gross substitute for potatoes? Or is it neutral? (1)_____ Are potatoes a **gross** complement or gross substitute for steak? Or are they neutral? (2)_____ Are steak and potatoes **net** complements, substitutes, or neutral? Explain. [Hint: in Chapter 5 you found that S is a normal good for Mead. What does this imply for the direction of the income effect on the demand for S from an increase in P_P? Given this effect and your answer to (1), what does this imply for the sign of the substitution effect on demand for S of an increase in P_P?]

(3)_____

_____

_____

_____

_____

b. Mead's utility function is a special case of the utility function $U = X^a Y^{1-a}$. What are the demand equations for X and Y corresponding to this more general function?

X = (1)_____   Y = (2)_____

Do your answers to (1) through (3) of **a** apply to this more general utility function? (3)_____

c. Do your answers to (1) through (3) of **a** apply to any "well-behaved" utility function of two goods? Why or why not?

(1)_____

_____

_____

(2)_____

_____

_____

(3)_____

_____

_____

Would any of the above answers change if there were other goods in the utility function? (4)_____

_____

_____

_____

d. In Chapter 5 you found Mead's compensated demand functions for S and P:

$$S^* = \frac{.4}{.51}\left(\frac{P_P}{P_S}\right)^{3/5} U \quad \text{and} \quad P^* = \frac{.6}{.51}\left(\frac{P_S}{P_P}\right)^{2/5} U$$

Use these to find the cross-price substitution effects:

$$\left.\frac{\partial S}{\partial P_P}\right|_{U=\text{constant}} = (1)\underline{\hspace{6cm}}$$

$$\left.\frac{\partial P}{\partial P_S}\right|_{U=\text{constant}} = (2)\underline{\hspace{6cm}}$$

Now, compare (1) and (2). What do you find?

(3)_____

e. Is your result in **d** a special feature of Mead's utility function, or would the same result be obtained for any well-behaved utility function? Why or why not? _____

_____

_____

_____

6.2. [Related to text problem 6.2.] If Sophie Stickate had more income she would drink less beer and more wine. While she views beer and wine as net substitutes, when the price of beer goes up, she buys less wine. On the other hand, if the price of wine goes up, she buys more beer. That is, wine is a gross

(1)_____ for beer, but beer is a gross

(2)_____ for wine. Explain how this can happen.

(3)_____

_____

_____

_____

_____

_____

_____

6.3. [Related to text problems 6.3 and 6.4.] Remember Hafta Match from Problem 5.5? She always buys a handbag (H) when she buys a pair of shoes (S), no matter what the prices of H and S happen to be. In that problem you examined how her demand for S responded to an increase in P_S.

a. If H and S are the only two goods in her utility function, how will her demand for H respond to an increase in P_S?

(1)_____

_____ How will her demand for

H respond to an increase in P_S if she is compensated so that she can attain the same level of utility as before the price increase? (2)_____

_____ For the remainder of this problem, you will examine her behavior when she spends her income on these goods plus a third good, clothes (C). Her utility function is:

$$U = C[\min(H, S)]$$

That is, to get her utility find the minimum of H and S and then multiply it by C. Note that in **a** and in Problem 5.5 we implicitly used $U = \min(H, S)$ as her utility function. Her budget constraint is:

$$P_H H + P_S S + P_C C \leq I$$

b. At her utility maximum point, what will the relationship between H and S be? Explain.

(1)_____

_____

_____

Now, use this relationship to reduce her new utility function to a function of C and H only.

U = (2)_____

Also use this relationship to eliminate S from her budget constraint.

(3)_____ $\leq I$

Notice that the price of H in this budget constraint is really $P_H + P_S$, since she has to buy a pair of shoes in order to get any enjoyment out of a new handbag. Her demand functions for H and C can be found by maximizing your answer to (2) subject to the budget constraint you found for (3). Confirm that they are:

$$H = .5I/(P_H + P_S) \qquad C = .5I/P_C$$

What is her demand function for shoes?

S = (4)_____

c. Find

$$\frac{\partial H}{\partial I} = (1)\underline{\hspace{3cm}} \qquad \frac{\partial H}{\partial P_S} = (2)\underline{\hspace{3cm}}$$

$$\frac{\partial H}{\partial P_S}\bigg|_{U = constant} = (3)\underline{\hspace{5cm}}$$

$$\frac{\partial H}{\partial P_C} = (4)\underline{\hspace{4cm}}$$

$$\frac{\partial H}{\partial P_C}\bigg|_{U = constant} = (5)\underline{\hspace{5cm}}$$

Based on the signs of these derivatives, are handbags gross substitutes or complements for shoes? (6)\underline{\hspace{3cm}} Net substitutes or complements for shoes? (7)\underline{\hspace{3cm}} Gross substitutes or complements for other clothes? (8)\underline{\hspace{3cm}} Net substitutes or complements for other clothes? (9)\underline{\hspace{3cm}} How does the compensated effect of an increase in P_S on Hafta's demand for H differ from what it would be if H and S were the only goods in her utility function? (10)\underline{\hspace{5cm}}

\underline{\hspace{9cm}}

\underline{\hspace{9cm}}

6.4. In Problem 5.2 you found the following "generalized" Slutsky equation for a change in the good's own price when the consumer originally had endowments of X^* and Y^*

$$\frac{\partial X}{\partial P_X} = \frac{\partial X}{\partial P_X}\bigg|_{U = constant} - (X - X^*)\frac{\partial X}{\partial I^*}$$

What is the corresponding generalization of the cross-price Slutsky equation? If the answer is not obvious, redo part **d** of Problem 5.2, replacing P_X wherever it appears with P_Y.

6.5. Remember Annie O'Brand from Problem 5.4? The demand function you drew for the case when she spends $10.00 on gas and $P_{Gulf} = \$2.00$ should look like the one drawn below,

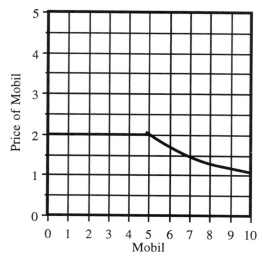

Illustrate how the demand curve would shift if P_{Gulf} increased to $3.00.

6.6. [Related to text problems 6.5 and 6.6.] Maple syrup comes in many grades. Suppose that grade A syrup sells for P_A dollars per gallon in Vermont—a major syrup producing state—and grade B sells for P_B dollars per gallon, which is less than P_A. In Florida, transportation costs of T dollars per gallon are added to the Vermont prices of both grades. Consider two consumers, one in Florida and one in Vermont, that have identical incomes and tastes. Which consumer will consume more maple syrup? [Hint: think of maple syrup as a composite commodity. For which consumer is the price of the composite commodity higher?]

(1)_____ Will the percentage of syrup consumed that is grade A be higher for the Florida consumer or the Vermont consumer? [Hint: examine the relative prices of the two grades in the two states.]

(2)_____ In general, how would you expect both the quantity and average quality of a good consumed to be related to the cost of transporting the good from the place of production to the place of consumption? Explain.

(3)_____

_____

_____

Harcourt Brace & Company

6.7. Suppose that barley (B) costs $1.00 per pound and that each pound yields 160 calories and 160 vitamins, and rice (R) also costs $1.00 per pound and yields 200 calories and 100 vitamins per pound.

a. On the graph below, find the point that represents the number of calories and vitamins purchased if an individual spends $100 on barley, and label it B*. Do the same for rice, labelling the point R*. Finally, draw in the line that represents the combinations of calories and vitamins that an individual can buy with $100 if rice and barley are the only goods purchased.

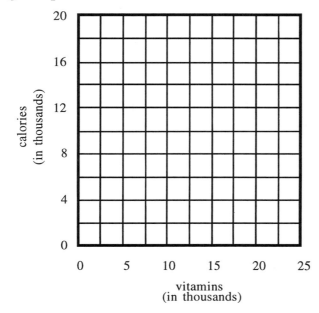

b. What is the implicit price of vitamins relative to the implicit price of calories? That is, suppose the consumer wants to buy one more unit of vitamins. How many calories must the consumer give up (holding expenditure constant)? [Hint: what is the slope of the line you drew in part **a**?]

c. Let P_C represent the implicit price of calories and P_V represent the implicit price of vitamins. Since a pound of barley costs $1.00 and yields 160 calories and 160 vitamins, we know that

_____ P_C + _____ P_V = 1.00

Harcourt Brace & Company

Now, use this equation and the implicit price ratio you found in part **b** to find P_C and P_V.

d. Let C represent calories and V represent vitamins, and suppose that a consumer has the utility function

$$U = C^{.7}V^{.3}$$

If the consumer has $100 to spend on rice and barley, how many calories and vitamins will she buy?

Indicate her choice on the graph in part **a** and label it A. What amounts of rice and barley must she purchase in order to get the required amounts of calories and vitamins? [Hint: let R* and B* represent the amounts you are trying to find. Set up an equation that requires the number of calories in R* and B* combined to be equal to the amount she chose. Set up a second equation for vitamins. Solve the two equations for R* and B*.]

e. Now, suppose that wheat costs $2.00 per pound and yields 300 calories and 500 vitamins per pound. On the graph in part **a**, indicate the calories and vitamins that would be obtained by spending $100 on wheat with W*. Add the line showing combinations of calories and vitamins that can be obtained by purchasing wheat and barley. Add the same line for wheat and rice. Explain why no consumer will want to purchase barley when the prices of the three grains are those given in the problem.

_____

_____

_____

_____

_____

CHAPTER 7

MARKET DEMAND AND ELASTICITY

price taker

KEY CONCEPTS

aggregation of individual demands to market demand:

horizontal sum

$$X_i = \sum_{j=1}^{m} X_{ij} = D_i(P_1, \ldots, P_n, I_1, \ldots, I_m)$$

where $\sum_{j=1}^{m} X_{ij} = D_{i1}(P_1, \ldots, P_n, I_1) + \ldots + X_{im}(P_1, \ldots, P_n, I_m)$

elasticity:

for $B = f(A \ldots)$, $\quad e_{B,A} = \dfrac{\text{percentage change in B}}{\text{percentage change in A}} = \dfrac{\partial A}{\partial B} \times \dfrac{A}{B}$

own price elasticity:

$$e_{PQ,P} = \frac{\partial PQ}{\partial P} \times \frac{P}{QP} = 1 + e_{Q,P}$$

own price elasticity and expenditure:

$$e_{PQ,P} = \frac{\partial PQ}{\partial P} \times \frac{P}{QP} = 1 + e_{Q,P}$$

elastic vs. inelastic demand

income elasticity:

$$e_{Q,I} = \frac{\partial Q}{\partial I} \times \frac{I}{Q}$$

luxuries vs. necessities

cross price elasticity:

$$e_{Q,I} = \frac{\partial Q}{\partial I} \times \frac{I}{Q}$$

Harcourt Brace & Company

relationships among elasticities (case of 2 goods, X and Y):

$$s_X e_{X,I} + s_Y e_{Y,I} = 1$$

$$e_{X,P_X} + e_{X,P_Y} + e_{X,I} = 0$$

substitution elasticities (own price and cross price):

$$e_{X,P_X}^s = \frac{\partial X}{\partial P_X} \frac{P_X}{X}\bigg|_{U = constant} \qquad e_{X,P_Y}^s = \frac{\partial X}{\partial P_Y} \frac{P_Y}{X}\bigg|_{U = constant}$$

Slutsky equations in elasticity form (own price and cross price):

$$e_{X,P_X} = e_{X,P_X}^s - s_X e_{X,I} \qquad e_{X,P_Y} = e_{X,P_Y}^s - s_Y e_{X,I}$$

identification problem

PROBLEMS

(Numbers in brackets at the beginning of problems below refer to related examples and problems in the text.)

7.1. [Related to text examples 7.1–7.4, and problems 7.1 and 7.3.] Once de'Leon and his brother Twice live on the island of Yewth. The only foods they consume are mangos, M, and coconuts, C, which they buy on their weekly trip to a neighboring island. Once and Twice have the same individual demand functions for M:

$$M = \frac{P_C I_i}{2P_M^2}$$

where P_C and P_M are the prices of C and M, respectively, and I_i is the individual's income—I_O for Once and I_T for Twice. Their incomes are weekly checks from the government of a large nearby country—compensation for the destruction of their mango and coconut trees by some explorers who were looking for a mythical fountain.

a. Suppose that $P_C = 1$, that Once has an income of 10, and that Twice has an income of 20. [Twice was born before the explorers destroyed the mango trees and Once was born later, but before the destruction of the coconut trees.] On the first two diagrams below, draw the mango demand curves for Once and Twice. Then add them horizontally to get their combined "market" demand curves.

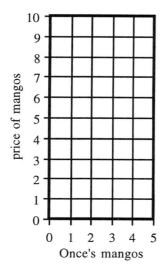

Once's mangos

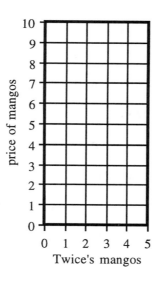

Twice's mangos

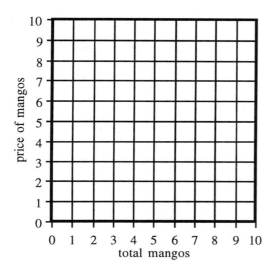

total mangos

Now, write the market demand function for M as a function of P_M, P_C, and the sum of the incomes of Once and Twice: I = I_O + I_T.

M = (1)_____.

Confirm that this is the equation depicted in the market graph when P_C = 1, I_O = 10, and I_T = 20. Find each of the following:

e_{M,P_M} = (2)_____

e_{M,P_C} = (3)_____

$e_{M,I}$ = (4)_____

Harcourt Brace & Company

Do any of these elasticities depend on P_M, P_C, I_O, I_T, or I?

(5)_____ If the price of mangos falls by 50%, by what percentage will the total quantity demanded increase? (6)_____% If the original price of mangos is $1.00, how many mangos does this represent? (7)_____ If the government imposes a sales tax of 5% on coconuts, by what percentage will the total quantity of mangos demanded change?

(8)_____% If the government doubles Once's income, leaving Twice's income unchanged, by what percentage will the total quantity of mangos demanded change? (9)_____% If the government redistributes income so that both Once and Twice get $15, by what percentage will the total quantity of mangos demanded change? (10)_____%

b. Now, suppose that Twice has the following demand function:

$$M = \frac{P_C I_i}{4P_M^2}$$

Once's demand function is unchanged. Again, graph the individual and market demand functions when $P_C = 1$, $I_O = 10$, and $I_T = 20$.

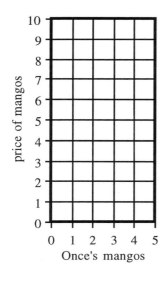

Once's mangos

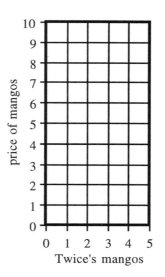

Twice's mangos

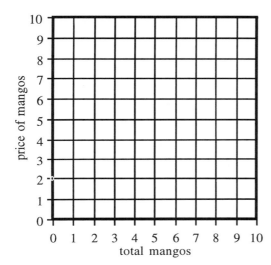

total mangos

Now, write market demand as a function of P_M, P_C, I_O, and I_T.

M = (1)_____

If possible, find each of the following:

e_{M,P_M} = (2)_____

e_{M,P_C} = (3)_____

$e_{M,I}$ = (4)_____

If you could not find any of the above, explain why.

(5)_____

_____

Harcourt Brace & Company

Now, suppose that the government redistributes income, giving Once and Twice each $15.00. Will this change the market demand curve? Explain. (6)_____

_____

_____

_____

If your answer is yes, sketch the new demand curve on the graph above and find the change in quantity demanded if P_M = $1.00. ΔM = (7)_____.

7.2. [Related to text problem 7.2.] Consider the following demand curve for boxes of paper clips per capita, C, where P_C is the price per box, P_S is the price of staples per box, and I is per capita income:

$$C = 100 - \frac{1000\, P_C}{2I + 5P_S}$$

a. If I = 10, P_S = 1, and P_C =.5, what will the quantity demanded of C be? (1)_____ What will quantity demanded be if I = 20, P_S = 2 and P_C = 1? (2)_____ Is this demand function homogeneous of degree zero in P_C, P_S, and I? Explain. (3)_____

_____

_____

_____

b. In the first column below write down the expressions for the elasticities indicated. In the second column put down their respective values whern P_C = $.50, P_S = $1.00, and I = 10.

e_{C,P_C}= (1)_____   (4)_____

e_{C,P_S}= (2)_____   (5)_____

$e_{C,I}$= (3)_____   (6)_____

c. As in **b**, assume P_S = $1.00 and I = 10, so C = 100 − 40 P_C. Find the value of P_C for which e_{C,P_C} = −1. [Hint: first, write down the general expression for this elasticity from **b.** Then substitute for P_S, I, and C; the elasticity will then be a function of P_C alone. Now, equate this expression to −1 and solve for P_C.]

Harcourt Brace & Company

$P_C = (1)$_____

Suppose that the demand function was $C = a - bP_C$. In terms of a and b, what value of P_C would yield $e_{C,P_C} = -1$?

$P_C = (2)$_____

7.3. [Related to text problem 7.5.] In the graph below, curve dd is a demand curve.

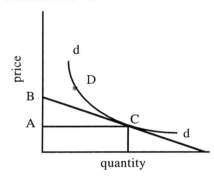

Consider the ratio AC/AB. In relation to the demand curve, what does this ratio represent? [Hint:remember, the curve graphed is actually the inverse of the demand function.]

(1)_____

_____

Now, consider the ratio A0/AC. In terms of the price and quantity of the good at point C, what does the ratio represent?

(2)_____

What does the product (AC/AB)(A0/AC) = A0/AB represent?

(3)_____ Is this demand curve elastic

or inelastic at point C? (4)_____

At point D? (5)_____ Find a point

on the demand curve where the elasticity is approximately equal to −1 and label it with an X. Finally, briefly discuss the following quotation:

"To determine whether a demand curve is elastic, examine its slope. Steep curves are inelastic, while curves that are not very steep are elastic."

(6)_____

_____

_____

Harcourt Brace & Company

7.4. [Related to text example 7.4.] Part **a** of this problem gives you practice in finding logarithmic derivatives. Part **b** reviews the connection between logarithmic derivatives and elasticities. This connection is utilized in parts **c** and **d**.

a. Consider the function $\ln(y) = a + b\ln(x) + c\,[\ln(x)]^2$, where a, b, and c are constants. Define $y^* = \ln(y)$ and $x^* = \ln(x)$, and rewrite the function as $y^* = a + bx^* + cx^{*2}$. The derivative of y^* with respect to x^* is $dy^*/dx^* = b + 2cx^* = b + 2c\ln(x)$. This is called the logarithmic derivative of this function. It is just the derivative of $\ln(y)$ with respect to $\ln(x)$: $d[\ln(y)]/d[\ln(x)] = dy^*/dx^*$. Logarithmic derivatives of many functions can be found by first converting the function to the form $\ln(y) = f[\ln(x)]$, or $y^* = f(x^*)$. Then take the derivative of y^* with respect to x^*. Find the logarithmic derivatives of the following functions:

(i) $\ln(y) = [2\ln(x) + 5]^2$

(ii) $y = 5x^{.5}$

(iii) $y = e^{3 + 2\ln(x) + 4\,[\ln(x)]^2}$

The same approach can be used to find partial logarithmic derivatives for functions of two or more variables. Write each of the following functions in the form $\ln(y) = f[\ln(x), \ln(z)]$ and find both $\partial[\ln(y)]/\partial[\ln(x)]$ and $\partial[\ln(y)]/\partial[\ln(z)]$:

(iv) $\ln(y) = a + b\ln(x) + c\ln(z) + d\ln(x)\ln(z)$, where a, b, c, and d are constants.

(v) $y = 3\,x^2\,z^5$

(vi) $y = 3\,x^4 e^{\left[1 + \ln(x) + 2\ln(z) - 5\ln(x)\ln(z)\right]}$

Harcourt Brace & Company

(vii) $y = 3 x^2 / z^5$

b. Consider the general function $y = f(x)$. Write the elasticity of y with respect to x, in terms of x, y, and the derivative dy/dx:

$e_{y,x} = $ (1)_____. Next,

differentiate ln(y): $d[\ln(y)] = $ (2)_____dy . In words, this last result says that if y changes by the small amount dy, the change in the logarithm of y will be the

percentage change in y. Similarly, $d[\ln(x)] = $

(3)_____dx. Now, use the last two answers to

write the ratio $d[\ln(y)]/d[\ln(x)]$ as a function of x, y, and

dy/dx:

$$\frac{d[\ln(y)]}{d[\ln(x)]} = (4)_____$$

Now, compare (4) and (1). If you have answered correctly, you should find that they are the same. Since the left-hand side of (4) is the logarithmic derivate, the result in words is that the elasticity of y with respect to x is equal to the logarithmic derivative of y with respect to x. This result extends straightforwardly to functions of several variables:

If $y = f(x, z)$, $e_{y,x} = \dfrac{\partial[\ln(y)]}{\partial[\ln(x)]}$ and $e_{y,z} = \dfrac{\partial[\ln(y)]}{\partial[\ln(z)]}$.

c. For the following functions, some of the own-price, cross-price and income elasticities are constant. That is, they don't depend on the prices, income, or the quantity demanded. Determine which elasticities are constant for each function and, if an elasticity is constant, state its value.

(i) (Illustration) $X = \dfrac{P_Y + I}{P_X}$

Answer: $X = P_X^{-1} (P_Y + I)$, so $\ln(X) = - \ln(P_X) + \ln(P_Y + I)$. We can easily find the partial logarithmic derivative of X with respect to P_X: $\partial[\ln(X)]/\partial[\ln(P_X)] = -1 = e_{X,P_X}$. However,

Harcourt Brace & Company

we can't easily find the partial logarithmic derivative of X with respect to either P_Y or I. We know that whatever the cross-price and income elasticities are, they are not constant because we could not write the function in the form $\ln(X) = a + b \ln(P_X) + c \ln(P_Y) + d \ln(I)$, where a, b, c, and d are constants. [To confirm that these elasticities are not constant, use the formula $e_{y,x} = (\partial y/\partial x)(x/y)$ to find expressions for them.]

(ii) $X = \dfrac{a\,I}{P_X}$ where $0 < a < 1$

(iii) $X = aP_X^{\,b} P_Y^{\,c} I^{\,d}$ where a, b, c, and d are constants

(iv) $X = 10\,P_Y\,I/(5 + P_X)$

Now that you have had some practice, can you spot the constant elasticities for the next function without finding logarithmic derivatives?

(v) $X = \sqrt{\dfrac{I + P_Y}{P_X}}$

d. In this part, logarithmic derivatives will be used to find the relationships between demand and expenditure elasticities.

    (i) (Illustration) Let total expenditure on a good be represented by $E = PQ$, where P is the good's price and Q is the quantity purchased. Show that the elasticity of E with respect to P equals one plus the own-price elasticity of demand.

        Answer: $\ln(E) = \ln(P) + \ln(Q)$. Hence

$$e_{E,P} = \frac{\partial[\ln(E)]}{\partial[\ln(P)]} = \frac{\partial[\ln(P)]}{\partial[\ln(P)]} + \frac{\partial[\ln(Q)]}{\partial[\ln(P)]} = 1 + e_{Q,P}$$

    Now, use the answer to determine conditions under which the expenditure elasticity is positive, negative, and zero.

    (ii) Show that $e_{E,P'} = e_{Q,P'}$ and $e_{E,I} = e_{Q,I}$, where P' is the price of another good and I is income.

7.5. Suppose that per capita demand for margarine in a particular year depends only on its price, P, according to:

$$Q = aP^b$$

where a is some unknown positive number and b is some unknown negative number.

a. You have data for two years:

	Q	P
year 1	100	$1.00
year 2	95	$1.10

Find values for the constants, a and b, that are consistent with these data. [Hint: $\ln(Q) = a + b \ln(P)$. Convert the data to logarithms, then use it to set up two equations in two unknowns—a and b. Now solve the equations for a and b.]

What is $e_{Q,P}$?

b. Now, suppose instead that per capita demand is determined by:

$$Q = aP^b I^c$$

where I is per capita income, in thousands of dollars. Suppose also that you observe Q, P, and I for 3 years:

	Q	P	I
year 1	100.00	$1.00	10.00
year 2	95.00	$1.10	10.45
year 3	95.65	$1.15	11.00

Set up a system of 3 equations that you could solve for a, b, and c. You don't need to solve them, but you should be able to demonstrate that (a = 10, b = −1, c = 1) solves the system.

Harcourt Brace & Company

What is $e_{Q,P}$? _____ Compare this to the elasticity you found in **a** and explain why they are different—even though the data for Q and P in years 1 and 2 are the same in both parts! _____

_____

_____

_____

_____

_____

_____

7.6. An economist estimates the following demand function for beef:

$$\ln(Q) = -8.30 - .68\ln(P_{beef}) + .35\ln(P_{poultry}) + .49\ln(P_{pork}) + 1.21\ln(I)$$

where Q is per capita consumption of beef and I is per capita income.

a. What is the own-price elasticity of demand for beef?

(1)_____ The cross-price elasticity with respect

to poultry? (2)_____ Pork? (3)_____.

Is demand for beef elastic or inelastic (4)_____

If the price of beef increased, would expenditures on beef

increase or decline? (5)_____ Is beef a gross

substitute or complement for poultry? (6)_____

Pork? (7)_____ Is beef a normal

good? (8)_____.

b. The economist also found that the average consumer spends about one percent of income on beef and half a percent each on poultry and pork. What is the compensated own-price elasticity of demand for beef? [Hint: use the elasticity version of the Slutsky equation.]

(1)_____ The

compensated cross-price elasticity with respect to poultry?

(2)_____ Pork?

(3)_____

Are the differences between the compensated and

uncompensated elasticities large? Why or why not?

(4)_____

_____

c. Is this demand function homogeneous of degree zero in
prices and income? Explain. [Hint: multiply the three
prices and I by a constant, k. What happens to quantity
demanded?]_____

_____

_____

_____

d. Suppose that each of the three prices and per capita income
are redefined to be nominal prices and income divided by the
Consumer Price Index. Would this function then be
homogeneous of degree zero in prices—including prices of
all other goods—and income? Explain.

_____

_____

_____

_____

_____

_____

7.7. [Related to text problem 7.10.] The elasticity of substitution, σ,
is a measure of the curvature of an indifference curve. It is
defined by:

$$\sigma = \left(\frac{d(Y / X)}{dMRS_{xy}} \times \frac{MRS_{xy}}{Y / X} \right) = \left(\frac{dMRS_{xy}}{d(Y / X)} \times \frac{Y / X}{MRS_{XY}} \right)^{-1}$$

a. In general, an elasticity is the "percent change in *variable
one* per percent change in *variable two*." What are *variable
one* and *variable two* in this case? _____

_____

_____

_____

b. Describe, in non-technical language, how the elasticity of substitution is related to the curvature of an indifference curve._____

_____

_____

_____

_____

c. In Problem 3.5 you found the following expression for the marginal rate of substitution for the CES utility function:

$$MRS_{XY} = \frac{\alpha}{\beta}\left(\frac{X}{Y}\right)^{\delta-1}$$

Find σ for this function. [Hint: use the second version of the definition of MRS_{XY}. Your answer should depend on δ only.]

d. What is the justification of the name for the Constant Elasticity of Substitution (CES) utility function?

_____

_____

_____

[Note: the CES is the only function that has this property.]

e. What is the elasticity of substitution for the Cobb-Douglas utility function? [Hint: remember that the Cobb-Douglas is a special case of the CES.]

f. What is the limit of σ as δ approaches 1? To what special case does this correspond?

_____

_____

g. What is the limit of σ as δ approaches $-\infty$? To what special case does this correspond?

_____

_____

CHAPTER 8

RISK AVERSION

probability:

$$0 \leq \pi_i \leq 1$$

$$\sum_{i=1}^{n} \pi_i = 1$$

expected value:

$$E(X) = \sum_{i=1}^{n} \pi_i X_i$$

fair games:

$$E(X) = 0$$

St. Petersburg Paradox

$$\text{expected utility} = \sum_{i=1}^{n} \pi_i U(X_i)$$

Von Neumann-Morganstern utility index

risk aversion:

$$U''(W) < 0$$

Pratt's measure:

$$r(W) = -U''(W)/U'(W)$$

relative measure:

$$rr(W) = -WU''(W)/U'(W)$$

maximum insurance (risk) premium of a fair bet, p:

$$E[U(W + h)] = U(W - p)$$

$$p \approx k\, r(W) \text{ where } k = E(h^2)/2$$

KEY CONCEPTS

Harcourt Brace & Company

state preference approach to choice under uncertainty:

states of the world

contingent commodity

independence of utility from states of the world

fair markets for contingent commodities

PROBLEMS

(Numbers in brackets at the beginning of problems below refer to related examples and problems in the text.)

8.1. [Related to text problems 8.3 and 8.5.] Suppose that you were offered the chance to play one of the following three games. You choose which one. You can only play once and you must pay $1000 before you can play.

Game A: The chance you will win is 50%. If you win you will receive $1100, for a net gain of $100. If you lose, you get back $900, for a net loss of $100.

Game B: The chance you will win is 75%. If you win you will again receive $1100, but if you lose you get only $700 back.

Game C: The chance you will win is 90%. If you win you will again receive $1100, but if you lose you get only $100 back.

a. Compute expected net winnings for each game.

Game A: _____

Game B: _____

Game C: _____

b. If you had to make a choice, which game would you prefer? [There is no correct answer here. Everyone has different preferences!]

c. Molly Malone's utility function is graphed below.

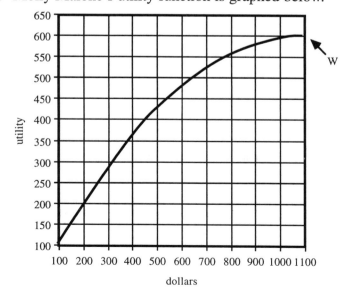

You are to determine which bet Molly would choose if forced to make a choice. Molly is an expected utility maximizer. If she wins the game she will have $1100, no matter which bet it is. Her utility, read off the graph, will be 600. The point on the graph that corresponds to this outcome is (1100, 600), which has been labeled with a W. Find the points on the graph that correspond to losing each of the three games. Label them A, B, and C, respectively. Next, draw a straight line connecting point C with point W. Then draw a vertical line over the amount of money she can expect to have if she plays game C. Find the intersection of these two lines. Molly's expected utility from game C is the vertical coordinate of the point of intersection. What is it? (1)_____ Now find Molly's expected utility from game B. (2)_____ From game C. (3)_____ Which game will she choose? (4)_____ Is Molly risk averse by the Von Neumann-Morganstern definition? Explain. (5)_____

_____

_____

Would any person who is risk averse make the same decision? Explain. (6)_____

_____

_____

What choice would a risk lover make? (7)_____ Recall your choice. Are you a risk averter or a risk lover? (If you found that you made the risk lover's choice but you have always thought of yourself as a risk averter, you might ask yourself whether the expected utility maximization model adequately characterizes your decision making. If not, why not?)

8.2. [Related to text problem 8.6.] Patty Khryminal has $100 dollars to spend on a shopping trip for clothes. To park legally, she would have to feed the meter with $2.10. However, she thinks there is only a 10% chance that she will get caught if she doesn't do it. If she does get caught, she will have to pay a $10.00 fine out of her shopping money. She is trying to decide whether to feed the meter or not. Patty is an expected utility maximizer. Her utility function is:

$$U = \log(W)$$

where W is the money she will be able to spend on clothes. Use base 10 logs in your computations and report answers to 4 decimal places in order to assure accuracy of subsequent results.

a. If Patty feeds the meter, what will her utility be?

b. If Patty does not feed the meter, how much money can she expect to have for other things? E(W) = (1)_____ If she had this amount with certainty, what would her utility be? (2)_____ What will her actual utility be if she doesn't get caught? (3)_____ If she does get caught? (4)_____ What is her expected utility? (5)_____ Compare your answer to (5) with your answer to (2). Which is larger? (6)_____ Why? (7)_____

_____

_____

_____

_____

Will Patty feed the meter? [Hint: compare your answer to (5) with your answer in **a**.] (8)_____

c. The mayor of Megalopolis is considering two proposals aimed at reducing the type of behavior that Patty exhibits. The first proposal would increase the fine for a violation to $20.00. If this proposal is adopted, how much money can Patty expect to spend on clothes the next time she brings $100 on a shopping trip, assuming that she doesn't feed the meter? (1)_____ What will her expected utility be? (2)_____ Will she change her behavior? (3)_____ The second proposal would increase the number of meter readers working the area by enough to increase the probability that a violator will be caught to .2. If this proposal is adopted, how much money can Patty expect to spend on clothes the next time she brings $100 on a shopping trip, assuming that she doesn't feed the meter? (4)_____ What

Harcourt Brace & Company

will her expected utility be? Will she change her behavior? (5)_____ Which proposal would you advise the mayor to adopt? (6)_____ Would your answer be changed or reinforced by the fact that the city will have to increase its meter reader budget in order to adopt the second proposal, whereas the first proposal can be implemented without cost? (7)_____

d. The utility function of another shopper with $100 to spend is depicted below. For this shopper you are to consider the following more extreme versions of the propositions that the mayor is considering.

	fine	chance of being caught	money left if caught	expected money left
Proposition 1	$10	0.5 (i.e., 50%)	(1)_____	(2) _____
Proposition 2	$50	0.1	(3)_____	(4)_____

Fill in the last two columns of the table. Now use the graph to determine the expected value of the shopper's utility under Proposition 1. Some lines have been drawn to help you. (5)_____

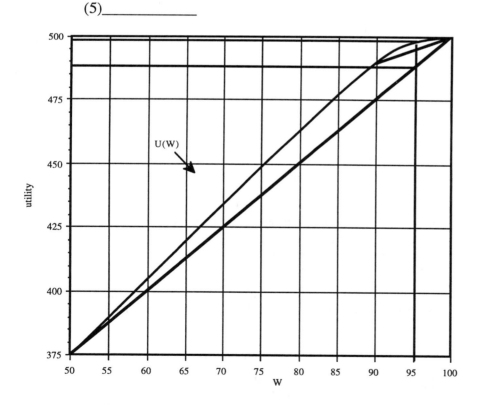

What is this shopper's expected utility under Proposition 2?

(6)_____ Which proposition will be more

effective in encouraging this shopper to feed the meter?

(7)_____ Do you think this result can be

generalized? That is, do you think the proposal that was more

effective in reducing this shopper's expected utility would

also be more effective in reducing the expected utility of

others who don't feed their meters, assuming they are risk

averse? Explain. (8)_____

_____

_____

_____

_____

Finally, can any general conclusions be drawn about the

relative effectiveness of enforcement and punishment in

detering crime? (9)_____

_____

_____

_____

_____

8.3. [Related to text examples 8.2, 8.3, and 8.4 and problem 8.5.] In Japan, golfers who get a "hole-in-one" are expected to give gifts to relatives, fellow workers, and friends. These gifts can cost them the equivalent of thousands of dollars. The cost is so great that there actually exists a market for "hole-in-one" insurance. This problem concerns a particular golfer and his decision about whether to buy such insurance.

Yoshitsugu Kanemoto, who is an expected utility maximizer, has the following utility function for annual income, I (measured in millions of yen):

$$U(I) = \ln(I - 1)$$

His annual income is 3 million yen (equivalent to about $25,000 U.S. at the time of writing). Yoshi figures (correctly) that he has a 1 in 1000 chance of getting a hole-in-one in a particular year. If he gets a hole-in-one, he expects to spend .25 million yen for gifts.

Harcourt Brace & Company

a. Is Yoshi risk averse? [Hint: find U"(I) and determine its sign.]

b. Compute Yoshi's expected utility. [Find the answer as accurately as your calculator permits—at least to seven decimal places. This is because his income is measured in millions, rather than units.]

c. Compute the maximum annual premium, p, that Yoshi would be willing to pay for an insurance policy that would pay him .25 million yen if he gets a hole-in-one. [Hint: Find the p for which $U(I - p)$ is just equal to the expected utility that you found in **b**. Round your answer to the nearest yen.]

d. If the actual premium charged was actuarially fair, how much would it be? [Hint: how much would the insurance company expect to pay Yoshi in any given year?]

Would Yoshi buy insurance at this price?

e. In fact, the actual premium is 260 yen. Will Yoshi buy the insurance?

f. Suppose that Yoshi's annual income was only 2 million yen, instead of three. What is the maximum premium that he would be willing to pay then?

Would he buy the insurance for 260 yen?

g. You should find that your answers to **e** and **f** are different. If not, you should try to correct your mistake before continuing. Check for rounding errors. The maximum premium in **f** should differ from the maximum premium in **c** by only about 20 yen. To understand the reason for this, find Pratt's measure of risk aversion for Yoshi.

8.4. Dr. Peter Priceless, M.D., trys every procedure available to treat his terminally ill patients, regardless of the cost. After all, it is not possible to place a dollar value on a life—or is it? Peter happens to be an expected utility maximizer. If he lives through the coming year, he expects his utility to be a particular amount, say u*, over the remainder of his life. He also has a utility function, which depends on his wealth, W. Let W* represent the amount of wealth that he would have to have with certainty in order to achieve utility level u*. That is:

$$u^* = U(W^*)$$

Of course, he may not live through the coming year. In fact, he knows that people like himself have a .00025 chance of dying in a year. He also knows that he could reduce this chance to .00020 if he chose to wear his seatbelt. But he chooses not to because it is not "worth the bother" to him. Specifically, he once calculated that it took him 10 seconds to buckle and unbuckle his seatbelt every time he drove his car. He figured that he averages two trips per day in his car, so over a year he would have to spend $2 \times 10 \times 365 = 7300$ seconds, or just over 2 hours, buckling and unbuckling. That would cost him about \$100 since he could be spending that time with patients for \$50 per hour (after expenses). Put another way, this would reduce the wealth he would have left for the remainder of his life by \$100. Using his utility function, he determined that

$$(1 - .00025)\,U(W^*) > (1 - .00020)U(W^* - 100)$$

and thereafter resolved not to wear his seatbelt.

a. Suppose that Peter is risk neutral. This would mean that his utility function is linear. Also suppose that he gets zero utility from zero wealth—the equivalent of being dead. Then his utility function must be of the form:

$$u = bW$$

where b is some positive constant. Use the inequality above to show that Peter's behavior implies that the value he puts on his own life is less than some finite, although large, number. [Hint: just plug the linear utility function into the inequality above, then solve for an upper bound on W*. The solution will not depend on the value of b.]

b. One of Peter's healthy patients, "Pop" Sanford, is a junk dealer who earns just $10.00 per hour. Suppose that Sam is also risk neutral, drives his battered pickup truck twice per day, has the same chance of surviving through the next year, and doesn't use his seatbelt. What maximum bound is Sam implicitly placing on his own life?

c. Suppose that Peter is not risk neutral, as was assumed in **a**, but instead is risk averse. Is the maximum value of his life that is implied by his behavior larger or smaller than you found in **a**? Give an intuitive explanation if you can. If you can't, illustrate by recalculating the maximum under the assumption that his utility function is $u = W^{.5}$.

_____

_____

_____

_____

_____

_____

_____

_____

_____

d. Do you think that a person who fails to wear a seatbelt is revealing something about the value of his or her own life?

(Feel free to criticize the explicit and implicit assumptions of the above analysis.)

_____

_____

_____

_____

_____

_____

_____

_____

8.5. [Related to text example 8.5.] The Mudville Strikers are scheduled to play their archrivals, the Titusville Turkeys, in the finals of the state slow-pitch softball tournament. In the bars of Mudville, the betting is heavy in favor of the Strikers—so heavy that to induce anyone to bet on the Turkeys they must be offered two to one odds. That is, if a bettor bets one dollar on the Turkeys, the bettor will lose the dollar if the Turkeys lose, but will receive two dollars if the Turkeys win.

Ernest Hardsell is an encyclopedia salesman and softball aficionado who has $100 from a successful sale in Mudville burning a hole in his pocket. He enters a Mudville bar and is offered the opportunity to bet.

a. On the diagram below, plot Ernie's budget constraint over the two states of the world—Strikers win and Turkeys win. Assume that he cannot bet more than his $100. Begin by finding the point that represents his outcomes if he doesn't bet. Label this point NB, for no bet. Let W_S represent his wealth if the Strikers win and let W_T represent his wealth if the Turkeys win. Now, fill in the following table:

bet	W_S	W_T
no bet	100	100
$10 on Turkeys	____	____
$20 on Turkeys	____	____
$X on Turkeys	____	____
$10 on Strikers	____	____
$X on Strikers	____	____

Now, plot Ernie's budget constraint.

Harcourt Brace & Company

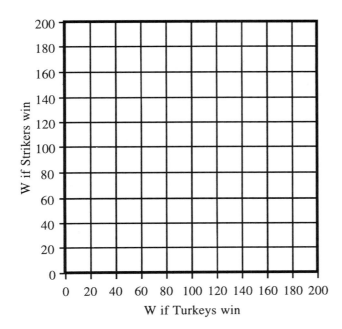

b. Ernie implicitly faces relative prices of the contingent commodities W_S and W_T. Let P_S and P_T represent these prices and let $P_S = 1$. What is P_T? [Hint: how are the relative prices related to the slope of the budget constraint you just drew?]

$P_T = (1)$_____

At these prices, what is the implicit value of Ernie's $100? That is, if he does not bet, he "buys" $100 of each contingent commodity. At the prices you found, what is the implicit cost of this purchase? [Don't be concerned if it does not equal $100. The choice $P_S = 1$ was arbitrary, and it was never said that price was measured in units of dollars.] implicit value = (2)_____ Now write an equation for Ernie's budget constraint in the form $aW_S + bW_T \leq c$, where a, b, and c represent constants that you are to provide values for. (3)_____

c. Ernie's utility function for wealth is $U = \ln(W)$, independent of who wins. Ernie is neither a Turkey or Striker fan and he thinks that the game is a toss-up: each side has a 50% chance of winning. Write his expected utility function below.

expected utility = (1)_____

What values of W_S and W_T will Ernie choose? Maximize his expected utility subject to his budget constraint. [Hint: Ernie's expected utility function should look like the logarithm of a Cobb-Douglas utility function. Would the answer be any different if Ernie maximized the Cobb-Douglas function subject to the same budget constraint?]

W_S = (2)_____

W_T = (3)_____ Plot his choice on the graph and label it **c**. In order to obtain this choice, he must bet (4)_____ dollars on the (5)_____. Explain why Ernie does not bet his full $100 on the Turkeys, even though the odds he is offered (two-to-one) exceed the odds that he believes are correct (one-to-one). (6)_____

_____

_____

_____

_____

_____

_____

d. The next day Ernie happens to be in Titusville. Betting there is heavy on the Turkeys—so heavy that two-to-one odds are offered for bets on the Strikers. Ernie is not able to sell any encyclopedias, so he has no additional money to make bets. However, Ernie's credit is good in Titusville, where he has been a regular at the bars for years. Suppose that he bets $10 on the Strikers. What will his wealth be if the Strikers win, after all of his bets are settled? (1)_____
What will his wealth be if the Strikers lose, after all his bets are settled? (2)_____ Plot this point on the diagram in part **a**. Now, draw his new budget constraint. Note that it will pass through the point you just plotted and the point that represents no additional bet. If $P_S = 1$ still, then P_T = (3)_____. The value of his contingent commodities if he chooses not to place an additional bet is (4)_____. The equation for his new budget constraint is (5)_____.

If he still believes that the actual odds are one-to-one, he will choose W_S = (6)_____ and W_T = (7)_____. Label this bundle in the diagram with **d**. To obtain this bundle of contingent commodities, he should place a bet of (8)_____ dollars on the (9)_____ in Titusville.

e. If Ernie has the opportunity to return to both Mudville and Titusville before the big game and if the odds in both towns remain the same, what bets could he place that would guarantee him post-game wealth of $200? Explain.

_____

_____

_____

_____

_____

_____

_____

_____

_____

CHAPTER 9

THE ECONOMICS OF INFORMATION

information:

    set

    value of

    asymmetry

    as a public good:

        nonrival

        nonexclusive

        patents

insurance:

    incomplete

    moral hazard

    adverse (self) selection

    risk pooling

    separating equilibria

    market signaling

(Numbers in brackets at the beginning of problems below refer to related examples and problems in the text.)

9.1. [Related to text example 9.1 and problem 9.1.] The Pisa Chamber of Commerce (PCC) thinks there is a 50/50 chance that the town's major tourist attraction, the famous Leaning Tower, will fall over sometime in the future unless some restoration is done. They think that if the tower falls, the present value of future profits from tourism for PCC members will fall right along with it—from about 20 trillion lira to 10 trillion. (At the time of writing, a U.S. dollar would purchase about 1,250 lira.)

    a. What does the PCC expect future profits to be if nothing is done?

b. Rafael's Renovations, a major construction firm, claims that it can keep the tower from falling for 6 trillion lira. If the PCC members pay for this project, what will their future profits be after subtracting renovation costs?

If the PCC members are, collectively, expected profit maximizers, will they be willing to pay for restoration?

c. Another firm, Allesandro's Architects (AA), claims that it can determine via substantial research whether the tower will stand even without renovation. Let P be the amount that AA will charge for the study. If the study shows that the tower will fall without renovation, net profits will be $20 - 6 - P = 14 - P$ if the PCC pays for renovation and $10 - P$ if they don't, so they would then choose to renovate. If the study shows that the tower will not fall, there will be no need to renovate and net profit will be $20 - P$. Thus, in terms of P, if the PCC pays for the study their expected profit will be (remember that they still believe there is a 50/50 chance that the tower will fall):

What is the largest amount that the PCC will agree to pay for the study? [Hint: equate the expression you just found to your answer in part **a** and solve for P.]

d. In part **c** it was assumed that AA could accurately predict whether the tower would fall. One of the PCC members is skeptical, so he talks to the past customers of AA and finds that AA's past predictions have been right 90% of the time and wrong 10% of the time. He then convinces the other members to use these percentages as probabilities in reassessing how much they would be willing to pay for the study. If AA predicts "fall," and the PCC members pay for renovations, the PCC's profit will be $14 - P$, but if no renovation is done, their expected profit will be (in terms of P) (1) _____. Therefore, if AA predicts "fall" the PCC (2) (will/will not) pay for renovation. If AA predicts "not fall", and the PCC members pay for renovations, the PCC's profit will again be 14 − P, but if no renovation is done, their expected profit will be (3) _____. Therefore, if AA predicts "not fall" the PCC (4) (will/will not) pay for renovation. Since the PCC currently thinks there is a 50/50 chance that the tower will fall, expected future profit if it pays for the study is (in terms of P) [Hint: you just found expected profits conditional on the predictions made by AA, and the PCC thinks that there is a 50% chance of each prediction being made.](5) _____.

Use your last answer to figure out the most that the PCC will agree to pay for the study. P = (6) _____.

This amount is (7) (less/greater) than the amount found in part **c**. The intuitive reason for this is (8) _____

_____

_____

_____

_____

_____.

9.2. [Related to text example 9.2 and problem 9.2.] An S&L becomes insolvent when its assets (primarily loans it has made and cash reserves) fall below its liabilities (the amount it owes to depositors). By definition, the difference between assets (A) and liabilities (L) is net worth, or equity (E). Equity is the value of the S&L to the owners (stockholders). When A falls below L, which may happen if many borrowers fail to pay back their loans, the S&L becomes worthless. Until 1990, a federal government agency called the Federal Savings and Loan Insurance Corporation (FSLIC) insured deposits at federally chartered S&Ls up to a limit of $100,000 per deposit. S&Ls paid insurance premiums to the FSLIC. If an S&L became insolvent, the FSLIC took it over, sold its assets, and paid off depositors with this money and additional money from a fund that was built up from past premiums. Since 1990 the Federal Deposit Insurance Corporation (FDIC) has taken over the FSLIC's job.

Inkcon Savings and Loan is on the verge of insolvency. Inkcon has assets of 500 million dollars and liabilities of 499 million dollars, so E is only (1) _____ million. The manager of Inkcon, Chuck Eaton, is approached by a developer who wants to borrow 100 million dollars and who is willing to pay a very high interest rate. The developer has been denied loans by several other institutions who think that his project is too risky. Chuck is attracted by the high interest rate. He figures that he can raise enough money to make the loan by offering a slightly higher interest rate to depositors. If he does this and the developer pays the loan off on schedule, the bank's net earnings (after paying off depositors, with interest) will be 5 million dollars. Then E will increase to (2) _____ million. The only catch is that Chuck thinks there is a 10% chance the developer will go broke and fail to pay back the loan (default), in which case Inkcon will lose 100 million in assets (the outstanding loan), will not be able to pay off its depositors, and will become insolvent. The owners equity will be zero. Hence, expected equity if he makes the loan is (3) _____ million. If Chuck is an expected E maximizer he (4) (will/will not) make the loan. The situation would be different if Inkcon's original equity were 50 million. Then, expected E if the loan were made would be (5) _____ and Chuck (6) (would/would not) make the loan. The situation would also be different if deposits were not insured. Then, Inkcon would not be able to attract enough deposits to make the loan because potential depositors would be afraid of losing their money. Because depositors are insured against losses, they allow Chuck to take big risks with their money. This is an example of (7) _____.

The problem illustrated by this example has been cited as a major cause of the Savings and Loan Crisis, in which hundreds of S&Ls became insolvent, the FSLIC used up its funds, and taxpayers had to foot the bill for over 200 billion dollars in losses. The crisis began in the early 1980s, when for several reasons S&L equity was very low. The government tried to prop up the industry in several ways, including raising the limit on deposit insurance from $40,000 to $100,000 per deposit. At the same time, the government relaxed regulations that had previously prevented S&Ls from making risky commercial real estate loans. How might the government change the deposit insurance system in order to reduce the problem illustrated by the example? [Hint: what do other types of insurers do to solve the same problem?] (8)_____

_____

_____

_____

_____

9.3. [Related to text examples 9.2 and 9.3, and problems 9.2 and 9.3.] In problem 8.3, you found that risk-averse golfers in Japan would be willing to pay more than the actuarially fair premium for hole-in-one insurance. In that problem it was assumed that the typical golfer had a 1 in 1,000, or .001, chance of getting a hole-in-one. Suppose instead that there are two kinds of golfers: "Good" golfers have a 1 in 1,000 (.001) chance of getting a hole-in-one, but "Bad" golfers have only a 0.5 in 1,000 (.0005) chance. Half of all golfers are Good and half are Bad. Both Good and Bad golfers must spend .250 million yen on gifts if they are "lucky" enough to get a hole-in-one. Assume that the typical golfer, Good or Bad, has an annual income of 3 million yen and has utility function $U(I - 1)$, where I is annual income.

a. If all golfers buy insurance, the number of golfers that will collect out of 1,000 is (1) _____, or (2) _____ percent. If all golfers pay the same premium, the actuarially fair premium is (3) _____ yen. If Bad golfers don't buy insurance, their expected utility is (4) _____, and if they buy insurance at the actuarially fair premium their utility, with certainty, is (5) _____. Therefore, they (6) (will/will not) want to buy. If Good golfers don't buy insurance, their expected utility is (7) _____, and if they buy insurance at the actuarially fair premium their utility, with certainty, is (8) _____. Therefore, they (9) (will/will not) want to buy. If golfers are free to choose whether to buy insurance, only (10) (Good/Bad) golfers will buy. They are the (11) (high/low) risk golfers.

Harcourt Brace & Company

This is an example of (12)_____ . The actuarially fair premium in this situation will be (13)_____, which is (14)(<u>higher/lower</u>) than when all golfers are required to buy insurance.

b. Suppose that complete insurance is sold by insurance companies for a premium of 250 yen, which is the actuarially fair premium for Good golfers. If Good golfers buy the insurance, their utility with certainty will be (1) _____ _____. The expected utility maximization hypothesis predicts that Good golfers (2) (<u>will/will not</u>) buy the insurance. If Bad golfers buy the insurance, their utility with certainty will be (3) _____. The expected utility maximization hypothesis predicts that Good golfers (4) (<u>will/will not</u>) buy the insurance.

c. Suppose insurance companies also offer an incomplete insurance policy. The maximum loss covered is .025 million yen, or one tenth of the .250 million loss, and the premium is the actuarially fair premium for Bad golfers of $.025 \times .0005 = .0000125$ million yen (or 12.5 yen). If bad Golfers buy this insurance their expected utility will be (1) _____ _____, so they (2) (<u>will/will not</u>) buy the insurance. If Good golfers buy this insurance their expected utility will be (3) _____, so they (4) (<u>will/will not</u>) prefer this insurance over the complete insurance described in part **b**. These two insurance policies create a (5) _____.

d. Suppose that all Japanese golfers, like many amateurs around the world, are rated by a "handicap" system: The higher your recent average scores, the higher your handicap is and you are allowed to subtract your handicap from your score when competing with others. (Note for non-golfers: the objective in golf is to complete the course with the fewest club strokes, and your score is just the number of strokes.) Bad golfers have high handicaps and Good golfers have low ones. Can handicaps serve as a signal to separate Good from Bad golfers for insurance purposes? Explain briefly. [Hint: is it

more costly for Bad golfers or Good golfers to get into the
high handicap (low risk) group?] _____

_____

_____

_____

_____

How, if at all, would this change the market equilibrium for
hole-in-one insurance? _____

_____

_____

_____

_____

e. In general, the only people who can verify a hole-in-one are
the golfer's playing partners. These partners are also foremost
among the beneficiaries of hole-in-one gifts. What problem
does this create for hole-in-one insurance? _____

_____

_____

_____

Any solutions?

_____

_____

_____

_____

_____

9.4. [Related to text problems 9.5 and 9.6.] A securities firm, Bull
and Bear, Inc., recruits new employees on college campuses
every spring. Their recruiter is trying to decide to whom to make
an offer: Jan Jones from Enormous State University (ESU) or
Megan Moffit from Small Private College (SPC). Jan and Megan
have identical grade point averages and otherwise appear to be
identical. B&B's recruiter does not know the SAT scores of the
two students, but if he did he would make an offer to the student
with the higher score. As B&B's recruiter knows, most high
school graduates can obtain admission to ESU, no matter what
their SAT scores are, and tuition is very low. Students must have
high SAT scores to get into SPC, and tuition there is very high.
Assume that neither school offers financial aid and that B&B's
recruiter believes that the education offered by both schools is
identical in quality.

a. Without further information, to whom will the recruiter make an offer? Explain? _____

_____

_____

_____

_____

b. Will a student who is admitted to both SPC and ESU be willing to pay more for an SPC education, even if she, like the recruiter, believes that the quality of education at the two schools is identical? Explain briefly. _____

_____

_____

_____

_____

_____

c. Suppose that SPC stops using SAT scores as an admission criterion. Instead, any student who is willing to pay for the "country club" atmosphere at SPC can be admitted. SPC sets tuition at the level that will just fill available spaces. Will this level be higher or lower than the old tuition—or can you tell? Explain briefly. _____

_____

_____

_____

_____

Harcourt Brace & Company

CHAPTER 10

GAME THEORY AND STRATEGIC EQUILIBRIUM

cooperative vs. noncooperative

players

strategies

payoffs

$G[S_A, S_B, U_A(a, b), U_B(a, b)]$

extensive form

normal form

dominant strategy

Nash equilibrium:

> A pair of strategies (a*, b*) represents an equilibrium solution to a 2-player game if a* is an optimal strategy for A against b* and b* is an optimal strategy for B against A*.

mixed strategies

Prisoner's Dilemma

cooperation and repetition

> two-period game
>
> infinite repetitions

sub-game perfect equilibrium

incomplete information

(Numbers in brackets at the beginning of problems below refer to related examples and problems in the text.)

10.1. [Related to text examples 10.1 and 10.2, and problems 10.1, 10.2, 10.7, 10.8, and 10.9.] At demolition derbies the object is survival. Drivers in old cars attempt to wreck each other's cars. The last car running wins. The best way to destroy another car without damaging your own too seriously is to back into its front end. Derby drivers spend a lot of time backing up, so it is not surprising that frequently pairs of drivers find themselves backing toward each other. Each has a choice of two strategies. The first is "Bull": continue backing straight toward the other. The second is "Chicken": swerve away and attempt to avoid being hit. If both drivers play Bull, they will collide and the chance that each will win the derby declines by 50%. If one plays Chicken and the other plays Bull, the chance that the Chicken will win declines by 20% and the chance that the Bull will win increases by 20%. If both play Chicken, their chances of winning will be unaffected by the close encounter.

a. Fill in the payoff matrix for this game.

		Driver B	
		Bull	Chicken
Driver A	Bull	A: B:	A: B:
	Chicken	A: B:	A: B:

b. Are there any dominant strategies for this game? Explain.

_____

_____

_____

_____

_____

c. Are there any Nash equilibria for this game? Explain.

_____

_____

_____

_____

_____

d. Let p stand for the probability that B plays Bull and let X represent the expected gain (loss if negative) to driver A of playing Bull. Write X as a function of p.

Plot this function on the diagram below.

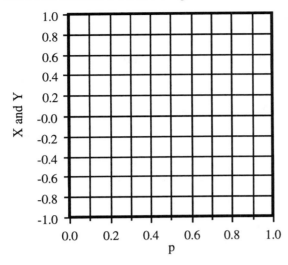

Let Y stand for the expected value to Driver A of playing Chicken. Write Y as a function of p and add the function to the graph.

e. Now, suppose that all drivers except A are the same and that each plays the following mixed strategy: Half the time they play Bull and half the time they play Chicken. What is the expected payoff to driver A of playing Bull all the time? [Hint: read the answer off the graph.] (1)_____

Chicken all the time? (2)_____ Bull half the time and Chicken half the time (3)_____

Which strategy should she pursue? (4)_____

Will other drivers continue to play Bull half the time?

(5)_____ What do you think will happen to the probability that each driver plays Bull if originally the

Harcourt Brace & Company

probability is 50%? Explain. (6)_____

_____

_____Will

an equilibrium value be reached and, if so, what is that

value? (7)_____ Is this equilibrium

stable? Explain. (8)_____

_____

_____

_____

_____

_____

10.2. [Related to text example 10.2 and problem 10.2.] The *Journal of Economic Perspectives* has a regular feature called "Puzzles." The following puzzle appeared in the Spring 1988 issue (Volume 2, Number 2, pp. 149–156) and originally appeared in Darrell Huff and Irving Geis, *How to Take a Chance*, (New York: Norton, 1959).

> Says Joe then: "It's a good night to play matching pennies—too hot for anything more strenuous. In fact, it's pretty warm to flip actual coins, so let's just lean back and say 'Heads' or 'Tails' instead." [*Assume these are called out simultaneously.*]
>
> "All right so far," you agree.
>
> "And to put a little variety into the game," Joe goes on, "I'll give you $3 when I call tails and you call heads. I'll give $1 when it is the other way around (i.e., I call heads and you call tails). And when we match, you give me $2 to make it even."

If you play against Joe, what do you expect to earn (and how would you play)? So would you play?

For a challenge, try to answer without further help. If you have difficulty, answer the questions below.

a. Suppose that Joe calls out Heads 50% of the time, at random—simulating a true coin flip. What would your expected winnings be if you play and call out Heads all of the time?

If you call out Tails all of the time?

What should you do?

b. Of course, Joe is no dummy. He knows what you just figured out and sets out to find a probability for playing heads that will minimize the expected value of your maximum expected value strategy. Write the expected value of your playing Heads, X, as a function of the probability, p, that Joe chooses.

Write the expected value of playing Tails, Y, as a function of p.

Graph these functions on the diagram below.

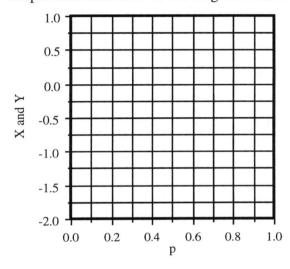

c. If Joe chooses p = .1, what is your maximum expected value strategy? [Hint: examine the graph.] (1)_____
What is the expected value of this strategy? (2)_____
If Joe chooses p = .9, what is your maximum expected value strategy? (3)_____ What is its expected value? (4)_____ Graph your maximum expected value as a function of p. [Hint the graph consists of two segments from the lines you already drew.] What value of p should Joe choose to minimize your maximum expected gain? (5)_____ If he chooses this value, what can you expect to win? (6)_____ Does it matter whether you choose Heads or Tails (7)_____
Should you agree to play? (8)_____

10.3. [Related to text examples 10.1 and 10.2 and problems 10.1 and 10.2.] The mother of Nick and Nack has discovered that five bags of her M&M's, which she purchased to give out on Halloween, have disappeared. She confronts each of them separately. "Did you and your brother take my five bags of

M&M's? If you both admit that the two of you took them, I am going to take five bags from each of you. But if one of you admits it and the other doesn't, I am going to take ten bags from the one who didn't admit it and give half of them to the one who did. Go to your room for five minutes and think about it by yourself." Each has 20 bags of M&M's.

a. Fill in the payoff matrix for this game.

	Nick	
	stonewall	confess
stonewall	Nack:	Nack:
	Nick:	Nick:
Nack		
confess	Nack:	Nack:
	Nick:	Nick:

b. Assuming that the twins cannot communicate while in their respective rooms, what do you think the outcome of this game will be? Explain. _____

_____

_____

_____

_____

_____

c. Suppose that the twins did not take the candy. The real culprit (unknown to them) was Sister Suzy! Does this change your answer to **b**? Explain. _____

_____

_____

_____

_____

d. What position would you expect prisoners' rights groups to take on the use of the prisoner's dilemma for obtaining confessions?_____

_____

_____

_____

10.4. The following is an adaptation of a "mating game" that appears in Gary Becker's *Treatise on the Family* (Cambridge: Harvard University Press, 1981, p. 69). Two women, Joyce and Cindy, and two men, Ralph and Dave, are the only people of their age in a remote town. These are very selfish people—all they care about is their own income. Nevertheless, there is some room for cooperation because a male-female pair can earn more together than the sum of their individual incomes. The excess of joint income over the sums for all possible pairs are displayed in the matrix below

	Cindy	Joyce
Ralph	8	4
Dave	9	7

For instance, suppose that Ralph "marries" Cindy. Their excess joint income will be 8. They are free to negotiate how the income will be split between the two of them. (All marriages are monogamous!)

To begin with, suppose that Cindy and Dave marry each other and split the excess income 50/50. Ralph and Joyce also marry and split their excess 50/50.

a. One day, Cindy and Ralph discover each other. Is there some marriage contract they could strike with each other which would make them both better off than under their current contracts? If so, give an example. _____
_____
_____
_____

b. Suppose that, as the world turns, Dave and Joyce also discover each other. What will happen: Will Dave make some counter-offer to Cindy, will Joyce make some counter-offer to Ralph, or will Dave and Joyce settle for each other? If you think they will settle for each other, what might be the terms of their contract? _____
_____
_____
_____
_____
_____
_____
_____

c. Which of the following sets of marriages, if any, is an equilibrium set? Explain.

Set A: Dave and Cindy; Joyce and Ralph

Set B: Dave and Joyce; Cindy and Ralph

_____

_____

_____

_____

_____

d. For which set of marriages is the total of excess income for the two marriages combined the largest?

e. If you found an equilibrium set in **c**, is it Pareto optimal in any sense? Explain. _____

_____

_____

_____

f. Suppose that there were more men and women. Do you think that a marriage market equilibrium would be Pareto optimal? Explain. _____

_____

_____

_____

_____

_____

_____

CHAPTER 11

PRODUCTION FUNCTIONS

production function:

$$q = f(K, L, \ldots)$$

marginal and average physical product of a factor of K and L:

$$MP_K = \partial q / \partial K = f_K \quad MP_L = \partial q / \partial L = f_L$$
$$AP_K = q/K \qquad AP_L = q/L$$

diminishing marginal product:

$$\partial MP_K / \partial K = \partial^2 q / \partial K^2 = f_{KK} < 0 \quad \partial MP_L / \partial L = \partial^2 q / \partial L^2 = f_{LL} < 0$$

relationship between marginal and average product of labor:

$$MP_L > AP_L \quad <=> \quad \partial AP_L / \partial L > 0$$
$$MP_L < AP_L \quad <=> \quad \partial AP_L / \partial L < 0$$
$$MP_L = AP_L \quad <=> \quad \partial AP_L / \partial L = 0 \ \text{ and } AP_L \text{ is at its maximum}$$

isoquant:

$$f(K, L) = q_o$$

marginal rate of technical substitution:

$$RTS(L \text{ for } K) = RTS_{LK} = - \frac{dK}{dL}\bigg|_{q = q_o} = \frac{MP_L}{MP_K}$$

law of diminishing marginal rate of technical substitution:

$$dRTS_{LK}/dL < 0$$

returns to scale:

$$f(mK, mL) = mf(K, L) = mq \quad <=> \text{ constant returns}$$
$$f(mK, mL) < mf(K, L) = mq \quad <=> \text{ decreasing returns}$$
$$f(mK, mL) > mf(K, L) = mq \quad <=> \text{ increasing returns}$$

elasticity of substitution:

$$\sigma = \frac{\text{percent } \Delta \, (K/L)}{\text{percent } \Delta \, RTS_{LK}} = \frac{d(K/L)}{d(RTS_{LK})} \frac{RTS_{LK}}{K/L}$$

common production functions:

linear: $q = aK + bL$ $a > 0, \; b > 0; \quad \sigma = \infty$

fixed proportions: $q = \min(aK, bL)$ $a > 0, \; b > 0; \quad \sigma = 0$

Cobb-Douglas: $q = AK^a L^b$ $a > 0, b > 0; \quad \sigma = 1$

CES: $q = \gamma[\beta K^\rho + (1-\beta)L^\rho]^{\varepsilon/\rho}$ $\gamma > 0, 0 \leq \beta \leq 1, \rho \leq 1, \varepsilon \geq 0;$
   $\sigma = 1/(1 + \rho)$

technical progress

sources of output growth:

$$G_q = G_A + e_{q,K}G_K + e_{q,L}G_L$$

PROBLEMS

(Numbers in brackets at the beginning of problems below refer to related examples and problems in the text.)

11.1. [Related to text examples 11.1 – 11.3 and problems 11.1, 11.2, and 11.4.] For each of the three production functions below, **(i)** find equations for MP_L and MP_K and determine whether they are both positive and diminishing in their respective factors (your answers may depend on the values of K and L), **(ii)** find equations for AP_L and AP_K, **(iii)** plot TP_L and, on a separate graph underneath, plot MP_L and AP_L, indicating on both plots where $MP_L = AP_L$, **(iv)** find RTS_{LK} and determine whether it diminishes in L, **(v)** graph a typical isoquant, and **(vi)** determine whether the function is homogeneous and, if so, determine whether returns to scale are constant, increasing, or decreasing.

a. $q = 10L^{.5}K^{.4}$

   (i) $MP_L =$ $MP_K =$

   (ii) $AP_L =$ $AP_K =$

   (iii) [Assume K = 1]

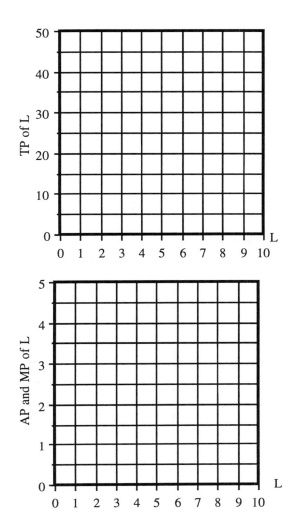

(iv) $RTS_{LK} =$

Does it diminish in L?

(v) [Assume q = 10.]

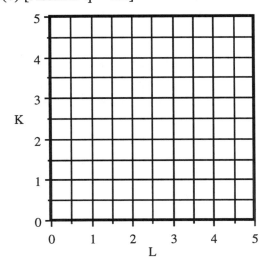

Harcourt Brace & Company

(vi) (homogeneity and returns to scale)

b. $q = KL + K + L$

(i) $MP_L =$ $MP_K =$

(ii) $AP_L =$ $AP_K =$

(iii) [Assume K = 1]

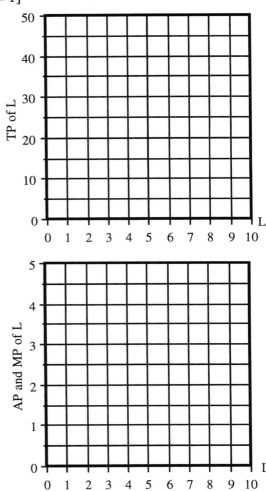

(iv) $RTS_{LK} =$ Does it diminish in L?

(v) [Assume q = 10.]

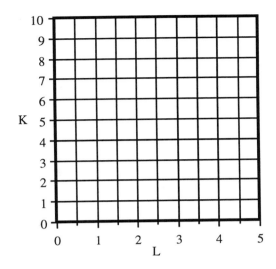

(vi) (homogeneity and returns to scale)

c. $q = \min(2L, K)$

   (i) If $L < K/2$, $MP_L =$ _____, but if $L \geq K/2$, $MP_L =$ _____.
   If $L < K/2$, $MP_K =$ _____, but if $L \geq K/2$, $MP_K =$ _____.

   (ii) If $L < K/2$, $AP_L =$ _____, but if $L \geq K/2$, $AP_L =$ _____.
   If $L < K/2$, $AP_K =$ _____, but if $L \geq K/2$, $AP_K =$ _____.

   (iii) [Assume $K = 5$]

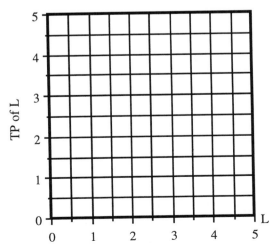

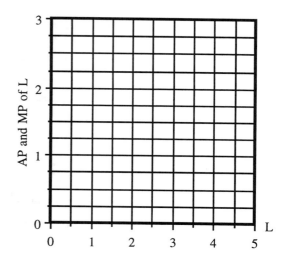

(iv) If L < K/2, RTS$_{LK}$ = _____, if L ≥ K/2,

RTS$_{LK}$ = _____.

Does it diminish in L?

(v) [Assume q = 10.]

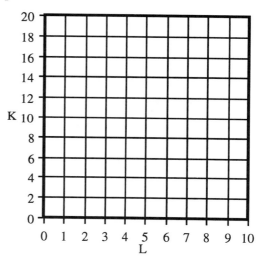

(vi) (homogeneity and returns to scale)

11.2. [Related to text problem 11.8.] Recall that the equation y = f(x, z) is said to be "homogeneous of degree k" if the following condition holds for any arbitrary constant, m:

$$f(mx, mz) = m^k f(x, z)$$

Harcourt Brace & Company

a. Use the chain rule to find the derivatives of both the left-hand and right-hand sides of this equation with respect to m and equate the derivatives to each other—they must be the same if the equation holds for any m. In taking the derivatives, treat x and z as constants. Your result is called the Euler condition.

b. A production function, q = f(K, L), is said to exhibit constant returns to scale if it is homogeneous of degree (1)_____. Write the Euler equation for a constant returns to scale production function: (2)_____ = (3)_____. Now, interpret the two sides of this equation. (4)_____

_____

_____

_____

_____

11.3. [Related to text problem 11.3.] The We-Haul Moving Company can load 10,000 pounds of furniture into a truck in 4 hours with 2 workers. If a third worker is added, loading time is reduced to 3 hours.

a. In the graph below, indicate the points representing the two different input combinations that can be used to produce the output "loading 10,000 pounds." Measure labor and truck input in hours of service.

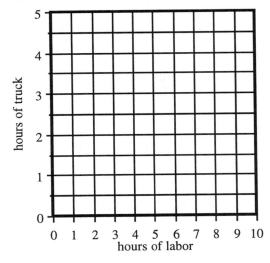

b. If there are constant returns to scale in loading a truck, how many hours of each input would be needed to load 5,000 pounds with two workers? L =

(1)_____hours   K = (2)_____hours.

With three workers? L = (3)_____hours K =

(4)_____hours. Indicate these two input

combinations on the graph.

c. Suppose that two workers load 5,000 pounds on a truck and
then a third worker helps them load an additional 5,000
pounds. How many hours of each input will be used? L =
(1)_____ K =(2)_____. Indicate this point
on the graph. Also, indicate the input combination that could
be used to load 10,000 pounds if the third worker only helped
after 7,500 pounds were loaded. Finally, draw a line that
indicates all input combinations that can be used to load
10,000 pounds if at least two and no more than three workers
are on the job at all times.

Draw a second line for 5,000 pounds.

d. For the range of input combinations considered above, the
rate of technical substitution of worker hours for truck hours
is (1) _____. Which is larger, the marginal
product of a worker hour or the marginal product of a truck
hour? Or are they the same? (2)_____ Now use
this answer and the fact that returns to scale are constant to
determine the actual marginal product of a worker hour.
[Hint: the result you obtained in the previous problem will
be useful.]

$\text{MP}_{\text{worker hour}}$ = (3)_____

11.4. [Related to text problems 11.5 and 11.6.] For a two input,
constant returns to scale production function it is relatively easy
to find the elasticity of substitution (σ) because, as shown in the
text, the rate of technical substitution depends only on the ratio
of the two inputs. Find σ for the following constant returns to
scale production functions.

a. (Illustration) $q = 10K^{.2}L^{.8}$

First, find the marginal products and then take their ratio to
get RTS_{LK}: $\text{MP}_L = 2(K/L)^{.8}$, $\text{MP}_K = 8(K/L)^{-.2}$, and RTS_{LK}
$= \text{MP}_L /\text{MP}_K = .25(K/L)$. Now, invert the last equation to get

the ratio K/L as a function of RTS_{LK}: $K/L = 4RTS_{LK}$.
Remember the definition of σ:

$$\sigma = \frac{\partial(K/L)}{\partial(RTS_{LK})} \frac{RTS_{LK}}{K/L}$$

The partial derivative in this expression refers to changing
K/L as RTS_{LK} changes, holding output constant (moving
along an isoquant). That is, it is simply the derivative of the
equation we just found with respect to RTS_{LK}, which
happens to be 4. Also, notice that for this function the ratio
$RTS_{LK}/(K/L) = 1/4$. Therefore,

$$\sigma = \frac{\partial(K/L)}{\partial(RTS_{LK})} \frac{RTS_{LK}}{K/L} = 4\frac{1}{4} = 1$$

[You may have noticed that σ is the elasticity of K/L with
respect to RTS_{LK} along an isoquant. For this particular
production function, $\ln(K/L) = \ln(4) + \ln(RTS_{LK})$ along an
isoquant. Since the coefficient of $\ln(RTS_{LK})$ in this equation
is this elasticity, it again is demonstrated that $\sigma = 1$.]

b. $q = 20K^{.4}L^{.6}$

c. $q = AK^aL^b$ where A, a, and b are positive constants and a +
b = 1. [This is the general form of the constant returns to
scale Cobb-Douglas function.]

d. $q = 2[.2K^{-2} + .8L^{-2}]^{-1/2}$

e. $q = \gamma[\beta K^{\rho} + (1-\beta)L^{\rho}]^{\varepsilon/\rho}$

CHAPTER 12

COSTS

costs:

    opportunity

    accounting

    economic

    of labor

    of capital (sunk vs. rental)

    of entrepreneurial services

    total cost = wL + vK

profit:

    accounting

    economic:

$$\pi = Pf(K, L) - wL - vK$$

cost minimization:

    Lagrangian:

$$\pounds = wL + vK + \lambda[q_0 - f(K, L)]$$

    first-order conditions:

$$w/v = RTS_{LK}$$

$$q_0 = f(K, L)$$

the dual to cost minimization, output maximization:

    Lagrangian:

$$\pounds = f(K, L) + \lambda(TC_0 - wL - vK)$$

    first order conditions:

$$w/v = RTS_{LK}$$

$$TC_1 = wL + vK$$

derived demand for inputs

expansion path

Harcourt Brace & Company

total, average, and marginal cost functions:

$$TC = C(v, w, q)$$

$$AC(v, w, q) = C(v, w, q)/q$$

$$MC(v, w, q) = \partial C(v, w, q)/\partial q$$

relationship between MC and AC:

$$MC > AC \iff \partial AC(v, w, q)/\partial q > 0$$

$$MC < AC \iff \partial AC(v, w, q)/\partial q < 0$$

$$MC = AC \iff \partial AC(v, w, q)/\partial q = 0 \text{ and AC is minimized}$$

effects of input price changes on costs:

TC, AC, and MC are homogeneous of degree one in input prices

partial elasticity of substitution:

$$s_{ij} = \frac{\partial(X_i/X_j)}{\partial(w_j/w_i)} \frac{w_j/w_i}{X_i/X_j} \quad \text{(Q and all other input prices are held constant)}$$

short run total, fixed, and variable costs:

$$STC(K_1) = SFC(K_1) + SVC(K_1) = vK_1 + wL$$

short run average total, average fixed, average variable, and marginal costs:

$$SATC(K_1) = SAFC(K_1) + SAVC(K_1)$$

$$SMC(K) = \partial STC(K_1)/\partial q = \partial SVC(K_1)/\partial q$$

relationships between short-run and long-run cost curves:

If q_1 is the level of output for which K_1 is the cost minimizing value of K, then:

for $q = q_1$, $STC(K_1) = TC$, $SATC(K_1) = AC$, $SMC(K_1) = MC$ and $\partial SATC(K_1)/\partial q = \partial AC/\partial q$;

for $q > q_1$, $STC(K_1) > TC$, $SATC(K_1) > AC$, $SMC(K_1) > MC$ and $\partial SATC(K_1)/\partial q > \partial AC/\partial q$;

for $q < q_1$, $STC(K_1) > TC$, $SATC(K_1) > AC$, $SMC(K_1) < MC$ and $\partial SATC(K_1)/\partial q < \partial AC/\partial q$.

PROBLEMS

(Numbers in brackets at the beginning of problems below refer to related examples and problems in the text.)

12.1. [Related to text examples 12.1 and 12.2, and problems 12.3 and 12.5–12.8.] Sedate Sedan, Inc., uses robots and workers to assemble automobiles. There is a diminishing rate of technical substitution between robots and labor: robots do well at tasks that are purely repetitive while labor does better at jobs that are less boring and require more thought. The various combinations of hours of robot use (R) and hours of labor use (L) needed to assemble sedans are described by a Cobb-Douglas production function:

$$s = A(RL)^{.5}$$

where A is a positive number. The company can rent all the robots it wants for r dollars per hour and hire all the workers it wants at w dollars per hour. It hires you to find its cost function.

a. First, state the two conditions that will be satisfied by the values of R and L that minimize C = rR + wL subject to the constraint that $s = A(RL)^{.5}$.

b. Now, you need to solve the conditions in **a** for R and L as functions of w, r, and s. The functions you will get are sometimes called the "output constant factor demand functions." First, verify that one of the conditions can be rewritten as:

$$R = (w/r)L$$

Now, substitute this result for R in the other condition, to eliminate R.

Finally, solve your last equation for L as a function of s, w, and r.

This is the output constant demand function for L. Now, find the function for R. [Hint: it should look the same as the result for L, except that r should be switched with w.]

c. Substitute your output constant factor demand functions into the cost definition where R and L appear:

$$C = w \left\{ \right\} + r \left\{ \right\}$$

Verify that this can be reduced to $C = 2A^{-1}(wr)^{.5}s$.

This is the desired cost function.

d. Recall Shephard's Lemma from Chapter 5: The partial derivative of the expenditure function with respect to a good's price is the compensated (utility constant) demand curve for that good. Since cost minimization subject to an output constraint is analogous to expenditure minimization subject to a utility constraint, Shephard's Lemma applies here, too. That is, the partial derivative of a cost function with respect to an input's price is the output constant demand equation for that input. To verify Shephard's Lemma, take the partial derivative of the cost function with respect to w and compare the expression you get with the output constant factor demand equation for L. Are they the same?

e. Now, write the average and marginal cost functions for s:

$AC = C/s =$

$MC = \partial C/\partial s =$

f. Note that this is a Cobb-Douglas production function with a = b = .5. Are returns to scale increasing, decreasing, or constant? (1)_____ Does AC increase, decline, or stay constant as q increases? (2)_____ Is MC larger, smaller, or the same as AC? (3)_____ How would your answers change if a + b exceeded one: returns to scale? (4)_____ AC increasing, decreasing, or constant? (5)_____ MC less than, greater than, or equal to AC? (6)_____ How would your answers change if a + b was less than one:

returns to scale? (7)_____ AC

increasing, decreasing, or constant? (8)_____

MC less than, greater than, or equal to AC?

(9)_____

g. Find the elasticities of marginal cost with respect to w and r.

$e_{MC,w} =$

$e_{MC,r} =$

12.2. It turns out that the parameter A in the production function for Sedate Sedan, Inc., is not a parameter at all. Instead, it is a function of s: $A = 1/(200 - 2s + .01s^2)$. Note that this does not affect the derivation of the cost function since s is treated as fixed in the cost minimization problem. However, MC and AC change because of the dependence of A on s. Suppose also that w = \$20.00 and r = \$5.00.

a. Show that the cost function is now $C = 4000s - 40s^2 + .2s^3$

Also, show that the production function can be written as
$.01s^3 - 2s^2 + 200s = R^{.5}L^{.5}$

b. Write the new average and marginal cost functions.

AC =

MC =

For what value of s is AC minimized?

Compute AC and MC at this point and compare their values.

What do you find?

At what point is MC minimized?

What is the value of MC at this point?

c. Graph the average and marginal cost functions over the range from 0 to 200.

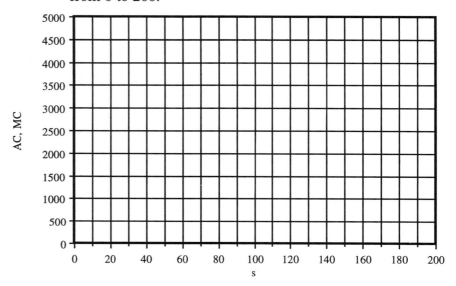

d. For some time Sedate has been assembling 50 sedans per week. What is MC? (1)_____ AC? (2) _____ Indicate these points on the graph. How many Robot hours have they been using? (3)_____ Labor hours? (4)_____ [Hint: to find R and L, use the output constant factor demand functions you found in the previous problem, after appropriate substitutions for A, r, and w.]

e. Now, suppose that Sedate wants to change its output level, but that it takes a week to hire and train a new worker. Furthermore, if they want to lay off a worker, they have to give a week's notice. Fortunately, Robots are readily available, require no training, and can be sent back to Roger's Robots, Inc., when not in use. Using the number of labor hours you found in **d**, find Sedate's short run cost function. The first step is to substitute your value for L into the production function, then invert the function to get the required R as a function of s.

$R =$

Next, substitute this function for R in $C = wL + rR$. Also, substitute your value for L and the actual factor prices. The result is the short run cost function.

$C_{50} =$

f. Explain how you would find short run average and marginal cost functions for C_{50}—but don't actually do it unless you like to play with messy expressions! _____

_____

_____

_____

_____

g. The table below gives total, average, and marginal costs for various levels of output based on C_{50}. Fill in the missing values.

s	C_{50}	SAC_{50}	SMC_{50}
40	109850	2746	1531
49	123499	2520	1502
50	_____	_____	_____
60	140007	2333	1514
70	155647	2224	1635
80	173256	2166	1916
84	181250	2158	2086
85	_____	_____	_____
90	194705	2163	2414

Harcourt Brace & Company

Allowing for numerical imprecision, for what value of s is

$SAC_{50} = AC$? (1)_____ $SMC_{50} = MC$?

(2)_____ $SAC_{50} = SMC_{50}$?

(3)_____ SAC_{50} minimized?

(4)_____ Use these observations and

the values in the table to add SMC_{50} and SAC_{50} to the graph

in **c**.

h. Explain why $SMC_{50} > MC$ at s = 60 and $SMC_{50} < MC$ at s

= 40. _____

_____

_____

_____

_____

_____

_____

_____

i. Explain why SAC_{50} has a negative slope at s = 50.

_____

_____

_____

_____

_____

_____

_____

j. Suppose that Sedate had been assembling 100 sedans per

week for some time. For what value of s will $SAC_{100} = AC$?

(1)_____ $SMC_{100} = MC$?

(2)_____ $SAC_{100} = SMC_{100}$?

(3)_____ SAC_{100} minimized?

(4)_____ Use these observations to sketch

SMC_{100} and SAC_{100} on the graph in **c**.

k. Suppose that Sedate had been assembling 150 sedans per

week for some time. For what value of s will $SAC_{150} = AC$?

(1)_____ $SMC_{150} = MC$? (2)_____

At this last point, which will be larger, MC or AC? (3)_____

Will the minimum of SAC_{150} be at a value of s greater than,

less than, or equal to 150? (4)_____ Relative

to this last value, will the value of s at which $SMC_{150} =$

SAC_{150} be larger, smaller, or the same? (5)_____

Use these observations to sketch SMC_{150} and SAC_{150} on the

graph in **c**.

12.3. [Related to text problems 12.7 and 12.8.] Timothy's Toothpicks,
Inc., is making plans for a new processing plant. Ernie's
Engineering, Inc., has been hired to estimate the cost of
producing t tons of toothpicks as a function of the area of the
plant, A. The engineers come up with:

$$C(t, A) = t^3/3 - t^2 + (300 - 6A)t + A^2$$

Once Timothy's has chosen A, this function will be its short-run
cost function.

a. Find short-run marginal and average cost functions. These
will be functions of A as well as t.

SMC =

SAC =

b. Find the plant size, A, that will minimize costs, as a function
of t.

Harcourt Brace & Company

c. Now use your result in **b** and the short-run cost function to find the "long-run" cost function, assuming that in the long run A is adjusted to minimize costs.

d. Find long run marginal and average cost functions.

MC =

AC =

12.4. The boiler in the heating plant at Arctic College is designed to burn either fuel oil or coal. Suppose that one ton of coal, C, produces as many BTUs as 100 gallons of fuel oil, F.

a. Draw a typical isoquant for BTU production.

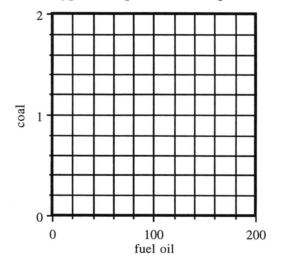

b. What is the elasticity of substitution between fuel oil and coal?

c. Suppose that fuel oil is $1.00 per gallon and coal is $90 per ton. Draw the output expansion path on the diagram above and describe the marginal and average cost curves.

_____

_____

_____

d. Repeat **c**, assuming that the price of coal has increased to
$110 per ton. _____

_____

_____

_____

12.5. [Related to text problem 12.4.] Fanny's Famous Fudge Factory
advertises that it carefully adheres to an old world recipe for its
fudge, which includes a Belgian chocolate liqueur and heavy
whipping cream. In fact, every pound of fudge includes "a"
ounces of liqueur, L, and "b" ounces of cream, C. The values of
"a" and "b" are tightly held secrets. Ignoring other ingredients,
the production function can be written as

$$F = \min(aL, bC)$$

a. Assume that the price of liqueur is $.50 per ounce and cream
is $.10 per ounce. Find Fanny's long-run total, average, and
marginal cost functions.

TC =

MC =

AC =

b. At the beginning of each month, Fanny's receives a shipment
of liqueur from Belgium. They can't get any more for
another month. If they don't use up the monthly purchase, it
can be saved until the next month at a storage cost of $.10
per ounce. They can always purchase as much cream as they
want at a local dairy. Suppose they receive a shipment of L =
1000a ounces and assume that the previous month's liqueur
was used up. If they produce 900 pounds of fudge, what will
total cost be—including the inventory cost of storing the
remaining 100a ounces of L? (1)_____

Harcourt Brace & Company

What is the average cost? (2)_____ What is the

marginal cost of the 901st pound? (3)_____

What is the cost of 1,000 pounds? (4)_____

The average cost? (5)_____ The marginal

cost of the 1000th pound? (6)_____

The 1,001st pound? (7) _____

Finally, sketch AC, MC, SMC_{1000}, and SAC_{1000} on the
diagram on the next page.

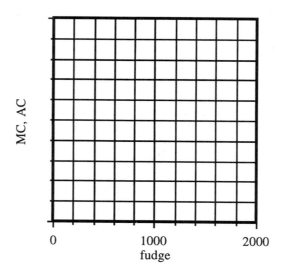

12.6. [Related to text problems 12.10 and 12.11.] This problem
illustrates the general proposition that every cost function
implies an underlying production function—although it is not
always as easy to find the latter as it is in this illustration.
Suppose that the cost function of a firm is given by $C = [v + 2(vw)^{.5} + w]q$, where v is the rental rate of capital, K, w is the
wage rate for labor, L, and q is output.

a. First, use Shephard's lemma (see Problem 12.1, part **d**) to
find the output constant demand functions for L and K.

L =

K =

b. Next, solve each of the two equations in **a** for $(w/v)^{.5}$.

From the L equation: $(w/v)^{.5}$ =

From the K equation: $(w/v)^{.5}$ =

c. Now, equate the right-hand sides of the two equations in **b** and solve the resulting equation for q as a function of K and L—the desired production function.

q =

d. The general form of the CES production function is q = $\gamma[\delta K^\rho + (1 - \delta)L^\rho]^{\epsilon/\rho}$, with $\sigma = 1/(1 - \rho)$. Compare the function you found in **c** to the CES. What do you find?

_____

_____

_____

What is the elasticity of substitution for the function you found? _____

e. Repeat **a** though **d** for the following cost function: C = $v^{.2}w^{.8}q$

CHAPTER 13

PROFIT MAXIMIZATION AND SUPPLY

revenue:

total revenue function: $TR(q) = P(q)\,q$

marginal revenue: $MR = dTR/dq = P + q(dP/dQ)$

profit maximization:

$\pi(q) = P(q)\,q - TC(q) = TR(q) - TC(q)$

first order condition: $MR = MC$

second order condition: $d^2p/dq^2 = d\pi'(q)/dq < 0$ at $q = q^*$

marginal revenue and elasticity:

$$MR = P\left(1 + \frac{1}{e_{q,P}}\right)$$

price taker:

first order condition: $P = MC$

short run supply: the positively sloped portion of MC that lies above AVC

profit maximization and input demand:

profit as a function of K and L: $\pi(K, L) = Pf(K, L) - (vK + wL)$

first order conditions:

$$\frac{d\pi}{dK} = P\frac{\partial f}{\partial K} - v = 0 \ \text{ and } \ \frac{d\pi}{dL} = P\frac{\partial f}{\partial L} - v = 0$$

$K^* = K^*(P, v, w)$ and $L^* = L^*(P, v, w)$

supply function:

$q^* = f[K^*(P, v, w), L^*(P, v, w)] = q^*(P, v, w)$

producer surplus:

short run

$\text{surplus} = \pi^* + FC$

long run

revenue maximization

contracts between managers and firms:

principle-agent problem

(Numbers in brackets at the beginning of problems below refer to related examples and problems in the text.)

13.1. [Related to text example 13.1 and problems 13.1 and 13.5.] Remember Sedate Sedan, Inc., from Problems 12.1 and 12.2? Sedate's demand curve is:

$$s = 300 - .025\ P$$

where P is the price of a Sedan.

a. Find Sedate's inverse demand curve and graph it in the diagram below.

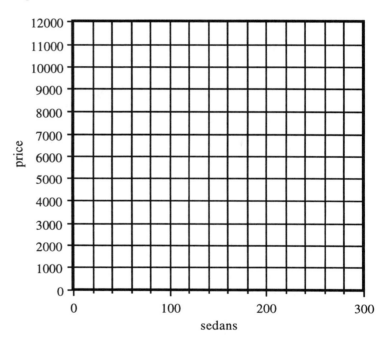

b. Use the inverse demand curve and the definition of total revenue (R = Ps) to find the revenue function, R(s).

c. Find the marginal revenue function for Sedate and graph it on the diagram for part **a.**

d. Now, examine the diagram. How large is the slope of MR relative to that of the inverse demand function? (1)_____. Now, choose a point on the vertical axis and compare the horizontal distance between the vertical axis and MR to the horizontal distance between the axis and the inverse demand curve for the value of P you chose. What is the ratio of the first distance to the second? (2)_____.

e. Consider a general linear demand function: $q = a - bP$, where both a and b are positive numbers. The inverse demand function is P = (1)_____. $R(q) =$ (2)_____. $MR =$ (3)_____. The slope of MR is (4)_____, the slope of the inverse demand function is (5)_____, and the ratio of the former to the latter is (6)_____. The horizontal distance between the vertical axis and the inverse demand curve at a given value of MR is q = (7)_____. [Hint: solve the MR function for q as a function of MR.] The horizontal distance between the vertical axis and the inverse demand curve at given P: q = (8)_____. If horizontal distances (7) and (8) are computed at the same point on the vertical scale, the ratio of the former to the latter is (9)_____. [Note: this result makes it easy to draw the MR curve for a linear demand curve. It will be linear, intersect the vertical axis at the same place as the inverse demand curve, and intersect the horizontal axis half-way between the origin and the horizontal intersection of the inverse demand curve.]

f. In Problem 12.2 you found the following long-run average and marginal costs curves for Sedate:

$$AC = 4000 - 40s + .2s^2 \quad MC = 4000 - 80s + .6s^2$$

Add these functions to the graph above. If Sedate maximizes profits, what level of output will it choose to produce?

Indicate the profit maximizing level of s on the graph. What will P be if this level of s is chosen?

Indicate the value of P on the graph. What will profits be? [Hint: compute average profit first, then multiply by the number of firms.]

Shade the area on the graph that represents this level of profits.

13.2. [Related to text problem 13.2.] The government decides to levy a tax on Sedate.

a. Suppose the tax is in the form of a lump sum, T, that does not depend on the number of sedans produced by Sedate. Sedate's after tax (net) profits can now be represented by:

$$R(s) - C(s) - T$$

Will Sedate's output level be affected by the tax? [Hint: this question can be answered without reference to Sedate's specific revenue and cost functions. What is the first order condition for maximizing net profits? How does it compare to the first order condition when T = 0?]

b. Suppose, instead, that profits are taxed at constant rate t. Net profits are $(1 - t)[R(s) - C(s)]$. Will this tax affect Sedate's output level?

c. For a progressive profits tax, the marginal tax rate increases with the level of profits. Under such a tax, net profits can be represented by $N(\pi)$, where $\pi = R(s) - C(s)$ is gross profit,

Harcourt Brace & Company

with $1 > N'(\pi) > 0$ and $N''(\pi) < 0$. The marginal tax rate is $1 - N'(\pi)$. Will such a tax affect Sedate's output level?

d. A unit tax on Sedate's output would leave Sedate with net profits of $R(s) - C(s) - ts$, where t is the tax per unit. How would this tax affect Sedate's output? [Hint: again, find the first order condition for the general revenue and cost functions. At the value of s that maximizes net profits, will MR be less than or greater than MC? Since MR falls with s and MC increases with s, will the value of s at such a point be larger or smaller than where MR = MC?]

e. Compare your answer to **d** with your answers to **a** through **c**. What conclusion can you draw? _____

_____

_____

_____

_____

_____

_____

_____

13.3. [Related to text examples 13.2 and 13.3.] The text shows two different ways to find a short-run supply function for a competitive, profit-maximizing firm. In the first method, the firm's short-run cost function is used to obtain the short-run marginal cost function, which is the inverse of the short-run supply function. In the second method, profit is first written as a function of the inputs and then profit-maximizing values of the variable inputs are found, as functions of input prices and the output price. These input demand functions are then substituted into the production function to find the supply function. In this problem you are to find a short-run supply function both ways, thereby demonstrating that the result is the same either way. Assume that the firm's production function is

$$q = K^{1/2}L^{1/4}M^{1/4}$$

where K is capital, L is labor, and M is materials. Assume that K is fixed at K^*. The firm can purchase any amounts of L and M that it wants to at wage rate w and price u, respectively, and it can sell any amount of q that it wants to at price P. The rental rate on capital is v, so fixed cost is vK*.

a. (using the cost function) Show that the short run total cost function for the firm is

$$STC = 2q^2K^{*-1}(uw)^{1/2} + vK^*$$

[Hint: you will need to find the values of L and M that minimize wL + uM subject to the constraint q = K*$^{1/4}$L$^{1/2}$M$^{1/4}$. You will obtain functions of u, w, q, and K*. Substitute these functions into Cost = wL + uM + vK* to get STC.]

Now, find SMC and equate your result to P.

Solve the above equation for q. Your answer is the short run supply function.

b. (using input demand functions) Find the values of L and M that maximize short-run profits:

$$PK^{*1/4}L^{1/2}M^{1/4} - wL - uM - vK^*$$

Your answers will be functions of K*, P, w, and u. These are the short run input demand functions for L and M.

Now, substitute your results into q = K*$^{1/4}$L$^{1/2}$M$^{1/4}$. Compare the result to the supply function you found in **a.**

c. The variables u, w, and K* appear along with P as arguments of the supply function. When these variables change, the supply function "shifts"; that is, a change in any of these variables changes the quantity supplied at any value of P. For each variable, determine whether the shift is backward (quantity supplied decreases) or forward (quantity supplied increases) and give an intuitive reason for your answer.

u and w:_____

_____

_____

_____

K*:_____

_____

_____

_____

_____

Now, explain why v does not affect short-run supply.

_____

_____

_____

_____

13.4. [Related to text examples 13.2 and 13.3, and problem 13.1.] Remember Timothy's Toothpicks, Inc., from Problem 12.3? Timothy's has a short run cost function given by:

$$C(t, A) = t^3/3 - t^2 + (300 - 6A)t + A^2,$$

where t is tons of toothpicks produced in a year and A is the floor area of the factory, in hundreds of square feet.

a. Timothy's current factory has a floor area of 4,500 square feet (i.e., A = 45). The toothpick industry is competitive. Show that Timothy's short run supply function is:

$$t = (P - 29)^{.5} + 1 .$$

[Hint: find the inverse supply function first (P as a function of T), then use the quadratic formula to solve for t as a function of P. Remember that the quadratic formula is a method of solving equations of the form $ax^2 + bx + c = 0$ for x.] The solution is

$$x = \frac{-b \pm \sqrt{b^2 - 4ac}}{2a} .]$$

Plot the supply function on the graph below. [Hint: note that the inverse of the function is $P = (t+1)^2 + 29$. Find P for a few values of t.]

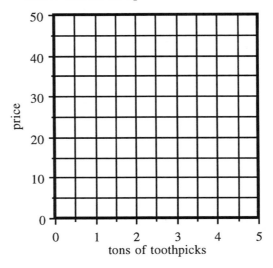

b. Find Timothy's short run average cost and average variable cost functions for A = 45.

SAC =

SAVC =

At what value of t is SAVC minimized?

What is the value of SAVC at this point?

What is SAC at this point?

Plot SAVC on the graph in **a**.

c. If P gets as low as the minimum of SAVC, what will Timothy's profits be? Will Timothy choose to stay in business? Explain. _____

_____

_____

_____

_____

13.5. [Related to text example 13.4 and problem 13.9] Suppose that a firm's short-run total cost function for T-shirts is:

$$STC = .05q^2 + 5q + 125$$

a. Find the firm's short-run supply function, with price on the left-hand side (i.e., the "inverse" supply function).

P =

Plot the function on the diagram below.

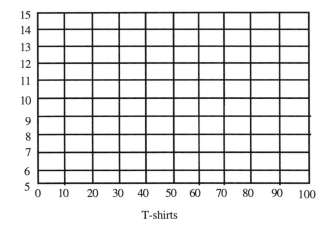

T-shirts

b. How many T-shirts will the firm produce if P = $10? Use the diagram in **a** to get your answer. Draw a horizontal line at P = $10 and a vertical line at the correct quantity.

q =

c. What is the firm's short-run producer surplus at P = $10? Shade the area in the diagram in **a** that represents your answer and calculate the value. Is this amount larger, smaller, or equal to the firm's profit at this price? Explain briefly.

_____

_____

_____

d. Develop a formula for this firm's short-run producer surplus as a function of P. [Hint: first write the formula for the area of the relevant triangle as a function of P and q, then use the inverse supply function to replace the q in the area formula with a function of P.]

13.6. Grimm's Grinders, Inc., faces the following inverse demand function for its gourmet grinders, G:

$$P = 200 - G$$

Grimm's has the following cost function:

$$C = 40G + G^2$$

a. Find each of the following functions for Grimm's Grinders:

R(G) = (1)_____ MR = (2)_____

AC = (3)_____ MC = (4)_____

π(G) = (5)_____

Plot the inverse demand, MR, AC, and MC functions on the diagram below.

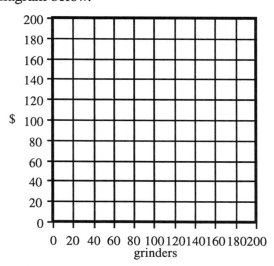

b. Find the profit maximizing values of G, P, AC, and π.

G* = (1)_____

P* = (2)_____

AC* = (3)_____

π* = (4)_____

Indicate G*, P* and AC* on the graph in **a**.

c. If Grimm's Chief Executive Officer (CEO) wants to maximize revenue, rather than profit, what level of output will she choose? [Hint: what does MR equal at the revenue maximizing output level?]

G** = (1)_____

Is this amount greater or less than the profit maximizing level of output that you found in **b**? (2)_____

Give an intuitive explanation of your answer. (3)_____

_____

_____

_____

_____

_____

Find P, AC, and π at output level G**.

P** = (4)_____

AC** = (5)_____

π** = (6)_____

Plot G**, P**, and AC** on the graph in **a**.

d. If Grimm's Board of Director's tells its CEO that she will be fired if the firm loses money, what level of output will the revenue-maximizing director choose? [Hint: begin by explaining why she will always choose to increase output if profits are positive. Then, figure out the value of G that will make profits exactly equal to zero.] (1)_____

_____

_____

_____

G*** = (2)_____ What will P be?

P*** = (3)_____ What will AC be?

AC***= (4)_____. Plot G***,

P***, and AC*** on the graph in **a.**

13.7. The Sticky Wicket Croquet Company produces croquet sets by the production function

$$q = L - .1L^2$$

where q is sets produced per hour and L is labor. SWCC can hire as many workers as it wants to for £4 (4 pounds) per hour. They can sell as many croquet sets as they produce at P pounds each.

a. Write profits as a function of P and L.

Find the first order condition for profit maximization.

If P = £10, how many workers should SWCC hire?

How many croquet sets will SWCC produce per hour with this number of workers?

Harcourt Brace & Company

Plot the profit-maximizing choices of L and q on the graphs below.

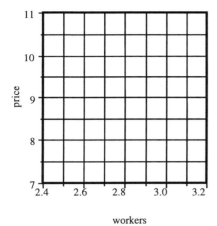

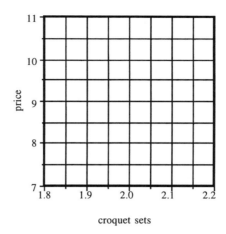

workers

croquet sets

b. How do profit-maximizing L and q change if P falls to £8?

Plot the new values on the graphs in **a**.

Now, suppose that hiring and firing at Sticky Wicket is a sticky business. When workers are hired they need training and often disrupt other workers with questions. When workers are fired they must be given severance pay and the morale of retained workers drops because they are fearful of being fired. All this adds up to adjustment costs. Let L_{-1} represent workers employed in the previous week and assume that adjustment costs per hour, A, are determined by:

$$A = .2(L - L_{-1})^2$$

c. Find marginal adjustment cost, dA/dL.

Does marginal adjustment cost increase or decrease as the size of the change increases?

d. Set up SWCC's new profit-maximization problem and find the first order condition.

e. Suppose that, as in **a**, P = 10 and w = 4. Assume that L_{-1} = 3. How many workers will SWCC hire and what output will it produce?

Compare your answers to your answers in **a**.

f. The next week P drops to £8. How many workers will SWCC hire now and what output will it produce?

Plot your answers on the graph in **a** and compare them to your answers in **b**. Give an intuitive explanation of the difference._____

_____

_____

_____

_____

g. If P continues to be £8 for a second week, what will happen to q and L?

Plot these answers in **a** and draw in the paths which q and L will follow if P continues to be £8 indefinitely.

13.8. Fair Share Legal Services, Inc., produces legal services, q, according to the following production function:

$$q = 1.5L - .1L^2$$

where L is the number of lawyers it hires. Assume that FSLS can hire as many lawyers as it wants at wage rate w and can sell as many services as it wants at price P.

a. If FSLS profit maximizes, how many lawyers will it hire—as a function of P and w? [Hint: find the first order condition for maximizing profits and solve for L as a function of P and w.]

How many lawyers will it hire if w = 5 and P = 10?

b. FSLS's wage bill is wL and its revenue is Pq = P(1.5L − .1L^2). The share of wages in total revenue, s, is

$$s = wL/Pq = wL/P(1.5L - .1L^2)$$

Suppose that FSLS is a revenue-sharing firm rather than a profit-maximizing one. That is, it hires lawyers up to the point where s is some prespecified value. Find its choice for L as a function of P, w, and s. [Hint: since s, w, and P are all determined, FSLS has nothing to maximize.]

What will L be if P = 10, w = 5 and s = .5?

Compare your answers to your answers in **a**.

c. Now, suppose that P drops to $8.00. What will happen to L under profit-maximizing if the wage rate is fixed by a contract with the lawyers union?

d. Continuing **c**, what will happen to w under revenue-sharing, assuming that L is fixed at the old level by contract?

e. Of course, FSLS might have a hard time getting lawyers to work at the wage rate you found in **d**. What is likely to happen?_____

_____

_____

_____

_____

_____

_____

13.9. Kolkhoz Korn is a collective popcorn farm in the Ukraine, USSR. It can sell as much popcorn as it can produce to the government's retail food bureau at a fixed price of P rubles. It has fixed costs of R rubles—rent it must pay the government for land and equipment. The production function for popcorn is $q = F(L)$, where L is labor. Assume that $MP_L > 0$ and $\partial MP_L / dL < 0$. Note that the second assumption implies $AP_L > MP_L$ for all $L > 0$. Each worker on the farm takes home an equal share of the net (after rent) revenue:

$$s = [P \cdot F(L) - R]/L$$

a. Suppose that Kolkhoz Korn chooses L to maximize net revenue per worker. Show that the first order condition for choosing L is

$$P \cdot MP_L = P \cdot AP_L - R/L$$

b. Capital Corn Company is a competitive, profit-maximizing popcorn farm in Iowa. Assume that it has the same production function as Kolkhoz Korn, pays the same amount in fixed costs, can sell as much corn as it can produce at the competitive price, P, and can hire as many workers as it wants at the competitive wage rate, w. What is the first order condition for its profit-maximizing choice of L?

Explain why Capital Corn will want to hire more workers if P increases. [Hint: what happens to MP_L when L increases?]_____

_____

_____

_____

_____

_____

_____

_____

c. Suppose that both farms happen to employ the same number of workers and face the same output price, P. You already know that Capital Corn will want to hire additional workers. Will Kolkhoz Korn want to hire additional workers, too? If so, which of the two farms will want to hire more? Explain. [Hint: which of the two sides of the first order condition in **a** increases by more when P increases?] _____

_____

_____

_____

_____

_____

_____

_____

_____

_____

13.10. Mr. Entrepreneur is the only decision maker in his firm. The profits of his firm depend solely on the number of hours, H, he spends on the job:

$$\pi = 20H - H^2$$

Profits decline if Mr. E works too much because he gets on the nerves of his employees.

a. Graph Mr. E's profit function below and indicate the value of H that maximizes profits.

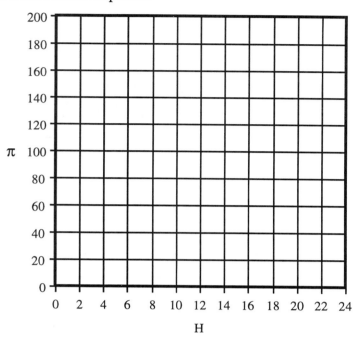

b. Mr. E likes leisure, L, as well as profits. The number of hours of leisure he gets in a day is L = 24 – H. His utility function is U = Lπ = (24 – H)π. Find the values of H and π that maximize his utility subject to his profit function. Indicate his utility-maximizing choice of H on the graph by writing H* at the appropriate spot on the horizontal axis and draw in the indifference curve that goes through this point. [Note that L is measured from right to left on the horizontal axis and ranges from 0 to 24. The indifference curve will have a positive slope in the diagram.]

Does his utility-maximizing choice also maximize his profits?

c. Marshall would exclude the portion of entrepreneurial income necessary to keep Mr. E in business from his profit. This amount is $\Pi* = \Pi - \Pi_{min}$, where Π_{min} is the minimum amount he would have to earn in order to be willing to stay in business and work the number of hours you found in **b.**

Harcourt Brace & Company

Suppose that the best job Mr. E can get if he goes out of business pays $75 per day and requires that he works 8 hours. Indicate this point on the graph above and draw the indifference curve that passes through this point. This is his "next best" indifference curve. Now examine the vertical distance between this curve and the horizontal axis at H*. What does this distance represent? (1)_____. Still at H*, what does the vertical distance between the next best indifference curve and the profit function represent? (2)_____. Is the vertical distance between this indifference curve and the profit function maximized at H*? (3)_____ Would your answer change if his indifference curves were vertically parallel? (4)_____.

CHAPTER 14

THE PARTIAL EQUILIBRIUM COMPETITIVE MODEL

very short-run supply

assumptions of perfect competition:

    large number of firms producing a homogeneous product

    all firms profit maximize

    all firms assume they are price takers

    transactions are costless

short-run market supply curves:

$$Q_S\,(P,v,w) = \sum_{i=1}^{n} q_i(P,v,w) = S(P,\beta)$$

    supply elasticity:

$$e_{S,P} = \frac{\partial Q_S}{\partial P}\frac{P}{Q}$$

market demand curve:

$$Q_D = D(P,\,\alpha)$$

short-run equilibrium:

$$Q_D = D(P,\,\alpha) = S(P,\,\beta) = Q_S$$

    demand shifts:

$$e_{P,\alpha} = \frac{e_{Q,\alpha}}{e_{S,P} - e_{S,P}}$$

long-run supply:

    entry and exit

    zero profits

    if all firms are identical, $P = MC =$ minimum value of AC for all firms

    constant, increasing, and decreasing costs

long-run equilibrium:

determination of the number of firms under constant costs

effect of demand shift

effect of an input price increase

long-run producer surplus

Ricardian rent

capitalization of rent

PROBLEMS

(Numbers in brackets at the beginning of problems below refer to related examples and problems in the text.)

14.1. [Related to text examples 14.1 and 14.2, and problem 14.1.] In Problem 13.4 you found the following short run supply function for Timothy's Toothpicks:

$$t = (P - 29)^{.5} + 1$$

Recall that the supply function was derived from a short run cost function in which the floor area of the plant was fixed at 4,500 square feet.

a. There are 100 firms in the toothpick industry, all having the same cost functions and floor area as Timothy's. Assuming that there are no interaction effects between the firms, find the short-run supply curve for the industry. Let T represent the total quantity of toothpicks supplied by all firms.

Graph the supply function on the diagram below. To make your task simpler, first find the inverse short-run supply function for the industry (P as a function of T).

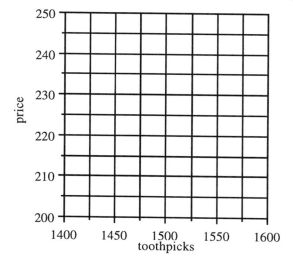

b. The inverse demand function for toothpicks is $P = - (T/100)^2$
$- .02T + 480$. Graph this function on the above diagram and
find the market equilibrium price and quantity. Confirm that
the price and quantity you determine mathematically is the
point where the two curves cross. [Hint: there are two
alternative ways to find the equilibrium price and quantity
mathematically. The first uses the demand and supply
function; equate quantity demanded to quantity supplied and
solve for P. The second uses the inverse demand and supply
functions; equate supply price to demand price and solve for
Q. For this particular problem the latter approach will be
simpler.]

14.2. Sketch supply and demand curves for vacations in Bermuda in
the diagram below. Indicate the equilibrium price and quantity
with P* and Q*, respectively.

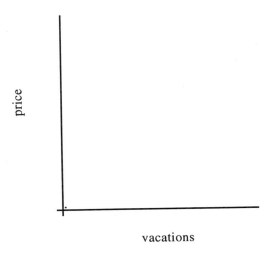

price

vacations

a. Suppose that the price of vacations in Florida increases. What
will happen to the demand curve for vacations in Bermuda?
Draw a new demand curve and indicate the new equilibrium
price and quantity with P** and Q**, respectively.

b. This part is concerned with quantifying the move from (Q*, P*) to (Q**, P**) by using elasticities. It will make use of the formula:

$$e_{P,\alpha} = \frac{e_{D,\alpha}}{e_{S,P} - e_{D,P}}$$

Suppose that the elasticity of demand for Bermuda vacations with respect to the price of Florida vacations is 0.5. What symbol is this represented by in the formula? (1)_____.
To illustrate the relationship between this elasticity and the graph, suppose that the price of Florida vacations goes up by 10 percent and the price of Bermuda vacations remains unchanged. By what percent will the quantity of Bermuda vacations change? (2)_____ On the graph, indicate what the new quantity would be under the old price with Q^+. Of course, the price of Bermuda vacations does not stay constant, so we need to figure out how much it changes and how that affects quantity demanded. Suppose that the supply elasticity of Bermuda vacations is 1 and the demand elasticity is –1. If the price of Florida vacations goes up by 1 percent, by what percent will the price of Bermuda vacations change? (3)_____ What will the percentage change be if Florida vacations go up by 5 percent? (4)_____
Suppose that P* = $1,000. If the price of Florida vacations goes up by 5 percent, what will P** be? (5)_____
What will the percentage change in the quantity of Bermuda vacations be? [Hint: notice that this is a movement along the supply curve. What elasticity is relevant?]
(6)_____ If Q* = 10,000, what is Q**? (7)_____

c. Now, imagine a different scenario: the original equilibrium is as depicted above. Airline fares on flights to Bermuda go up by 10%. Since half the cost of the vacation is the air fare, the price of vacations goes up by 5%. What happens to the supply curve for Bermuda vacations?
(1)_____ Using the relevant elasticites from **b**, by what percentage will the price increase?
(2)_____ What will the new equilibrium price be? (3)_____

By what percentage will equilibrium quantity change?

(4)_____ What will the new equilibrium

quantity be? (5)_____

14.3. [Related to text problem 14.3.] The bird seed industry is
perfectly competitive. The demand function for bird seed is

$$Q = 200,000 - 20,000P$$

There are 100 identical firms in the bird seed industry.   In a
particular year each firm produced 1,000 tons of seed. Since
seed takes a year to produce and rots if it is not used within a
year, the supply of seed in this particular year is fixed at 100,000
tons.

  a. Calculate the equilibrium price.

  b. Calculate the elasticity of demand at the market equilibrium

     point.

  c. Suppose that one firm has an extra ton of seed to sell while

     all other firms continue to supply 1,000 tons. What will the

     price be then?

d. In **c**, when the single firm increased its quantity sold by

(1)_____ percent, the price went down by

(2)_____ percent. Therefore, the elasticity

of demand facing this single firm (assuming output of other

firms is fixed) is about (3)_____.

e. Now, suppose that the short-run supply curve of each firm is
$q = 200P$. Assuming no interactions between the 100 firms,
what is market supply?

Calculate equilibrium price and quantity.

f. Continuing **e**, suppose that one firm decides to sell one more
ton, whatever the price. Its supply function is now $q = 200P + 1$. Calculate the new equilibrium price and quantity,
assuming that the supply functions of other firms remain
unchanged.

g. Continuing **f**, what is the elasticity of demand facing the
individual firm now?

h. Suppose that, in the long run, the bird seed industry exhibits constant costs. What will the elasticity of demand facing an individual firm be then?

i. Under what condition(s) is it reasonable to assume that a firm faces an infinitely elastic demand for its product?

_____

_____

_____

_____

_____

_____

14.4. [Related to text example 14.4, and problems 14.4–14.6 and 14.8.] This problem is a continuation of Problems 13.4 and 14.1. Be sure that you have answered those problems correctly before proceeding. In 13.4 you found that in the long run Timothy's should have a factory with an area equal to three times the number of tons of toothpicks produced in a year. This implied that Timothy's long run total, marginal and average cost functions are:

$$C = t^3/3 - 10T^2 + 300T$$
$$MC = t^2 - 20t + 300$$
$$AC = t^2/3 - 10t + 300$$

a. Find Timothy's long run supply function.

b. In Problem 14.1 you should have found an equilibrium price of $225. At this price, what are Timothy's profits?

Remember that A = 45 originally and that Timothy's produces 15 tons in the short run equilibrium. [Hint: is Timothy's on its long-run cost function?]

Are there any incentives that would lead Timothy's to either reduce or expand production in the long run, or lead other firms to either enter or exit the industry? Explain.

_____

_____

_____

_____

_____

c. Assuming that there are no interaction effects, describe the long-run supply curve for the industry. Assume there is free entry and exit and that potential competitors have the same cost functions. _____

_____

_____

_____

Add the long-run supply curve to the following graph, which already shows the short-run supply curve and the demand curve from 14.1.

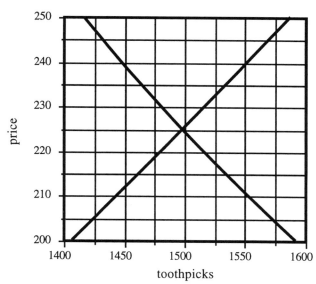

14.5. [Related to text problem 14.7.] In a remote northern state there are N bush pilots, all operating independently. All pilots face the same costs. Costs are measured in thousands of dollars per year, depend on thousands of miles flown in a year, m, and include the pilot's implicit salary, S (the amount left over after all other expenses are paid, in thousands of dollars):

$$C = m^2 - m + S$$

The number of pilots who are willing to set up operations depends on S:

$$N = 8S$$

Total demand for miles flown, in thousands of miles, is:

$$M = (20/P)^3$$

a. In the short run, the supply of pilots is fixed. Suppose that N = 40. The short-run supply function of each pilot is m = (1)_____. Assuming that there are no interactions between the supply curves of individual pilots, the market short-run supply function is M = (2)_____. Verify that the short-run equilibrium price is about 4.242 thousand dollars. How many thousands of miles will each pilot fly? m = (3)_____. Nonsalary costs for each pilot are (4)_____. The implicit salary is S = (5)_____ thousand dollars. The number of pilots willing to work for this salary is N = (6)_____.

b. Now we want to find the long-run supply function. Long-run equilibrium requires that S = (1)_____. Hence
$$\underset{\text{(a function of N)}}{}$$
the long-run cost function of each pilot is also a function of N: C = (2)_____. Even though long-run cost depends on N, long-run marginal cost does not depend on N: MC = (3)_____. However, long-run average cost does: AC = (4)_____.

Each pilot will equate P to MC in the long run. Hence the supply of each pilot will be m = (5)_____.

Market supply will be N times this function of P, but N itself depends on P. Would you expect N to increase or decrease as

P increases? Why? (6)_____

_____

_____

To find the mathematical relationship between N and P, first

recall that long-run equilibrium requires MC = AC. Why?

(7)_____

_____

_____Use this

condition to find long run N as a function of m: N =

(8)_____. Now, substitute your

answer from (5) for m to get N as a function of P: N =

(9)_____.Now, multiply this by your answer to (5)

to get total M supplied in the long run as a function of P

alone: M = (10)_____. Explain in

your own words why this long-run supply function is flatter

than the short run supply function you found in **a**, but not

horizontal. (11)_____

_____

_____

_____

_____

_____

c. Use the results in **b** to find long-run equilibrium values for

the following:

P =

m =

N =

Harcourt Brace & Company

M =

S =

AC =

d. Will pilots be earning any accounting profits in long run

equilibrium? (1)_____ Any economic

profits? (2)_____

14.6. Suppose that average costs of each firm in the microcomputer industry are given by:

$$AC = f(q, w, v, t)$$

where q is the firm's output, w and v are factor prices, and t is time. Suppose that over time $\partial AC/\partial t < 0$; that is, over time average costs fall due to technical change. Assume that the industry is competitive.

a. If the industry exhibits constant costs, what will happen to

microcomputer prices over time? (1)_____

_____ What will determine the rate at

which output expands? (2)_____

_____.

b. How are your conclusions in **a** affected by the observation

that industry expansion increases demand for labor with the

technical skills needed to assemble micros, driving up their

wage rates?

(1)_____

(2)_____

CHAPTER 15

APPLIED COMPETITIVE ANALYSIS

welfare loss

$$\text{welfare loss} = 1/2(P_D - P_S)(Q^* - \overline{Q})$$

price controls

shortages

black markets

tax incidence analysis

tax wedge

$$\frac{dP_D}{dt} = \frac{e_S}{e_S - e_D}$$

$$\frac{dP_D / dt}{dt / dt} = -\frac{e_D}{e_S}$$

deadweight loss

$$DW \approx -1/2\left(\frac{dt}{P_0}\right)^2 \left[e_D e_S / (e_S - e_D)\right]P_0 Q_0$$

marginal vs. average burden

transactions costs

effects on attributes of transactions

trade restrictions

gains from trade

tariff

quota

implicit tariffs

KEY CONCEPTS

PROBLEMS

(Numbers in brackets at the beginning of problems below refer to related examples and problems in the text.)

15.1. [Related to text example 15.1 and problem 15.1.] The inverse demand curve for baby-sitting in Suburbia is given by:

$$P_D = 10 - H/20$$

where H is number of hours demanded per week and P is price, in dollars per hour. The supply curve for baby-sitting is:

$$P_S = H/20$$

Assume that the market is competitive.

a. Draw the supply and demand curves in the diagram below, and indicate the market equilibrium price and quantity.

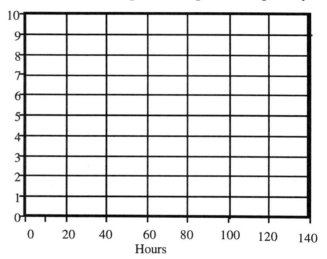

b. Calculate consumer surplus and producer surplus in the competitive equilibrium. [Hint: These are each represented by triangular areas in the graph, and the area of a triangle is equal to .5 × height × width.]

CS =

PS =

c. The members of the Parent and Teachers Association (PTA) at Suburbia High School think that high school students— their own teenagers—are spending too much time baby-sitting and not enough time studying. They agree to restrict the hours that each of their teenagers can baby-sit per week to 5 hours. The effect of this restriction on the market is to reduce the total quantity of hours supplied to 80. The hourly price consumers (parents of young children) are willing to pay for this amount of baby-sitting is (1)_____. Teenagers, independent of their parents preferences, are willing to supply this amount of care at an hourly rate of (2)_____. Since there is no restriction on price, the market price will (3) (increase/decrease) to (4)_____ per hour. Consumer surplus is reduced by (5)_____. The amount of consumer surplus that is transferred to producers is (6)_____. [Hint: a rectangular area on the graph.] The remaining loss in consumer surplus is a deadweight loss of (7)_____. [Hint: a triangular area on the graph.] There is also a deadweight loss of producer surplus (8)_____ [Hint: another triangular area]. Thus, the net change in producer surplus (i.e., the transfer from consumers minus the deadweight loss to producers) is (9)_____, and the total deadweight loss is (10)_____.

15.2. [Related to text problems 15.1 and 15.4] Demand and supply (both long and short run) of apartments in Megalopolis are depicted in the diagram below.

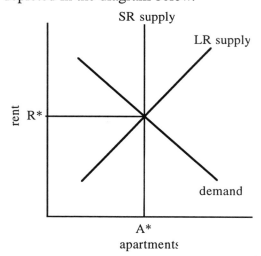

a. Why would you expect the long-run supply curve to be upward sloping, as depicted? _____

_____

_____

b. Over time rents have been rising due to increases in demand. A "renters revolt" occurs and, in response, the city council decides to impose a ceiling on rents at their current level. Draw a line representing the ceiling in the diagram. Demand continues to increase. Draw a new demand curve, representing such an increase. Indicate on the diagram the rent that, in the absence of the rent ceiling, would clear the market in the short run with R_S. Indicate the new quantity demanded at rent R* with A**. Indicate the long-run market clearing rent with R_L and the long-run number of apartments with A_L.

c. What does the horizontal distance between A** and A* represent? _____

_____

d. The vertical distance between R_S and R* represents the difference between the amounts tenants would be willing to pay landlords for A* apartments and how much they have to pay. State some ways in which competition between tenants for apartments could make the implicit rent payed by those

Harcourt Brace & Company

that are successful in getting apartments greater than R*. Do these extra expenses benefit landlords?

_____

_____

_____

_____

_____

_____

_____

_____

_____

e. If the rent ceiling is maintained and landlords receive no other compensation, what will happen in the long run, when new apartments can be built and old ones renovated or destroyed? Compare this to what would happen in the absence of the rent ceiling. What will be the next crisis for Megalopolis?_____

_____

_____

_____

_____

_____

_____

_____

_____

f. Shade the area on the diagram that represents the long-run deadweight loss from the rent ceiling. Cross-hatch the area that represents the amount of surplus transferred from landlords to renters in the long run.

15.3. [Related to text problems 15.5–15.7] The inverse demand curve in the toothpick industry is given by:

$$P = 600 - T/4$$

where T is tons of toothpicks and P is price. The inverse short-run supply curve is given by:

$$P = -150 + T/4$$

The long-run supply curve is horizontal at a price of $225.

These curves are depicted in the diagram below. Note that the industry is in both long-run and short-run equilibrium.

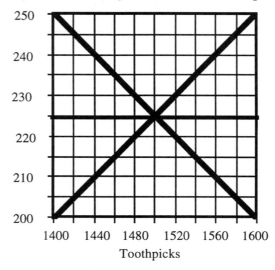

a. The Surgeon General issues a report on oral cancer in which toothpicks are implicated as a cause. As a result, the inverse demand curve shifts to

$$P = 580 - T/4$$

Draw this new demand curve on the diagram. In the short run, what will equilibrium price and quantity be? [Read the answers off the diagram.] P = (1)_____ T = (2)_____ In the long run, when some toothpick plants are closed due to the lower prices, what will equilibrium price and quantity be? P = (3)_____ T = (4)_____ Draw the new short-run supply curve (assume that the new short-run supply curve is parallel to the old curve).

b. The toothpick labor union is up in arms about the loss of jobs from the plant closings caused by the Surgeon General's report. Most of the factories are in Maine, Oregon, and Washington. The Congressmen from these states manage to include an industry subsidy in the next federal budget bill. Their fellow Congressmen would never support a direct subsidy to toothpick buyers because of the Surgeon General's report. It is, however, difficult to fight support for employment, so it is agreed that the government will pay each toothpick firm $20.00 per month for each worker employed. Since the production technology requires one month of labor per ton of toothpicks, this subsidy amounts to $20 per ton. This shifts the short-run supply function to:

P = (1) _____

The long-run supply function also shifts downward by the same amount, and is now horizontal at P = (2)$_____. Add these new supply functions to the diagram. In the short run, immediately after this change is implemented, what price will consumers pay and how many toothpicks will they buy? P = (3)_____ T = (4)_____ How much of the unit subsidy will be received by ("shifted on to") consumers, in the form of a lower equilibrium price? (5)_____ How much will be retained by producers? (6)_____. In the long run, what will price and quantity be? P = (7)_____ Q = (8)_____. How much of the subsidy will be shifted on to consumers? (9)_____ Retained by producers? (10) _____ What do you think of the Congressmen's rationale for the employment subsidy? (11)_____

_____

_____

_____ Would the long-run results be any different if consumers were given a direct subsidy equivalent to $20 per ton of toothpicks? If so, how? (12)_____

_____

_____

_____

[Remark: the only thing absurd in this example is the use of toothpicks, as anyone familiar with the history of the government's support of the tobacco industry will recognize.]

15.4. [Related to text example 15.3 and problems 15.8 – 15.10.] The information in the graph below summarizes the findings of a 1985 study on the sugar industry.[1] The domestic demand and supply curves are shown in the graph, along with information

---

[1] Rachel Dardis and Carol Young, "The Welfare Loss from the New Sugar Program," *Journal of Consumer Affairs*, vol. 19, no. 1, Summer 1985, 163-176.

about the world price of sugar, the U.S. tariff on imported sugar, and the U.S. quota on imported sugar. The domestic price of sugar is $.22 per pound, but the world price is only $.09 per pound, and the tariff is $.02. Thus, to sell sugar on the U.S. market, foreign producers have to give up $.11 per pound—$.09 of sales in other markets plus $.02 in taxes—but are compensated $.22 per pound by buyers. The size of the quota is represented in the graph by the distance from Q_2 to Q_3. The sizes of various areas have been indicated in the graph and will be used to answer the questions below. Assume that the foreign supply to the domestic market is perfectly elastic; the world price of $.09 per pound does not depend on the quantity of sugar imported into the United States.

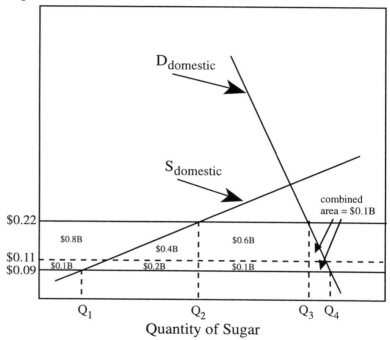

a. Domestic sugar producers gain from the trade restrictions relative to their position in the absence of trade restrictions. The value of their gain in domestic producer surplus is estimated to be (1)_____. At the same time, U.S. consumers lose a total of (2)_____ in consumer surplus.

b. The loss of consumer surplus is in part transferred to other parties, including: the transfer of surplus to domestic producers (see **a**); the transfer of tariff revenue of (1)_____ to the U.S. government; and the transfer of (2)_____ to foreign producers. In addition, there is a deadweight loss of (3)_____.

Harcourt Brace & Company

c. Explain why the loss in consumer surplus from trade restrictions such as these must exceed the gain in domestic producer surplus. _____

_____
_____
_____
_____

d. Sugar quotas are given out to carefully selected countries. In what sense could these quotas be viewed as implicit "foreign aid" to the selected countries? _____

_____
_____
_____
_____ Would consumers as a group be better off or worse off if the government dropped the quotas, raised the tariff to $.13, and gave the additional tariff revenue to the same countries? Explain.

_____
_____
_____
_____
_____ Why might the government prefer to use the quota to provide foreign aid rather than the higher tariff and explicit foreign aid?

_____
_____
_____
_____
_____

e. Up to this point it has been assumed that the supply of imported sugar is perfectly elastic. Suppose, instead, that the elasticity is positive; as more sugar is imported, the world market price increases. Would the gain in consumer surplus that could be achieved by eliminating the trade restrictions be larger or smaller than the loss in consumer surplus that you reported in **a**? Explain. _____

_____

_____

_____

_____Would the loss
in producer surplus that would result from eliminating the
trade restrictions be large or smaller than the gain reported in
a? Explain. _____

_____

_____

_____

CHAPTER 16

GENERAL COMPETITIVE EQUILIBRIUM

interactions between markets

efficiency in the allocation of inputs to production processes:

$$RTS_{LK}^{X} = RTS_{LK}^{Y}$$

production possibility frontier (PPF):

rate of product transformation:

$$RPT_{XY} = -dY/dX \text{ (along PPF of X and Y)} = MC_X/MC_Y$$

opportunity cost

relative capital intensity

conditions satisfied in general competitive equilibrium:

production is on the PPF

$$RPT_{XY} = P_X/P_Y = MRS_{XY}$$

tariffs and relative factor prices

existence of equilibrium prices:

excess demand functions (in an economy with fixed supplies):

$$ED_i(P) = D_i(P) - S_i \text{ where } P = (P_1, \ldots, P_n)$$

Walras' Law:

$$\sum_i P_i ED_i(P) = 0$$

Brouwer's Fixed-Point Theorem: Any continuous mapping [F(X)] of a closed, bounded, convex set into itself has at least one fixed point (X*) such that F(X*) =X*

transactions demand for money

(Numbers in brackets at the beginning of problems below refer to related examples and problems in the text.)

16.1. [Related to text problem 16.1.] The production possibility frontier for red pencils (R) and blue pencils (B) is

$$R + B = 100$$

a. Graph this function on the diagram below.

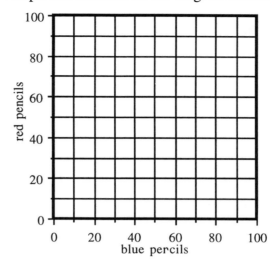

b. Each person in this competitive economy has the same amount of money to spend on pencils and has the following utility function for pencils:

$$U = RB$$

How many pencils will be produced under competitive equilibrium? Indicate this point on the graph.

c. What price ratio (P_R/P_B) would prevail in **b**?

d. How would your answers to **b** and **c** change if half the people in this economy had twice as much money to spend on pencils as the other half?

e. How would your answers to **b** and **c** change if half the people in this economy had the utility function $U = R^{.75}B^{.25}$ and the other half had $U = R^{.25}B^{.75}$?

16.2. [Related to text examples 16.1 and 16.2, and problem 16.2.] Suppose that fish (F) and mangos (M) are produced by the following production functions:

$$F = L_F^{.5} \quad \text{and} \quad M = L_M^{.5}$$

where L_F and L_M are labor used in production of F and M, respectively. Total labor available is 100 units, so:

$$L_F + L_M = 100$$

a. Verify that the production possibility frontier is $F^2 + M^2 = 100$. [Hint: start by solving the production functions for L_F and L_M as functions of F and M, respectively.]

Plot the PPF on the diagram below. [Hint: the PPF is a quarter of a circle. Where is the center of the full circle? What is the circle's radius?]

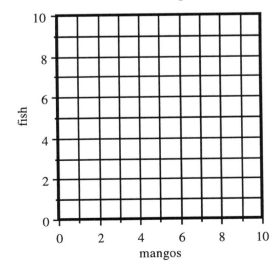

b. Find RPT_{MF}. [Hint: start by differentiating the equation for the PPF. Your answer will be a function of M and F.]

c. The representative consumer in this competitive economy has the following utility function:

$$U = F^{.75}M^{.25}$$

Find MRS_{MF} for the representative consumer.

d. Use the PPF and your results from **b** and **c** to find the amounts of F and M that are produced in a competitive equilibrium. [Hint: what two conditions must hold in equilibrium? Write down the two equations that represent these conditions for this problem.]

Plot this point on the diagram in **a** and sketch the indifference curve that passes through it.

e. What will the price ratio (P_M/P_F) be in the competitive equilibrium?

f. How much labor will be allocated to F production? To M production?

16.3. [Related to text problems 16.3 and 16.4.] This problem shows you how to find the PPF for an economy with two goods and two inputs when the production functions for both goods are of the Cobb-Douglas variety. The general results will be useful in solving the problems in the text. The production functions are

$$X = K_X^{\alpha} L_X^{\beta} \quad \text{and} \quad Y = K_Y^{\gamma} L_Y^{\delta}$$

Total factor supplies are fixed at levels K and L. Since the marginal products of each factor are positive no matter how much of each factor is used, all factors will be employed in a competitive equilibrium. Hence, the following full-employment conditions will be satisified:

$$K_X + K_Y = K \qquad L_X + L_Y = L$$

The following definitions will be useful: $b = \beta/\alpha$, $d = \delta/\gamma$, $s = L_X/L$, $k_X = K_X/L_X$, $k_Y = K_Y/L_Y$, and $k = K/L$.

a. Efficiency requires that RTS_{LK} be the same for both goods. Use this condition to find a relationship between k_X and k_Y under competitive equilibrium.

Suppose that b is larger than d. Which good is relatively capital-intensive? [Hint: which must be lower, k_X or k_Y?]

b. Show that $sk_X + (1 - s)k_Y = k$. [Hint: substitute the definitions of s and the various capital-labor ratios and then show that this condition reduces down to one of the full-employment conditions.]

c. Now, verify that the equations in **a** and **b** can be solved to get:

$$k_Y = bk/[b + (d - b)s]$$

[Hint: solve the equation in **a** for k_X as a function of k_Y, then substitute your result for k_X in the equation in **b**. Finally, solve the resulting equation for k_Y.]

Find a similar result for k_X.

d. The definition of s implies that $L_X = sL$ and the definition of k_X implies that $K_X = k_X L_X = k_X sL$. Use these along with your results from **c** to show that

$$X = \left(\frac{d}{b+(d - b)s}\right)^\alpha K^\alpha L^\beta s^{\alpha+\beta}$$

[Hint: begin with the production function for X, substitute the definitions for K_X and L_X, then substitute for k_X, then substitute the definition of k, and then simplify.]

Now, find a similar expression for Y. [Be careful: $L_Y = (1 - s)L$.]

e. Your results in **d** can be used to find all efficient combinations of X and Y (points on the PPF) that can be produced with a given K and L by considering all values of s between 0 and 1, once you know the values of the parameters. To illustrate, suppose K = 100, L = 200, $\alpha = \beta$ = .5, $\gamma = 1/3$, and $\delta = 2/3$, so b = 1 and d = 2. The equations are then:

$$X = [2/(1+s)]^{.5}(141.42)s$$
$$\text{and}$$
$$Y = [2/(1+s)]^{1/3}(158.74)(1 - s)$$

Use these to fill in the blanks in the following table:

s	X	Y
0.0	0	200
0.25	45	139
0.5	_____	_____
0.75	113	41
1.0	_____	0

Plot these points on the diagram below and sketch the entire PPF.

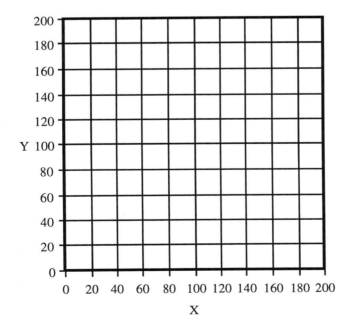

16.4. [Related to text problem 16.5.] A small country produces tape recorders and cameras to sell on the world market. Its production functions for these goods are both Cobb-Douglas with two inputs, capital, and labor. The country is so small that it can sell as many cameras and automobiles as it wants on the world market without affecting world prices. Total capital and labor devoted to production of these goods is fixed. The locus of efficient input allocations and the production possibility frontier are depicted below.

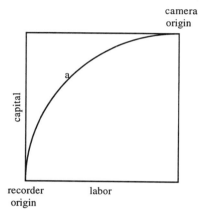

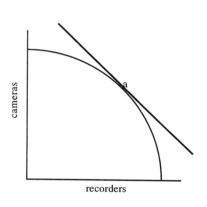

A. Locus of Efficient Input   B. Production Possibility
   Allocations   Frontier

Initially, international trade opportunities are described by the straight "trade" line in diagram B. Production is at point "a" and the allocation of inputs is at point "a" in diagram A.

a. Which good is relatively capital intensive?

b. What will happen if the world price of cameras rises relative to the world price of recorders? Draw a new trade line on diagram B and label the new choice "b". What happens to output of cameras? (1)_____ Of recorders? (2)_____ What happens to the allocation of capital and labor? (3)_____ _____ Label the new allocation on diagram A with "b". What happens to the capital-labor ratio in the recorder industry? (4)_____ The camera industry? (5)_____ What happens to the price of labor relative to the price of capital? (6)_____ Explain .(7)_____

_____

_____

_____

_____

_____

_____

16.5. [Related to text example 16.4 and problem 16.7.] Visitors to Walras Park purchase tickets for a fixed price per ticket. Each day the manager sets a price which he hopes is just low enough to sell 10,000 tickets.   There are three rides in the park. The number of tickets a person must purchase for each ride varies. The number of tickets needed for each ride are T_1, T_2, and T_3. Let $t_2 = T_2/T_1$ and let $t_3 = T_3/T_1$. The manager wants to choose values of T_1, T_2, and T_3 that will keep all three rides busy all of the time. If there is excess demand for a ride, refunds are given. Excess supply exists if some seats on a ride are vacant.

a. Let X_i^D represent the number of rides demanded on the ith

ride by visitors in a typical day. If all 10,000 tickets are

bought, the budget constraint for all visitors is:

$$T_1 X_1^D + T_2 X_2^D + T_3 X_3^D = 10{,}000$$

Let X_i^S represent the maximum number of rides on the ith

ride that the park can offer in a day. Ideally, the manager

chooses prices such that his "budget constraint" is satisfied:

$$T_1 X_1^S + T_2 X_2^S + T_3 X_3^S = 10{,}000$$

Use these equations to show that:

$$T_1 ED_1 + T_2 ED_2 + T_3 ED_3 = 0$$

where $ED_i = X_i^D - X_i^S$.

Is Walras' Law satisfied at Walras Park?

Harcourt Brace & Company

b. When all 10,000 tickets are sold, the excess demand functions for rides two and three are

$$ED_2 = -t_2 + 2\,t_3 - 1$$

$$ED_3 = 2\,t_2 - 3\,t_3$$

Are these excess demand functions homogeneous of degree zero in prices?

c. Use Walras' Law to find ED_1.

Is ED_1 homogeneous of degree zero in prices?

d. Find the values of t_2 and t_3 that make ED_2 and ED_3 both zero.

e. Will ED_1 be zero at the values of t_2 and t_3 found in **c**? Explain. _____

_____

_____

_____

f. Suppose $X_1{}^S = 2{,}000$, $X_2{}^S = 1{,}000$, and $X_3{}^S = 2{,}000$. What must T_1, T_2, and T_3 be in order to satisfy the manager's budget constraint and the relative values found in **d**?

16.6. [Related to text problem 16.9.] In problem 16.2 you found an equilibrium price ratio for mangos and fish. In this problem you are given additional information that will allow you to determine the levels of these two prices as well as the wage rate. There are 100 people in this economy and each supplies one unit of labor per period. Hence $L = 100$, as before. The government has issued 1,000 tokens to be used as money. The representative consumer is willing to hold a stock of money equal to 10% of the value of transactions made each period.

a. What will the money wage rate (w) be in equilibrium? [Hint: in equilibrium, the representative consumer doesn't save or dissave (i.e., add or subtract from her stock of tokens), so a token earned is a token spent. Hence, her stock of tokens must equal 10% of her wages.]

b. What will the nominal prices be? [Hint: the representative consumer's budget constraint can be written as $(P_F/P_M)P_M F + P_M M = w$. You already know the equilibrium values of P_F/P_M, F, M, and w.]

c. The government decides to retire some of the tokens. To do so it levies a 10% tax on wages for one period. The tokens it collects from the tax are destroyed. How many tokens will be collected? (1)_____ What will the money supply be then? (2)_____ When a new equilibrium is reached, what will nominal prices and the wage rate be? P_M = (3)_____ P_F = (4)_____ w = (5)_____ What is the effect on the representative consumer's equilibrium consumption of F? (6)_____ M? (7)_____ Stock of tokens? (8)_____ Has any nominal saving or dissaving occurred? (9)_____ Has any real saving or dissaving occurred? (10)_____

16.7. At Enormous State University half of the student seats in the football stadium are "reserved" and the other half are "open admission." There is one seat for each student at ESU and open admission seats are free to all students on a first-come first-serve basis. Students must pay a fee for the more desirable reserved seats. Assume that all ESU students plan to come to each game.

a. If the fee for reserved seats is set too low, there will be an excess supply of (1)_____ seats and excess demand for (2)_____ seats. If the fee is too high, there will be an excess supply of (3)_____ seats and excess demand for (4)_____ seats.

b. Under what condition(s) will there exist a fee at which excess demand for both types of seats will be zero (or at least within two or three seats from zero)? _____

_____

_____

_____

_____

c. Will the condition(s) be satisfied if fraternities, sororities, and other large groups of students go to games in "blocks"—each group choosing the type of seating for all of its members, with the choice depending on the fee? Explain.

_____

_____

_____

_____

_____

16.8. Brouwer's Fixed Point Theorem states that a mapping of a set onto itself will have a fixed point if four specific conditions are satisfied. The diagram below illustrates a case where the conditions are satisfied. The fixed point is x*. In **a** through **d**, illustrate how a function may have no fixed point if the condition listed is violated.

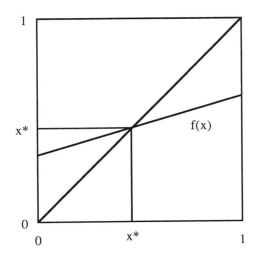

a. The mapping (function) must. be continuous

b. The set must be convex.

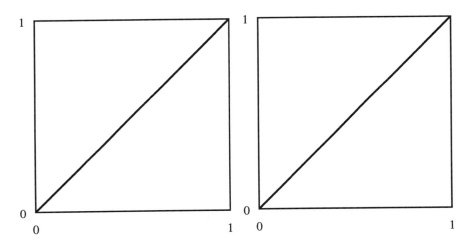

c. The set must be closed.

d. The set must be bounded

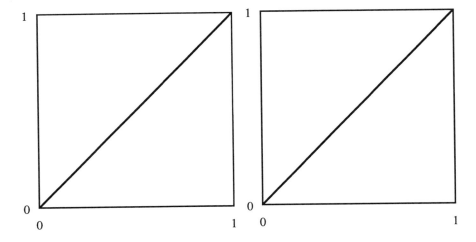

CHAPTER 17

THE EFFICIENCY OF PERFECT COMPETITION

Pareto efficiency

productive efficiency:

efficient input allocation within a firm:

RTS between any input pair must be the same for all outputs

$RTS_{LK} = w/v$ for all outputs under perfect competition

efficient input allocation among firms:

MP of any input in the production of an output must be the same for all firms

$MP_L = P/w$ for all firms under perfect competition

efficient choice of outputs by firms:

RPT between any pair of outputs must be the same for all firms

$RPT_{XY} = MC_X/MC_Y = P_X/P_Y$ under perfect competition

comparative advantage

transformation function:

$T(X_1, X_2, \ldots, X_n) = 0$

Lerner's rule:

$$\frac{dX_1^A}{dX_2^A} = \frac{dX_1^B}{dX_2^B}$$

efficiency in product mix:

RPT for all firms = MRS for all consumers, for any pair of goods

$RPT_{XY} = MC_X/MC_Y = P_X/P_Y = MRS_{XY}$ under perfect competition

laissez-faire

departures from perfect competition:

imperfect competition (market power):

Harcourt Brace & Company

RPT ≠ MRS

externalities:

   social rate of product transformation (SRPT)

   SRPT > RPT = MRS

public goods:

   nonexclusive

   free rider

market adjustment and information:

   Walrasian tâtonnement process (price adjustment)

   $dP/dt = k[ED'(P^*)] \cdot (P - P^*)$

   stability requirement: $ED'(P^*) < 0$

   Marshallian quantity adjustment:

   $dQ/dt = k[D^{-1}(Q) - S^{-1}(Q)] = k[ED^{-1}(Q)], k > 0$

disequilibrium pricing:

   cobweb model:

   $Q_t^S = a + bP_{t-1}$

   $Q_t^D = c - dP_t$

   $Q_t^D = Q_t^S$

   price prediction:

   $P_t = (P_0 - P^*) (-b/d)^t + P^*$

   stability requirement: $b < d$

rational expectations

information and inefficient equilibria:

   asymmetric information and the lemons model

distribution in an exchange economy:

   gains from trade

   terms-of-trade

   Pareto efficient allocation

   Edgeworth Box:

      condition for efficiency in exchange between persons A and B:

      $MRS_{XY}^A = MRS_{XY}^B$

   contract curve

   core

   offer curve

Harcourt Brace & Company

(Numbers in brackets at the beginning of problems below refer to related examples and problems in the text.)

17.1. [Related to text problem 17.1.] Robinson Crusoe produces and consumes fish (F) and goat's milk (M). Since he doesn't have much else to do, he spends 100 hours (H) per week producing F and M. His production functions are:

$$F = \sqrt{H_F} \qquad\qquad M = \sqrt{H_M}$$

where H_F and H_M are hours spent in F and M production, respectively. His utility function is

$$U = F^{.75}M^{.25}$$

a. Find Robinson's PPF. [Hint: see Problem 17.2.]

A portion of Robinson's PPF is drawn in the diagram below.

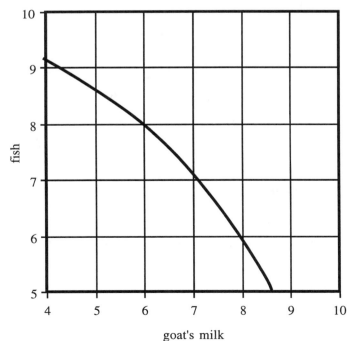

fish

goat's milk

What is Robinson's RPT_{MF}?

What is Robinson's MRS_{MF}?

b. Robinson can only consume what he produces. Suppose that he spends 36 hours producing F and 64 hours producing M. Find F and M and plot them on the graph. F = (1)_____ M = (2)_____ What is Robinson's utility level at this point? U = (3)_____. What is Robinson's RPT_{MF} at this point? (4)_____ His MRS_{MF}? (5)_____ Sketch the indifference curve that passes through this point, being careful that your sketch is consistent with answers (4) and (5). Label the curve with your answer to (3). Explain why Robinson is not at the highest utility level he can achieve on his own at this point. (6)_____

_____

_____

_____

What condition must hold for Robinson to be at his highest utility level? (7)_____

_____

_ Use this condition and the equation for his PPF to determine the point on his PPF that will maximize his utility. M = (8)_____ F = (9)_____ At this point U = (10)_____ Plot this point on the graph, sketch the indifference curve that passes through it, and label it with answer (10).

c. Suppose that Robinson is given the opportunity to trade with the rest of the world at prices for M and F of $1.00 and $3.00, respectively. This means that if he sells a fish, he can get (1)_____ units of goat's milk in return. Draw a line on your graph that represents the choices now available to him if he continues to produce at the point that maximized his

Harcourt Brace & Company

utility in the absence of trade. What is the equation for this line? (2)_____ Find the point on this line that maximizes his utility. F = (3)_____ M = (4)_____ His utility at this point is U = (5)_____ Plot this point on the graph, sketch the indifference curve that passes through it, and label it with answer (5). Describe the transactions that Robinson would make in order to obtain this point.

(6)_____

_____

_____

d. In **c**, is Robinson's production efficient? Explain.

(1)_____

_____

Is his exchange with the rest of the world efficient? Explain.

(2)_____

_____

_____

Given your (presumably correct) answers, explain in your own words why Robinson's production and consumption decisions are nevertheless not the best he could make.

(3)_____

_____

_____

_____ What condition must hold for his production decision to be best?

(4)_____

_____

_____ Use this condition and the equation for his PPF to find his optimal production levels.

F = (5)_____   M = (6)_____

Plot this point on the graph and draw in the line that now represents the consumption choices available to him through trade. Find the equation for this line.

(7)_____

Find his optimal consumption levels.

F = (8)_____   M = (9)_____ His utility will be U = (10)_____. Plot this point on the graph, sketch the indifference curve that passes through it, and label it with answer (10).

17.2. King Oscar thinks that sardines, S, and reindeer meat, R, are perfect substitutes. His utility function for these two commodities is

$$U_K = S + 2R$$

Queen Sophia also thinks that sardines and reindeer are perfect substitutes, but has a somewhat different utility function:

$$U_Q = 2S + R$$

At dinner, Oscar is served 4 sardines and an 8 ounce reindeer steak. Sophia, who is much smaller of the two, is served half as much.

a. Draw the Edgeworth Box for this situation on the graph. The first step is to determine the appropriate dimensions for the box. How are these related to the endowments? _____

_____

_____

Choose appropriate scales for the horizontal (R) and vertical (S) axes. Measure Oscar's endowment from the lower left-hand corner and plot it on the graph. Measure Sophia's endowment from the upper right-hand corner. You should find that it is represented by the same point as Oscar's endowment. Label the point E.

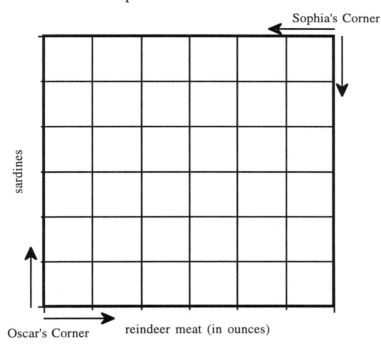

Draw the two indifference curves—one for Oscar and one for Sophia—that pass through the endowment point. Shade in the area that represents servings that would make at least one of them better off without making the other worse off.

b. Describe the contract curve. _____

_____

_____

_____

_____

c. Describe the core. _____

_____

_____

_____

_____

d. Describe the trade(s) Oscar would be willing to make if Sophia promises to give him 1 ounce of R for every 2 S he gives her. (1)_____

_____

_____

_____

What trade(s) would he be willing to make if Sophia promises to give him 1 ounce of R for every S he gives her?

(2)_____

_____ What trade(s) would he be willing to make if Sophia promises to give him 2 ounces of R for every S he gives her? (3)_____

_____ Answers (1) through (3) describe various points on Oscar's offer curve. Indicate this curve on the Edgeworth Box.

e. Indicate Sophia's offer curve on the Edgeworth Box.

f. What price ratio(s), P_R/P_S, would lead Oscar and Sophia to make a trade that would leave them in the core?

_____

_____

17.3. Remember Noah Fect from Problem 5.6? His utility function for beer (B) and soft drinks (S) is

$$U = S + \ln(B)$$

Noah has a twin brother, Sayma, who has identical preferences. Noah has a six-pack of beer and Sayma has a six-pack of soft drinks.

a. Draw the Edgeworth Box for this situation on the graph below. Choose appropriate scales for the horizontal (B) and vertical (S) axes. Measure Noah's endowment from the lower left-hand corner and plot it on the graph. Measure Sayma's endowment from the upper right-hand corner. You should find that it is represented by the same point as Noah's endowment. Label the point E.

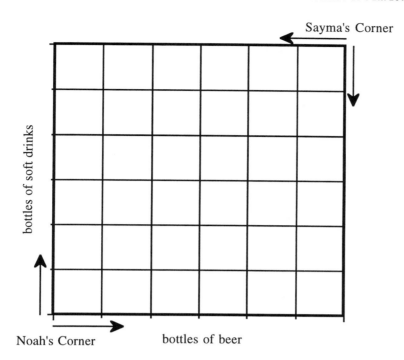

Sayma's Corner

bottles of soft drinks

Noah's Corner   bottles of beer

b. Carefully draw the two indifference curves that pass through the endowment point.

c. In general, what condition must hold for an allocation of B and S to be Pareto Optimal? (1)_____

_____

Use this relationship to find a relationship between B_N and B_S—beer allocated to Noah and Sayma, respectively—that will hold at all Pareto Optimal points. (2)_____

_____

Combine this relationship with the fact that $B_N + B_S = 6$ to find the amount of B each twin will get at all Pareto Optimal points. (3)_____

_____

Draw the contract curve on the diagram in **a** and label the endpoints of the core with A and B.

d. What price ratio, P_B/P_S, would lead Noah and Sayma to trade to an allocation that is in the core? (1) _____

_____

What trade would they make? (2)_____

_____

Would the price ratio be different if the original allocation of beer and soft drinks had been different? Why or why not?

(3)_____

_____

e. Assuming that utility can be compared across the two twins, who will have more utility after the trade described in **d**?

(1)_____ Give an intuitive explanation of why they are not equally well off, even though they have identical tastes and each has a six-pack at the outset.

(2)_____

_____

_____

_____

_____

f. Suppose that Noah originally has two six-packs of beer, instead of one. What price ratio would lead to an allocation in the core now? (1)_____ Compare this ratio to the ratio you found in **d**. Which is less? (2)_____ Give an intuitive explanation of why. (3)_____

_____

_____

_____

_____

_____

_____

g. Suppose that Noah has just one six-pack of beer, but Sayma has two six-packs of soft drinks. What price ratio would lead to an allocation in the core then? (1)_____

Compare this ratio to the ratio you found in **d**. Which is less?

(2)_____ Give an intuitive explanation of why.

(3)_____

_____

_____

_____

17.4. [Related to text example 17.5, and problems 17.5–17.7.] Once and Twice (see Problem 7.1) get shipwrecked on their return from their weekly shopping trip. Each of them has managed to salvage some coconuts, C, and mangos, M from the ship. Once has $C_O = 75$ coconuts and $M_O = 25$ mangos, while Twice has $C_T = 25$ coconuts and $M_T = 75$ mangos. Both have preferences described by:

$$U = (CM)^{.5}$$

[You may notice that this utility function is not consistent with the demand functions that were specified in Problem 7.1. Attribute this to writer's license! Ignore the previous demand functions.]

a. Draw the Edgeworth Box for this situation on the graph below. Choose appropriate scales for the horizontal (M) and vertical (C) axes. Measure Once's endowment from the lower left-hand corner and plot it on the graph. Measure Twice's endowment from the upper right-hand corner. You should find that it is represented by the same point as Once's endowment. Label the point E.

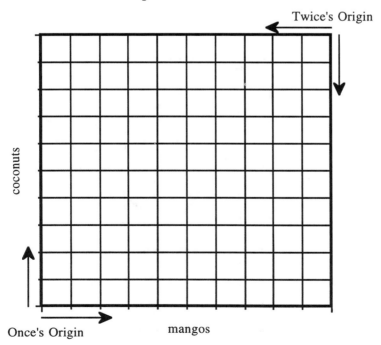

b. Draw in the two indifference curves that pass through E. Shade in the area that represents allocations of C and W that would leave both Once and Twice at least as well off as they are at point E.

c. Find a relationship between the ratio of coconuts to mangos for Once, C_O/M_O, and the ratio of coconuts to mangos for Twice, C_T/M_T, that must hold for all allocations that are Pareto Optimal.

All Pareto Optimal points also satisfy $C_O = 100 - C_T$ and $M_O = 100 - M_T$. Use these and the ratio condition to find an equation for the contract curve. The equation will be a relationship between C_O and M_O.

Draw the contract curve on the Edgeworth Box. Label the endpoints of the core with A and B.

d. The diagram below is a blow up of a section of the Edgeworth Box, including the lens space (the set of allocations where both Once and Twice are at least as well off as at E).

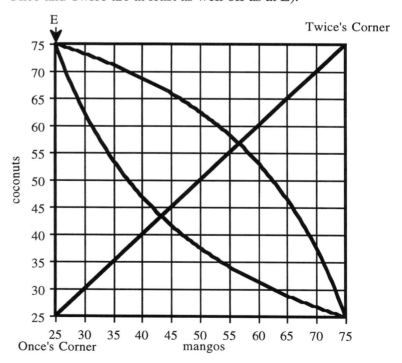

You are to find Once's offer curve. First, suppose that Twice makes the following proposition to Once: "I'll give you two mangos for every coconut you give me, for as many as you want to trade." Draw the line that represents the set of allocations that Twice is now making available to Once. Write the equation for the line below, in the form $aM + bC = c$, where a, b, and c are constants.

(1)_____

How many mangos and coconuts would Once choose? [Hint: think of the above constraint as a standard budget constraint, where a is the price of M, b is the price of C, and c is income.]

M_O = (2)_____ C_O = (3)_____

Plot this point on the diagram and sketch the indifference curve that Once would be on at this point.

Now, suppose that Twice makes the following proposition to Once "I'll give you X mangos for every coconut you give me, for as many as you want to trade," where X stands for a specific number. Write the equation that describes the allocations now available to Once. It will depend on X.

(4)_____ How many mangos and coconuts will Once choose, as a function of X?

M_O = (5)_____ C_O = (6)_____

Fill in the following table.

X	M_O	C_O
1.0	_____	_____
.75	_____	_____
0.5	_____	_____

Plot these points on the diagram. What allocation would Once choose if 1/X just equalled his MRS_{MC} at the endowment point? (7)_____ Draw a smooth curve through the points that you have plotted. This is Once's offer curve. What does this curve describe?

(8)_____

_____

_____

Now sketch Twice's offer curve. This is not difficult to do because of the symmetry of this problem.

e. For what terms of trade would the market "clear"? That is, for what terms of trade would the number of coconuts that Once would choose to give up be just the number that Twice would want in exchange for the mangos he would have to give to Once? (1)_____ Describe the trade that would take place. (2)_____

_____

_____ Is the resulting allocation on the contract curve? (3)_____ In the core? (4)_____

Suppose there were 1000 people just like Once on this island (same tastes and endowments) and another 1000 just like Twice. All are free to trade with one another, each Once-type knows all trades being offered by Twice-types and vice-versa. Explain why Once and Twice would agree to make the trade which you just described, and no other. (5)_____

_____

_____

_____

_____

_____

_____

_____

_____

_____

_____

f. Suppose that Twice, being the elder of the two, gets to choose the terms of trade. Once gets to choose the quantities traded under those terms. That is, Twice gets to maximize his utility, subject to the constraint that the allocation must be on Once's offer curve. Twice's utility can be written as a function of Once's choice, using the fact that total C and M both equal 100:

Harcourt Brace & Company

$$U_T = [(100 - C_O)(100 - M_O)]^{.5}$$

Use your answers for (5) and (6) of **d** to write Twice's utility as a function of X. Then find the value of X that maximizes this function.

X* = (1)_____ For X*, M_O = (2)_____ and C_O = (3)_____. Plot this point on the graph. Which curve is steeper at this point, Once's offer curve or Twice's indifference curve (the latter is not yet drawn)? (4)_____ Sketch the two indifference curves—one for Once and one for Twice—that pass through the point you found. [Note that both of these indifference curves also pass through the point where the values of M_O and C_O are reversed.] "If a single agent in an economy is allowed to set prices, the resulting allocation of commodities will be inefficient." Use this example to explain the meaning of this quotation. (5)_____

_____

_____

_____

_____

_____

g. Suppose that Once and Twice have made the trade that you found in **f**. Twice again is given the opportunity to choose terms of trade, while Once may choose the quantities traded at those terms. Will another trade occur? (1)_____ If you answered no, explain why. If you answered yes, what will prevent such trades from going on indefinitely? (2)_____

_____

_____

_____ What trading strategy

should Twice follow in order to obtain an allocation that is arbitrarily close to the intersection of Once's original indifference curve with the contract curve—the allocation in the lens space where Twice's utility is at its maximum?

(3)_____

_____

_____

_____

"A price-setter that can perfectly price discriminate does not cause economic inefficiency, but instead captures all of the available gains to trade." How is this quotation illustrated by the above example? (4)_____

_____

_____

_____

_____

_____

_____

17.5. Twins Nick and Nack have been trick-or-treating. Each has returned with large quantitiesof peanuts and M&Ms. They are now engaged in trading. Their situation is represented in the following Edgeworth Box diagram.

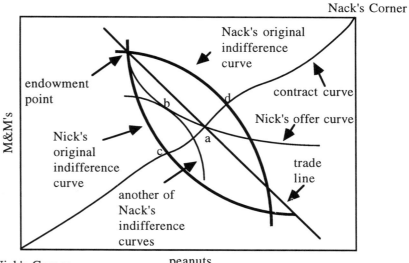

a. Suppose that Nick and Nack are with a large group of friends who are also trading. Among these friends terms-of-trade have been established and are represented by the slope of the trade line that is drawn in the picture. If Nick and Nack could trade with these friends, as well as with each other, and their quantities of peanuts and M&Ms are a small fraction of the quantity that the whole group possesses, which point will they trade to: a, b, c, or d? Explain why and state whether this point is Pareto efficient.

_____

_____

_____

_____

_____

_____

_____

b. Now suppose that the twins are alone and that Nack is much more assertive than Nick. He knows that Nick will accept any terms-of-trade that he dictates, although Nick will still decide for himself how much he is willing to trade. In short, Nack behaves like a monopolist. If Nack knows Nick's offer curve, which point will they trade to: a, b, c, or d? Explain why and state whether this point is Pareto efficient.

_____

_____

_____

_____

_____

_____

_____

_____

c. Continuing **b**, suppose that Nack thinks he can state terms-

of-trade, trade the amount Nick chooses, state new terms-of-

trade, trade again, etc. That is, Nack now behaves like a

price-discriminating monopolist. Which point will they

eventually trade to? Explain why and state whether this point

is Pareto efficient.

_____

_____

_____

_____

_____

_____

_____

_____

17.6. [Related to text problem 17.2] On Paradise Island there are 100
acres of land (A), suitable for growing either Mangos or
Coconuts (but not much else), and 100 people (L). The
production functions for Mangos and Coconuts are both of the
fixed-proportions variety:

$$M = \min(.5A_M, L_M) \qquad C = \min(A_C, .5L_C)$$

where A_M is A used in producing M, etc.

a. Draw a box diagram of the isoquants for M and C

production on the graph on the next page. Note that L is on

the horizontal axis, A is on the vertical axis, inputs used in

M production are measured from the lower left-hand corner,

and inputs used in C production are measured from the

upper right-hand corner. At the point marked by the + there

are 100/3 units of L and 200/3 units of A allocated to M

production. How many are allocated to C production at this point? $A_C = (1)$_____ $L_C =$ (2)_____ What is M at this point? (3)_____ Draw in the M-isoquant that passes through this point and label it with the number you just found. What is C at this point? (4)_____ Draw in the C-isoquant and label it with this value.

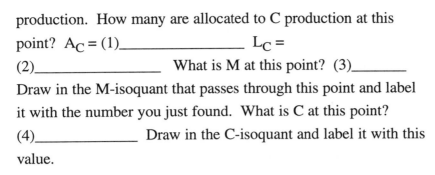

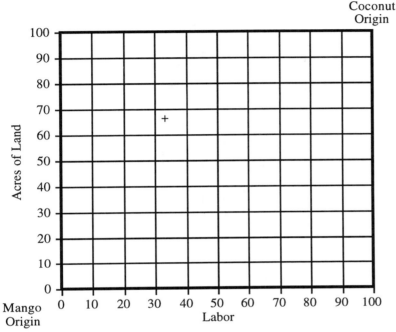

Coconut
Origin

Acres of Land

Mango
Origin

Labor

What is the ratio A_M/L_M equal to at the **+** point? (5)_____ Draw a line through the Mango Origin that has this value as its slope. What is the ratio A_C/L_C at the **+** point? (6)_____ Draw a line through the Coconut Origin that has this value as its slope. Now, sketch two more isoquants for each good—one each to the left of the **+** point and one each to the right. Shade in the area that represents the set of efficient allocations of the two inputs. You should find that there is only one allocation for which all of both A and L will be utilized. What allocation is it? (7)_____ Indicate an efficient allocation for which there is excess (unutilized) A with **A+**. Indicate an efficient allocation for which there is excess L with **L+**.

b. Suppose that there were an unlimited amount of A on Paradise Island. If all L was used in growing M, how many

M would be grown? (1)_____ If all L was used in growing C, how many C would be grown? (2)_____ If C output is reduced by one unit, how much L becomes available to increase M? (3)_____ By how much would M be increased? (4)_____ Use answers (1)–(4) to draw the PPF for this situation in the following diagram.

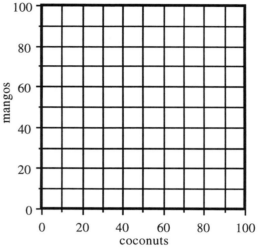

Now, suppose that there are only 100 acres, but that L is unlimited. Draw the PPF for this case on the same graph. Finally, indicate what the PPF will be for the case when both L and A equal 100 by darkening the appropriate segments of the two lines you have just drawn. Indicate the point on this PPF that corresponds to the + point in **a** with **a+**, indicate an excess L point with **L⁺** and indicate an excess A point with **A⁺**. Explain why this function is concave to the origin.

(5)_____

_____

_____

_____

_____

c. The economy of Paradise Island is perfectly competitive. (What did you expect in Paradise?) In a competitive equilibrium with C = 20 and M = 40, what would the price ratio be? P_C/P_M = (1)_____ Why? (2)_____

_____

_____

_____

_____

What would the price ratio be for C = 40 and M = 20?

P_C/P_M = (3)_____ Explain why the amounts of C

and M produced would be the same for any price ratio

between your answers to (1) and (3).

(4)_____

_____

_____

_____

d. Since coconuts remain edible for very long periods of time,
while mangos spoil easily, coconuts are used as money in
Paradise. Hence, P_C = 1 always. Thus, when C = 20 and M
= 40, P_M = (1)_____ [refer to answer (1) in **c**].
What will be the rental rate for land? [Hint: what is the value
of the marginal product of land in C production?]
(2)_____. What will be the wage rate?
(3)_____ What problem might arise in the
labor market, and how would you expect it to be resolved?

(4)_____

_____

_____

17.7. [Related to text example 17.2 and problem 17.3.] In the country
of Ruritania there are two regions, A and B. Two goods (X and
Y) are produced in both regions. Production functions in region
A are given by

$$X_A = \sqrt{L_{X_A}} \qquad Y_A = \sqrt{L_{Y_A}}$$

where L_{X_A} and L_{Y_A} are the quantities of labor devoted to X and
Y production, respectively. Total labor available in region A is
100 units. That is,

$$L_{X_A} + L_{Y_A} = 100$$

a. Find Region A's production possibility frontier and plot it on the following graph. [Hint: see Problem 17.1.]

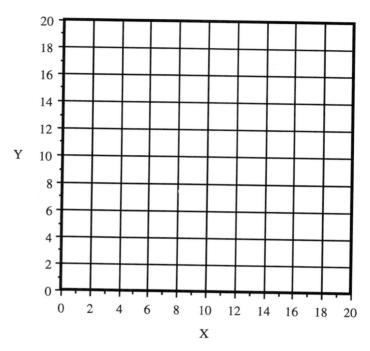

b. In region B the production functions are:

$$X_B = \frac{1}{2}\sqrt{L_{X_B}} \qquad Y_B = \frac{1}{2}\sqrt{L_{Y_B}}$$

Region B also has 100 units of labor. Find region B's PPF.

$Y_B = $ _____

Add Region B's PPF to the graph, labelling it PPF_B. Now, suppose that $X_A = 10$ and $X_B = 2$, so $X = X_A + X_B \equiv 12$ units. Under these circumstances, how many units of Y can be produced in Ruritania? $Y_A = (1)$_____

$Y_B = (2)$_____ $Y = (3)$_____

Plot (X, Y) on the graph and label it with **b**.

c. Let RPT_A and RPT_B be the rates of product transformation in the two regions. In the graph above, RPT_A is minus the (1)_____ of PPF_A. The mathematical expression for

RPT_A is obtained by taking the derivative of PPF_A with respect to X_A and multiplying by -1.

$RPT_A = (2)$_____

$RPT_B = (3)$_____

d. Assume that labor cannot be moved between regions. What condition must hold to guarantee that production is allocated efficiently between the two regions (i.e., that the country as a whole is producing as much Y as possible given its total X production)? (1)_____ Suppose that two units of X are produced in A for every unit of Y produced in A. If the efficiency condition is to be satisfied, it must also be that (2)_____ units of X are produced in B for every unit of Y produced in B. Is this condition satisfied when 10 units of X are produced in A and 2 units of X are produced in B, as in **b**? (3)_____ Given that 12 units of X are to be produced, should the amount produced in A be greater than, less than, or equal to 10? Explain. (4)_____

_____

_____

_____

_____

e. Now, we want to find the PPF for all of Ruritania, again assuming that labor cannot be moved. This can be done fairly easily for this problem because of the simple shapes of PPF_A and PPF_B. If your answers to **a** through **d** are correct, you should find that the point (6, 8) is on PPF_A and the point (3, 4) is on PPF_B. In addition, you should be able to verify that these points satisfy the efficiency requirement from **d**. [If not, you should check the answers and find your error(s) before proceeding.] Indicate these points on your graph. Total X production in the two regions combined is (1)_____. Total Y production is (2)_____. Indicate on the graph the point that represents total X and Y production. This point is on the country's PPF. Notice that all three of these points lie on a ray drawn from the origin.

Harcourt Brace & Company

The slope of this ray is the ratio of Y to X production in each region, as well as in the entire country.

Now, draw another ray from the origin and examine the points where it intersects PPF_A and PPF_B. Is the efficiency requirement satisfied at these points? (3)_____ Find a point on the same ray that is on the country's PPF. This exercise can be repeated with additional rays to trace out the country's entire PPF. Repeat it until you can determine from examining the graph what the equation for the country's PPF must be. It is Y = (4)_____ Use the country's PPF to determine the maximum Y that can be produced if X = 12. Y = (5)_____ Compare this to your last answer in **b**. Which is larger, and why? (6)_____

_____

_____

_____

f. Find expressions for the marginal products of labor in X production for the two regions.

$MP_L^{X_A}$ = (1)_____ $MP_L^{X_B}$ = (2)_____

What are the values of these marginal products when $X_A = 9$ and $X_B = 3$, as in **e**?

$MP_L^{X_A}$ = (3)_____ $MP_L^{X_B}$ = (4)_____

Explain how you could increase total X production in Ruritania without changing Y production in either region if you were allowed to move labor between regions.

(5)_____

_____

_____

_____

What condition must hold if labor used in X production is to be allocated efficiently between the two regions?

(6)_____ This condition implies that L_{X_A} must equal (7)_____ times L_{X_B}. Verify that the same must be true for labor used in Y production. _____

_____

_____

_____ Since

there are 200 units of labor in all of Ruritania, the only way to

achieve these ratios is to place (8)_____

units in region B and the remaining (9)_____ units in

region A. Given this allocation of labor, the new PPFs in

regions A and B are:

A: (10)_____

B: (11)_____

These can be combined to get the country's new PPF:

(12)_____ Add the new

PPF for the country to your graph. If 12 units of X are

produced in Ruritania, how many units of Y can be produced?

(13)_____ Compare this answer to your last answer

in **e**. Which is larger and why?

(14)_____

_____

_____

17.8. The two markets depicted below both have negatively sloped
supply curves. In Market A the demand curve is steeper than the
supply curve, but in Market B the reverse is true. Initially, the
price is P* and quantity sold is Q*. Assume that quantity sold is
always the smaller of quantity demanded and quantity supplied.

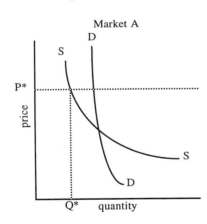
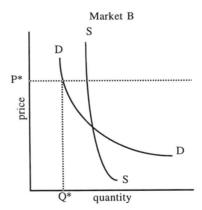

   a. If prices adjust according to the Walrasian tâtonnement

   process, what will happen to P in Market A? Explain.

   (1)_____

   _____

   _____

   If prices adjust according to the Marshallian quantity model, what will happen to Q in Market A? Explain. (2)_____

_____

_____

_____Is this

market stable? Explain. (3)_____

_____

_____

_____

b. Repeat **a** for Market B.

(1)_____

_____

_____

(2)_____

_____

_____

_____

(3)_____

_____

_____

17.9. [Related to text problem 17.8.] Suppose that demand for gyroscopes, G, is

$$G = 75 - 14P$$

and that supply is

$$G = 80 - 20P + P^2$$

a. Draw these curves on the diagram below.

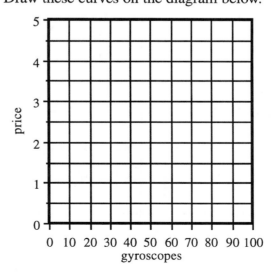

b. There are two equilibria in this market. Find them.

c. Which of these equilibria is (are) stable under Walrasian adjustment? [Hint: see Problem 17.5]

Under Marshallian adjustment?

17.10. [Related to text example 17.4 and problem 17.9.] Suppose that the annual demand function for soybeans (in millions of bushels) is

$$Q_t^D = 6 - 2P_t$$

and that supply is

$$Q_t^S = 4 + P_{t-1}$$

a. Draw the demand and supply curves on the graph below.

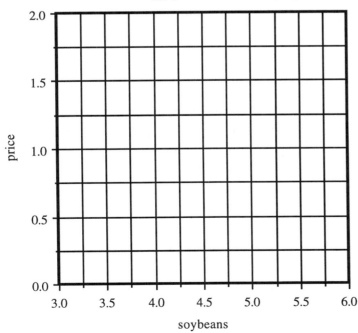

b. Is this market stable?

c. What is the equilibrium price? [Hint: in the long run $P_t = P_{t-1}$.]

Quantity?

d. Suppose that the market has been in equilibrium, but that a drought causes the supply curve to shift up to:

$$Q_t^S = 3 + P_{t-1}$$

Draw this new supply curve on the diagram and determine the new quantity supplied. [Be careful: the original price is the relevant price for determining quantity supplied. Draw a horizontal line from the original equilibrium to the new supply curve.]

At this quantity, what price will clear the market? [Hint: since quantity is fixed for the year, the short-run supply curve is vertical at the quantity you just found.]

Plot the original and new prices and quantities on the diagrams below. Let $t = 0$ be the pre-drought year and $t = 1$ be the year of the drought.

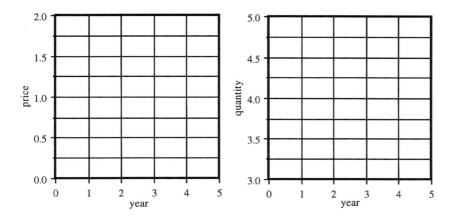

e. Suppose that the drought continues for a second year. What quantity will be supplied in year 2? [Hint: be sure to use the price from period 1. Draw a horizontal line at this price from the demand curve to the supply curve.]

What will the price be? [Hint: draw a vertical line at the quantity supplied from the supply curve to the demand curve.]

Plot these values on the diagrams in **d**. If the drought continues, at what values will price and quantity eventually stabilize?

f. Repeat **e** for years 3 and 4, adding a horizontal and vertical line for each year in the original graph. Plot the prices and quantities on the diagrams in **d**.

g. Solve explicitly for P_t as a function of the initial equilibrium price. [Hint: a formula for this function is given under Key Concepts. Be sure to use the new supply curve in finding this function.]

Show that this function predicts the same values for P_t in periods 1, 2, and 3 that you found above.

17.11. [Related to text example 17.4.] Continuing Problem 17.10, suppose there is a 50% chance of a drought every year—no matter what the weather was like in the previous year. Also suppose that farmers know the supply curves for both types of years and the demand curve. Each year they expect the price to be the average of the long-run equilibrium prices for good and bad years. Call this average E(P). The supply curves for good and bad years, respectively, are now

$$Q_t^S = 4 + E(P) \qquad Q_t^S = 3 + E(P)$$

a. What is E(P)?

b. Draw the demand curve and the two supply curves on the following diagram. [Hint: the supply curves will be vertical.]

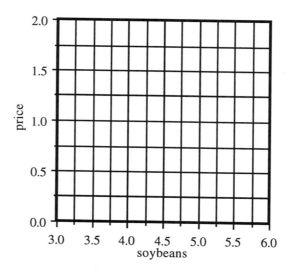

Harcourt Brace & Company

c. What will price and quantity be in a good year?

In a bad year?

d. Are farmers' expectations rational? Explain.

_____

_____

_____

_____

_____

_____

e. Suppose that year zero is a good year, year one is a bad year, year two is a good year, year three is a bad year, etc. Plot the paths of price and quantity on the diagrams below.

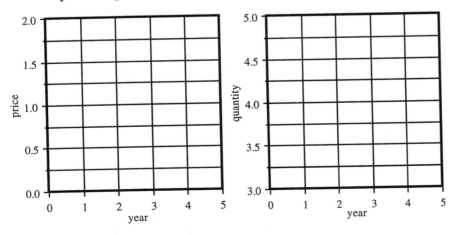

f. Now, return to the cobweb model of Problem 17.3. When a good year is followed by a bad year, the price for that year can be determined by using the price prediction equation from part **g** of that problem: $P_t = (P_{t-1} - 1)(-.5)^1 + 1 = 1.5 - P_{t-1}$. Find the comparable equation for the case when a bad year is followed by a good year. [Hint: the only difference is that the "good year" long-run equilibrium price, 2/3, is now relevant.]

Write down the equations for quantity supplied in bad and good years.

Now, use these equations to calculate the prices and quantities for the same sequence of years that you considered in **e**.

t	P_t	Q_t
0	_____	_____
1	_____	_____
2	_____	_____
3	_____	_____
4	_____	_____

For which model is price more stable? _____
What do you think is the reason? _____
_____
_____
_____ For which model is quantity more stable?_____ What do you think is the reason?_____
_____
_____
_____

17.12. Economists have found strong evidence that more people enter law school when lawyers' salaries rise at a faster rate than salaries in other professions. They also have found strong evidence that lawyers' salaries rise at slower rates when the number of lawyers entering the profession increases. How would you expect salaries of lawyers to behave over a 15-year period following the adoption of a federal law that severely limited maximum awards in medical suits?

_____

_____

_____

_____

_____

_____

17.13. [Related to text problem 17.10.] At High Tech University all incoming students buy a particular type of personal computer. They may either buy new machines or used machines from older students. Suppose that there are 1,000 machines available on the used market. The value of these machines varies from $1,001 to $2,000 dollars—in fact there is one machine worth $1,001, a second worth $1,002, and so forth. However, their value is related to factors like hours of use, which are known to the seller but can't be verified by the purchaser. Hence, all machines sold are sold for the same price. Assume that no seller will sell his or her machine if that price is below the machine's value.

   a. What is the supply function?

   b. Suppose that the demand function is

$$Q^D = 1.5 \ E(V) - P$$

   where E(V) is the expected (average) value of all used machines. What will E(V) be (to the nearest dollar)?

   c. What will the equilibrium price and quantity be?

   d. Now, suppose that incoming students are aware that only the worst machines are sold. Assume that E(V) is the expected

Harcourt Brace & Company

value of just those machines that are sold. Given the price you found in **c**, what will E(V) be?

For this value, what will equilibrium price and quantity be?

Explain why this is not a full equilibrium. [Hint: is the value of E(V) you used equal to the average value of machines sold?]_____

_____

_____

_____

_____

e. Now, find an equilibrium in which E(V) equals the value of machines actually sold. As a first step, write E(V) as a function of P.

Now, substitute the result into the demand function.

Equate this demand function to the supply function and solve for P.

What will quantity sold be at this price?

17.14. Johnny Washenwax spends every Saturday morning working on his car, trying to keep it in "good-as-new" condition. He thinks

this is a valuable use of his time since it will increase the value
of his car when he sells it.

a. What do you think? _____

_____

_____

_____

_____

b. What does the Akerlof lemon model imply about incentives

to maintain durable goods? _____

_____

_____

_____

Is this economically efficient? Explain. _____

_____

_____

_____

_____

c. A criticism of the lemon model presented in the text is that it
is not realistic to suppose that people sell their automobiles
only when the price exceeds its value. Many people may be
willing to accept the loss just because they want to buy a new
car. Suppose there is some chance that each car with a value
greater than the market price will be sold at the market price,
but this chance becomes smaller as the car's actual value
increases. Will Akerlof's basic conclusion—that the average
used car sold will be of lower value than the average value of
all used cars—still be valid? Explain.

_____

_____

_____

_____

CHAPTER 18

MODELS OF MONOPOLY

barriers to entry:

    technical

    legal

    creation of

profit maximization rule for a monopolist:

    MR = MC

nonexistence of supply curves in monopoly markets

market separation and price discrimination:

    $MR_1 = MC = MR_2$

    the market with more inelastic demand will have a higher price

    perfect price discrimination

efficiency of monopoly:

    deadweight loss

    under perfect price discrimination

monopoly regulation:

    two-tier pricing

    "fair" rate of return and over-capitalization

possible benefits of monopoly:

    research and innovation incentives

    lower planning costs

    lower advertising costs

(Numbers in brackets at the beginning of problems below refer to related examples and problems in the text.)

18.1. [Related to text example 18.1 and problems 18.1 and 18.8.] The Selectpersons of Smalltown have granted Doug's Dogs, Inc., the exclusive rights to hot dog vending on Main Street. Assume that the marginal variable cost of producing hot dogs is constant at

Harcourt Brace & Company

$1.00 and, at least at first, assume that fixed costs are zero. Daily demand for hot dogs is:

$$Q = 100 - 20P$$

[Note: this function does not depend on the income of consumers; that is, the effect of a change in income on demand for hot dogs is zero. Hence, this is both the ordinary and compensated demand function for hot dogs. This assumption simplifies the computation of consumer surplus. As review, you should think about how your answers to the consumer surplus questions would change if hot dogs were an inferior good!]

a. Find Doug's inverse demand curve and his marginal revenue function.

inverse demand: P =

MR =

b. Depict Doug's profit maximization problem in the diagram below. That is, draw in the (inverse) demand curve, MR, MC and AC. Let P range from 0 to 5 and let Q range from 0 to 100. Indicate by Q* his profit-maximizing output. Indicate the corresponding price by P*. Outline the area that represents his profits with bold lines and label it Π*. Outline the area that represents consumer surplus, at price P*, with bold lines and label it CS*.

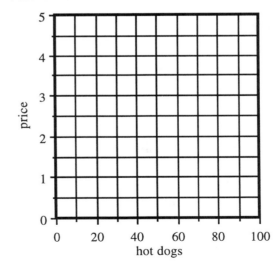

c. Explain why Doug will maximize profits where MR = MC.

_____

_____

_____

Now, use this rule to actually compute Q*.

Q* =

Now, compute P* and profits at Q*, Π*.

P* =

Π* =

Also, compute consumer surplus at price P*. [Hint: the formula for the area of a triangle having base length b and height h is area = bh/2]

CS* =

Explain, in your own words, what this surplus represents.

_____

_____

_____

Suppose that, in addition to giving Doug exclusive vending rights, the Selectpersons tell Doug he cannot charge more than $1.00 per hot dog. How many hot dogs will he sell?

d. Suppose the Selectpersons open up Main Street to any vendor that wants to compete. Assuming that other vendors, like Doug, can produce hot dogs at a constant MC of $1.00, what will the new equilibrium price and quantity be?

P_C =

Q_C =

What will consumer surplus be now?

CS_C =

Compare this amount to the sum of Π* and CS*. Determine which is greater and explain what the difference between the two represents. _____

_____

_____

_____

Use bold lines to outline the area on the graph that represents the difference and label it DWL for deadweight loss.

How many vendors will there be—or is it impossible to tell? Explain._____

_____

_____

_____

e. Of course, there are fixed costs, which we have ignored so far. Suppose that each potential vendor can rent the necessary equipment for $5.00 per day. How would this affect your answers to part **c**, assuming again that Doug's has exclusive rights? _____

_____

_____

_____

_____   _____

_____

Now, examine the competitive outcome again, assuming this time that fixed cost for each potential vendor is $5.00. It is no longer appropriate to think of a vendor's MC as constant, at least in the long run. If a vendor rented equipment and just sold one hot dog, total cost would be (1)_____. This is also MC for the first hot dog. The total cost of selling two hot dogs is (2)_____, so MC for the second (and each additional) hot dog is (3)_____. Thus, this is a case of declining MC. Suppose that Doug is the only vendor. Counting his fixed cost, his average cost (as a function of Q) will be AC = (4)_____ . If, for given Q, the price falls below this level, his profits will be negative and he will go out of business. Of course, the price customers are willing to pay is P = (5)_____. Equate these two and solve for Q. [You will need to use the quadratic formula; round your answer to the nearest integer value—you can't buy just part of a hot dog!] Q = (6)_____. If Doug sets his price so that this many hot dogs are sold, he will break even. His "breakeven"

price (rounded to the nearest cent) is $P_b =$
(7)_____. Suppose that Doug sells hot dogs at
price P_b. Along comes Frank's Franks, Inc. What will
happen to Frank if he sells at a *higher* price?
(8)_____ Can Frank sell
at the *same* price without losing money and/or putting Doug
out of business? Explain. [Hint: if both sell at price P, what
will their combined revenue be? Their combined costs?]
(9)_____

_____

_____

Can Frank sell at a *lower* price without losing money?
(10)_____

_____

Hence, only one of them at most can break even if Doug
continues to sell at P_b. Now, suppose that both of them
collude and raise their price to $1.25. If you were the owner
of Wendy's Weiners, what would you do?
(11)_____
Would your answer be any different if Doug was the only
vendor and he charged $1.25? (12)_____ Based on this
discussion, describe the long-run competitive equilibrium. Be
sure to state how many vendors there will be, what their
profits will be, how many hot dogs will be sold and what the
price will be. (13)_____

_____

_____

_____

_____

Finally, comment on the following statement: "A natural
monopolist will always make excess profits if left untaxed
and unregulated." (14)_____

_____

_____

_____

_____

_____

f. Return again to the case where Doug has exclusive vending rights, with no fixed costs. The town decides to charge Doug a license fee. Find the largest fee that Doug will agree to and determine whether or not the fee will affect his choice of output level. _____

_____

_____

g. Back to the free entry case. The Selectpersons decide to charge each vendor t dollars for every hot dog sold. As a result, marginal cost to the vendors is $1.00 + t. This is depicted in the graph below.

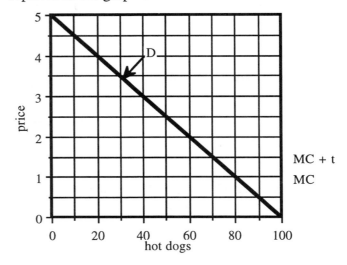

Indicate on the graph the equilibrium level of output for the illustrated tax rate by Q_t. Also, shade in the area on the graph that represents tax revenue to the town. Finally determine what value of t will maximize tax revenue. [Hint: your results in **c** are relevant. What area on the graph would a profit-maximizing monopolist try to maximize?]

_____

_____

_____

h. If the objective of the Selectpersons is to maximize revenue to the town, does it matter to either them or their constituents whether they license a single vendor or apply a unit tax and allow free entry? _____

_____

_____

_____

_____

_____

_____

18.2. [Related to text problems 18.3 and 18.4.] Consider a monopolist whose average and marginal costs are both constant at $1.00.

a. If the inverse market demand curve is $P = 5 - .05Q$, what will the profit-maximizing price and quantity be?

b. If the demand curve shifts to $P = 9 - .1Q$, what will the profit-maximizing price and quantity be? [Note that this is a nonparallel shift.]

c. If the inverse demand curve now shifts to $P = 3 - .025Q$, what will the profit-maximizing price and quantity be?

d. Plot the three price-quantity pairs you found in **a–c** on the graph below.

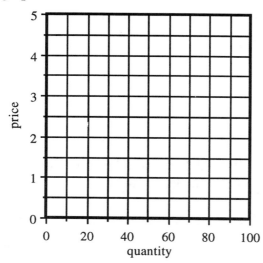

e. What is the set of price-quantity combinations that could conceivably be chosen by this monopolist? Shade in the area on the graph that is included in this set.

P ≥ _____ Q ≥ _____

f. In a competitive industry, each time the demand curve shifts it intersects a different point on the supply curve, in effect tracing the supply curve out. Explain why the three points you just plotted are not on the monopolist's supply curve and why, in fact, the concept of a monopolist's supply curve is not meaningful. _____

_____

_____

_____

_____

_____

_____

18.3. [Related to text problem 18.5.] A Better Mouse Trap, Inc., holds a patent on a mouse trap that electronically senses the presence of a mouse, emits an odor that attracts the mouse into the trap, closes the door on the mouse, and humanely asphyxiates it with ether, then beeps to signal the owner. Demand for ABMT traps is:

$$Q = (100 - 10P)M$$

where P is price, Q is quantity and M is some unknown "shift" factor that does not depend on P or Q. ABMT's costs are given by:

$$TC = Q + 1000$$

a. Write down ABMT's revenue function, which will depend on Q as well as M.

R(Q, M) = (1)_____

Now, find MR, which will also be a function of both Q and M. Assume that M is fixed. MR = (2)_____

Given Q, does an increase in M increase or decrease MR? (3)_____ As a function of M, what level of output will maximize ABMT's profits?

$Q^* = (4)$_____

At this level of output, what price will ABMT charge? $P^* =$ (5)_____ Does this price depend on M? (6)_____ [Note: this is not the usual case. It happens here only because the elasticity of demand does not depend on M. This particular form of a shift factor was chosen for simplicity.] Now, substitute Q^* and P^* into the definition of profits to find a function of M that tells how profits depend on M, assuming that the profit-maximizing levels of Q and P are chosen. $\Pi^* =$

(7)_____

b. Hard Sell Advertising, Inc., promises ABMT that it can help ABMT obtain a favorable value of M. Specifically, if ABMT pays HSA A dollars to advertise its product, HSA promises to deliver $M = 20A - .01A^2$. Use this and your maximum profit function from the first part [Π^*] to write ABMT's profits, net of advertising costs, as a function of A alone.

$\Pi_{net} = \Pi^* - A =$

Now, show that ABMT should buy advertising up to the point where the marginal gross profit from advertising is just equal to \$1.00—which happens to be the marginal cost of advertising—if it wants to maximize Π_{net}.

Give an intuitive explanation of this result.

_____
_____
_____
_____

Find the value of A that maximizes Π_{net}. Also, compute the corresponding values of P, Q, Π_{net}, and Π^*.

Comment on the following statement: "All consumers pay for advertising, regardless of whether they were influenced by the advertising." _____

_____

_____

_____

_____

18.4. [Related to text example 18.2 and problem 18.7.] Dr. Thomas "Fat" Wallet, D.D.S., has two kinds of patients, insured and uninsured. Their respective demand curves for teeth cleaning are:

$$Q_I = 200 - 4\,P_I \qquad Q_U = 200 - 8\,P_U$$

where P_I and P_U are the prices he charges insured and uninsured patients, respectively. His marginal cost for cleaning teeth is upward sloping; the more time he spends cleaning teeth the less time he has for golf, and the value of his forgone leisure increases the more of it he forgoes. Specifically, his marginal cost function is:

$$MC = 0.1\,(Q_U + Q_I)$$

a. Find his revenue and marginal revenue functions for insured and uninsured patients.

$R_I(Q_I) =$

$MR_I =$

$R_U(Q_U) =$

$MR_U =$

b. Show that to maximize profits, defined as $R_U(Q_U) + R_I(Q_I) - C(Q_U + Q_I)$, Fat should choose Q_U and Q_I such that MC = $MR_U = MR_I$.

Explain in words why these conditions must hold for profit to be maximized. _____

_____

_____

_____

_____

_____

_____

c. Now, use your conditions from **b** and the expressions for MC, MR_U, and MR_I to set up two equations in two unknowns, Q_U and Q_I. [Note: there are three possible equations, but you only need any two of the three. The third is redundant and will automatically be satisfied if the other two are.] Then, solve the equations for the profit-maximizing quantities. Round your answers to the nearest whole numbers.

$Q_U = (1)$_____ $Q_I = (2)$_____

What prices will Fat charge? $P_U = (3)$_____
$P_I = (4)$_____ Assuming that insurance covers only 80% of charges to insured patients, how much will the insurance company have to pay out? (5)_____

d. Find the insured and uninsured elasticities of demand at the profit-maximizing quantities and prices. $e_{Q_U,P_U} = (1)$
_____ $e_{Q_I,P_I} = (2)$ _____ Is the more elastic demand associated with the larger price or the smaller price? (3)_____ Is this always the case with price discrimination? Explain. (4)_____

_____

_____

_____

_____

_____ Is demand by either group inelastic at the equilibrium? (5)_____ Is this always the case with price discrimination? [Hint: what would MR in either market be if demand in that market was inelastic?] (6)_____

_____

_____

e. Fat knows which patients are insured only because he submits their bills directly to the insurance company. Suppose the insurance company stopped accepting bills directly from dentists. Assuming that Fat had no other way of distinguishing between patients, what would the new equilibrium prices and quantities be? [Hint: when producers can't charge discriminatory prices, market demand is just the sum of demands for all consumer groups.]

$P_U = (1)$_____ $P_I = (2)$_____

$Q_U = (3)$_____ $Q_I = (4)$_____

Find the elasticities of demand at the new equilibrium.

$e_{Q_U, P_U} = (5)$ _____ $e_{Q_I, P_I} = (6)$_____

What are insurance payments now, again assuming 80% coverage? (7)_____ Did insurance payments increase or fall? (8)_____ Can it be argued that this result does not depend on the particular demand function chosen for insured patients, as long as it is less elastic than for uninsured patients? [Hint: what did you find out about the elasticity of demand for insured patients under discrimination? What is the relationship between elasticity and the effect of a reduction in price on expenditure? Is it necessarily the case that insured demand will become inelastic when discrimination is not allowed, as it did here?] (9)_____

_____

_____

Based on this analysis, who would you expect to oppose price discrimination by health care professionals? Insurers? Uninsured patients? Insured patients? (10)_____

_____

_____

_____

_____

_____

Harcourt Brace & Company

f. What philanthropic justification might Fat use to mollify a critic who takes a dim view of his pricing practices? [Hint: how would you expect the typical insured customer to differ from the typical uninsured customer?] _____

_____

_____

_____

_____

g. One characteristic of the market for teeth cleaning is that you can't sell your cleaning to someone else! Of what relevance is this to the existence of price discrimination in markets for professional services? _____

_____

_____

_____

_____

CHAPTER 19

MODELS OF IMPERFECT COMPETITION

pricing under homogeneous oligopoly:

    quasi-competitive (price-taking) model:

        $P = MC_i(q_i)$

        competitive solution

    cartel model:

        $MR(Q) = MC_i(q_i)$

        monopoly solution

        incentive to chisel

    Cournot (quantity-taking) model:

        $P + q_i\, \partial P/\partial q_i = MC_i(q_i)$

        solution lies between the quasi-competitive and cartel solutions

    conjectural variation model:

$$P + q_i\left(\frac{\partial P}{\partial q_i} + \sum_{j \neq i}\frac{\partial P}{\partial q_j}\frac{\partial q_j}{\partial q_i}\right) = MC_i q_i$$

    price leadership model

    Stackelberg leadership model

product differentiation:

    product group

    first order conditions for profit maximization:

        $P_i + q_i\, \partial P_i/\partial q_i = \partial TC_i/\partial q_i$

        $q_i\, \partial P_i/\partial z_i = \partial TC_i/\partial z_i$

    Hotelling's model of spatial differentiation

entry:

zero-profit equilibrium: barriers:

excess capacity   brand loyalty

contestable markets: brand proliferation
$n = Q^*/q^*$ strategic pricing

irreversible investments

slow demand adjustment

industrial organization:

market structure: firm conduct

concentration ratios   industry performance:

economies of scale   static efficiency

strategic behavior   dynamic efficiency

mergers: equity

horizontal   employment and wages

vertical   political influence

conglomerate

PROBLEMS

(Numbers in brackets at the beginning of problems below refer to related examples and problems in the text.)

19.1. [Related to text examples 19.1 and 19.2, and problems 19.1 and 19.2.] This problem continues Problem 20.1. Recall that demand for hot dogs on Main Street in Smalltown is:

$$Q = 100 - 20P$$

Assume that there are no fixed costs and, as before, that MC = $1.00. The purpose of this problem is to examine duopoly equilibria in this market (different behavioral assumptions lead to different equilibria) and to compare these equilibria to both the competitive and monopoly equilibria as well as to each other.

a. The demand and MC functions are graphed below. Indicate the competitive price and quantity with P* and Q*. Indicate the monopoly price and quantity with P_M and Q_M. [See your answers from the previous chapter.] As you proceed through the problem, you will be adding additional solutions to this diagram.

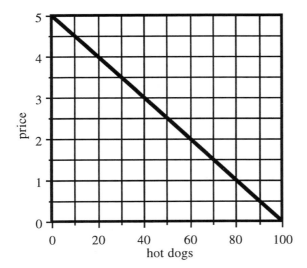

b. The town grants vending rights to Doug's Dogs and Frank's Franks, at no charge. Other vendors are excluded. Assume for now that both Doug and Frank are Cournot Duopolists— they take each other's production as fixed and adjust their own to maximize their profits. Let Q_D represent Doug's production and Q_F represent Frank's: $Q = Q_D + Q_F$. Write Doug's profits as a function of Q_D and Q_F. [Hint: as a first step, invert the demand function and replace Q with $Q_D + Q_F$.]

$\Pi_D = (1)$_____

Suppose that Doug knows Q_F. If he assumes that this will not change once Frank knows Q_D, what value of Q_D should Doug choose to maximize his profits as a function of Q_F?

$Q_D = (2)$_____

This is Doug's "reaction function." Draw it on the diagram below.

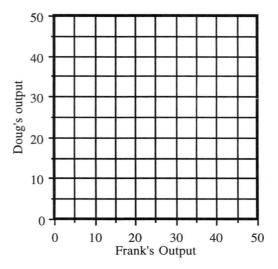

Now, find Frank's reaction function and add it to the diagram.

Q_F = (3)_____

Suppose that Doug had been producing at the monopoly solution before Frank arrived on the scene. Indicate his output level on the reaction function graph. What output would Frank initially choose to sell? (4)_____
Explain why this would not be an equilibrium, and describe what would happen.

(5)_____

_____

_____

_____

_____

_____ Draw the path that output would follow toward the new equilibrium on the reaction function diagram. What would equilibrium P, Q_D, Q_F, and Q be?

P = (6)_____ Q_D = (7)_____ Q_F = (8)_____ Q = (9)_____ Doug's profits are Π_D = (10)_____ and Frank's profits are Π_F = (11)_____. Their combined profits are Π = (12)_____. Plot P and Q on the graph in **a** and label them P_C and Q_C (C for Cournot).

c. Explain why the behavior of both Frank and Doug in **b** is naive. (1)_____

_____

_____

_____

_____

Assume that Frank continues to behave naively, but that Doug figures out that Frank is reacting to his decisions. Specifically, Doug knows that Frank's choice of Q_F is a function of his own choice of Q_D, as you found in **b** (Frank's reaction function). Doug takes this into account by substituting Frank's reaction function into his own profit equation, to get: Π_D = (2)_____

Find Doug's new profit-maximizing choice of Q_D.

Q_D = (3)_____ . Frank will choose Q_F = (4)_____ . Total quantity produced is Q = (5)_____. The price is P = (6)_____. Doug's profits are Π_D = (7)_____ and Frank's profits are Π_F = (8)_____. Their combined profits are Π = (9)_____. Plot the new Q and P on the graph in **a**, labelling them P_{LF} and Q_{LF} (LF for Leader-Follower). Also, plot the point (Q_D, Q_F) on the reaction function diagram in **b** and label it LF.

Harcourt Brace & Company

d. In **c** it was assumed that Frank continued to be naive. Suppose instead that he figures out Doug's behavior at the same time that Doug figures out his own. That is, they both simultaneously decide to lead, mistakenly thinking that the other will follow. His choice of output level will then be Q_F = (1)_____. [Hint: does his problem differ in any way from Doug's in **c**?] Total output will be Q = (2)_____ and the price will be P = (3)_____. Doug's profits are Π_D = (4)_____ and Frank's profits are Π_F = (5)_____. Their combined profits are Π = (6)_____ . Plot the new Q and P on the graph in **a** and label them Q_{LL} and P_{LL}. Also, plot the point (Q_D, Q_F) on the reaction function diagram in **b** and label it LL.   Finally, what do you speculate will happen once they both realize that the other is not following? (7)_____

_____

_____

_____

_____

e. Compare the outcomes in **b** through **d** with both the competitive and monopoly outcomes.   What do you find?_____

_____

_____

_____

_____

What general conclusions, if any, can be drawn from this example?_____

_____

_____

_____

_____

_____

_____

19.2. [Related to text example 19.4 and problem 19.2.] There are N service stations in Smalltown, each at a different location. Each has fixed costs of $5,000 per month and can purchase gasoline from its supplier for \$1.00 per gallon. Even though the gasoline sold at all stations is identical—and consumers know it—their products are differentiated by their locations. The typical firm (firm i) faces the following demand function for its gasoline, q_i, measured in thousands of gallons:

$$q_i = -.2(N - 1)p_i + .2(p_1 + ... + p_{i-1} + p_{i+1} + ... + p_N) + 1000/N$$

where p_i is the price it charges and the $p_1, ..., p_{i-1}, p_{i+1}, ..., p_N$ are the prices charged by its $N - 1$ rivals.

a. Each service station maximizes its profits, taking both the number and prices of its rivals as being fixed. Write an expression for the typical station's profits as a function of its output, the prices at the other stations, and N. [To make the notation simpler, define $S = p_1 + ... + p_{i-1} + p_{i+1} + ... + p_N$. Then, as a first step, invert the firm's demand function to get q_i as a function of p_i, S, and N.]

$\Pi_i =$

Find the value of q_i that maximizes Π_i (another function of the other prices [or S] and N).

$q_i =$

Now, find the price that the station will charge at this output level (yet another function of the other prices [or S] and N).

$p_i =$

b. As is evident from the last function you found in **a**, each station reacts to the prices chosen by all other stations. Prices will adjust until each station charges the price that all other stations expect it to charge when they are choosing their own prices. This will be an equilibrium—prices will stay constant unless there is some change in demand or marginal cost.

Since all stations have the same demand functions and costs, it must be the case that all prices are identical in such an equilibrium. This is a convenient feature of this problem because it allows you to easily find the equilibrium prices and quantities as functions of N. Set each of $p_1, ..., p_N$ (including p_i) equal to a common value p^* in your price equation for the typical station. [If you have used S, as suggested above, replace it now with $(N-1)p^*$.] Then, solve this equation for p^* as a function of N.

$p^* =$

Find each firm's equilibrium output (a function of N).

$q^* =$

Find each firm's equilibrium profit (a function of N):

$\Pi^* =$

c. There are no barriers to entry (e.g., zoning laws) to service stations in Smalltown. Anyone can set up a station and face the same costs and demand functions as other stations. The only change that occurs if a new station enters is that N increases by 1. What will determine the number of service stations in Smalltown in the long run? [Hint: what will happen if $\Pi^* > 0$? If $\Pi^* < 0$?] (1)_____

_____

Show that the long-run value of N is 101.
(2)_____

_____

For this value of N, $p^* = $ (3)_____ and $q^* = $ (4)_____

Harcourt Brace & Company

Graph the long-run equilibrium demand, marginal revenue, marginal cost, and average cost curves for the typical firm in the diagram below.

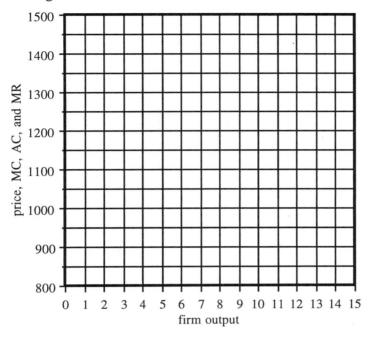

Which is greater, p* or MC? (5)_____ Is AC minimized? (6)_____ Compare your answers for (5) and (6) to what you would find in long-run equilibrium under perfect competition. (7)_____

_____

_____

19.3. [Related to text problem 19.7.] Suppose that the personal computer industry is characterized by a very large producer, Enormous Personal Computer, Inc., and 10 other firms in a competitive fringe that produce clones of EPC's computers. Demand for personal computers is given by:

$$Q = -10P + 35000$$

EPC can produce PCs at a constant marginal cost of $1,000, while firms in the competitive fringe face increasing marginal costs, given by:

$$MC = q + 500$$

a. Assume that each member of the competitive fringe acts as a price taker. Find each firm's supply function.

Graph the supply curve for all fringe firms combined in the diagram below. Also, graph market demand.

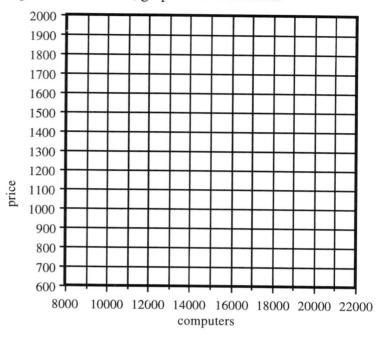

b. EPC knows the supply functions of the competitive fringe firms. Let m represent EPC's output. Find EPC's demand curve, taking into account the behavior of fringe firms. To begin, replace Q in the market demand function with m + $10q_i$. Then, substitute the supply function for the typical fringe firm and solve for m as a function of P.

m = (1)_____ EPC's inverse

demand function is: P = (2)_____

Add EPC's demand function to the graph in **a**. Find EPC's marginal revenue function and add it to the graph in **a**.

MR = (3)_____

What value of m will maximize EPC's profit?

m* = (4)_____

If EPC chooses m*, what will P be? P* =

(5)_____

Harcourt Brace & Company

How many PCs will be supplied by each competitive fringe firm? q* = (6)_____

What will the total quantity be? Q* = (7)_____ Indicate the values of P*, m*, Q*, and 10q* on the graph in **a**. Also, indicate the area that represents consumer surplus, under the assumption that the ordinary demand curve is identical to the compensated demand curve.

c. Assume that there is free entry and exit for fringe firms and that the equilibrium you found is a long-run equilibrium. What must average costs be for fringe firms?

(1)_____ If EPC priced at marginal cost, what would happen to P, Q, m, q, the number of firms on the fringe, and consumer surplus? (2)_____

_____

_____

_____

_____

d. If EPC left the market, what would happen to P, Q, m, and consumer surplus in the short run when the number of firms is fixed? _____

_____

_____

_____

What will happen in the long run when more identical firms can enter and exit, assuming that this is a constant cost industry? [Hint: if the equilibrium you depicted in the diagram is the long-run equilibrium when EPC is a leader, what must average cost be for the fringe firms?]

_____

_____

_____

Harcourt Brace & Company

Does it matter to consumers whether EPC, which has lower costs of production than the fringe firms, is in the industry or not?_____

_____

_____

_____

19.4. [Related to text example 19.3.] In Problem 19.1 it was assumed that the hot dogs sold by different vendors were identical. In fact, however, they are differentiated by the location of the vendors. Suppose that Main Street is 200 yards long, that the Selectpersons have assigned Doug's Dogs to a location 50 yards from the west end, in front of the town office, and Frank's Franks to a location 30 yards from the east end, in front of the police station. As before, both vendors have constant MC of $1.00. The situation is depicted in the following diagram:

```
<—-50 yards——><————120 yards——————><-30 yards->

west end _____D_____F_____ east end

         <————————————————— 200 yards ——————————————>
```

There are 100 shoppers on Main Street who wish to buy hot dogs, no matter what the price. In deciding which vendor to buy from, all shoppers consider both the vendors' prices and the distance they must walk. Each shopper is willing to pay a penny for each yard of walking he or she can avoid—it's a hot day!

a. One shopper, located somewhere between Doug and Frank, can't make up his mind which way to go. The problem is that Doug's price, P_D, plus the implicit cost of walking the X yards to Doug's stand, $.01X$, is just equal to Frank's price, P_F, plus the implicit cost of walking the $Y = 120 - X$ yards to Frank's stand. Find the values of X and Y as functions of P_D and P_F. [Hint: begin with the equation $P_D + .01X = P_F + .01Y$, then substitute for Y and solve for X.]

b. Suppose also that there is a hungry shopper located in every two-yard interval along Main Street. Write Doug's profits as a function of P_D and X. [Hint: Doug's customers are all those to the west of point X.]

Now, substitute the equation you found in **a** for X to get Doug's profit as a function of the two prices.

Find the analogous equation for Frank.

c. Assume that each vendor takes the other's price as fixed. Find Doug's profit-maximizing price as a function of Frank's price. [Hint: first find the first order condition, then solve for P_D as a function of P_F.]

Find the analogous equation for Frank.

d. Now, solve the two equations you found in **c** for the equilibrium prices.

Which vendor charges the higher price?_____
Why?_____

_____

Harcourt Brace & Company

_____

_____

_____

e. Explain what would happen if the Selectpersons allowed Doug and Frank to locate anywhere they wished. Be sure to mention what would happen to prices and comment on whether this would be efficient. _____

_____

_____

_____

_____

_____

_____

19.5. Do you think the market for Intermediate Microeconomic Theory textbooks is best described as oligopolistic, contestable, or perfectly competitive? Explain. _____

_____

_____

_____

Most successful textbooks get revised every three or four years by their authors—even if their subject matter has not changed substantively over that period. Why do you suppose this is so?

_____

_____

_____

_____

Would this happen if the market was perfectly competitive? Explain._____

_____

_____

_____

What other goods are frequently "revised"?

_____

_____

_____

CHAPTER 20

GAME THEORY AND MODELS OF PRICING

Stackelberg equilibrium

Bertrand equilibrium

two-stage price games and the Cournot equilibrium

tacit collusion in repeated games

entry, exit, and strategy:

>   sunk costs and commitment

>   first mover advantages and entry deference

>   limit pricing and incomplete information

>   predatory pricing

games of incomplete information:

>   player types and beliefs

>   Bayesian Nash equilibrium

>   Bayesian Cournot equilibrium

(Numbers in brackets at the beginning of problems below refer to related examples and problems in the text.)

20.1. [Related to text problem 20.1.] Demand for bottled water is given by:

$$W = 1000 - 100P.$$

Krystal Klear and Nature's Nurture can produce bottled water at a constant marginal cost of 10 cents (.10) per bottle. Consumers are indifferent between the two waters and will buy the one that has the lowest price. If both firms charge the same price, each gets half the sales.

a. If KK charges 15 cents per bottle, what will NN's profit be if it also charges 15 cents? (1) _____ If it charges 14 cents? (2) _____ Therefore, NN would choose a price of (3) _____ cents. KK's

profit would then be (4) _____, so KK would then reduce its price to (5) _____. NN would retaliate by (6) _____ and this process would continue until both had reduced their prices to (7)_____ cents. This is a (8) _____ equilibrium. Each firm's profit would be (9) _____.
The outcome (10) (is/is not) Pareto efficient.

b. NN discovers a new, more accessible source for its water. The effect of the discovery is to reduce NN's marginal cost to 8 cents per bottle. KK is stuck with its old source and marginal cost of 10 cents per bottle. If NN leaves its price at the equilibrium level from part **a**, their profit will now be (1) _____, and if they reduce it to 9 cents it will be (2) _____. Therefore, NN will price its water at (3) _____ cents. If KK keeps its old price, its sales will be (4) _____ and its profits will be (5) _____, but if it matches NN's new price, its profits will be (6) _____. Hence, KK will (7) _____. The new equilibrium thus achieved (8) (is/is not) Pareto efficient.

20.2. [Related to text problem 20.3.] In Problem 18.1 you examined the behavior of two hot dog vendors, Doug's Dogs and Frank's Franks, when they behaved under each of the following situations: (a) both are Cournot quantity-takers, (b) one is a Stackelberg leader and the other remains a quantity-taker (follower), and (c) both try to be leaders. Their profits under each of the pairs of behaviors are displayed in the matrix below.

		Doug's Behavior	
		leader	follower
Frank's behavior	leader	DD: $0.00 FF: $0.00	DD: $40.00 FF: $20.00
	follower	DD: $20.00 FD: $40.00	DD: $35.55 FF: $35.55

Assume that there are no other behaviors for them to choose from.

a.. Is there a Nash equilibrium in this game?

b. What does your answer to **a** suggest about the stability of prices in a noncooperative duopoly?

20.3. [Related to text problem 20.3.] In Problem 19.4 the Selectpersons assigned places on Main Street to the two hot dog vendors, Doug's Dogs and Frank's Franks. Recall that Main Street, depicted below, is 200 yards long, and that every two yards there is a hungry shopper.

west end _____ east end

<————————— 200 yards —————————>

Suppose now that the Selectpersons allow Doug and Frank to choose their own spot either at the middle of Main Street or 50 yards from either end. Both can choose the same location and if they do they each get 50 customers.

a. Suppose that Doug chooses 50 yards from the west end and Frank chooses 50 yards from the east end. How many customers will each get? Enter the answers in the upper right-hand box of the following payoff matrix after the appropriate vendor's initials.

		Frank's Location		
		50 yds. from west	center	50 yds. from east
	50 yds. from west	DD: FF:	DD: FF:	DD: FF:
Doug's Strategies	center	DD: FF:	DD: FF:	DD: FF:
	50 yds. from east	DD: FF:	DD: FF:	DD: FF:

Fill in the rest of the matrix appropriately with either 50, >50, or <50.

b. Which outcome, if any, is an equilibrium? Explain.

_____

_____

_____

_____

_____

_____

20.4 [Related to text example 20.4 and problems 20.2, 20.5 and 20.9.] In problem 20.1, Krystal Klear and Nature's Nurture both set their prices, then sold as much as they could. Suppose, instead, that they set production levels each month and then sell everything they produce in that month – nobody wants to buy "skunky water." Remember that the demand function is

$$W = 1000 - P.$$

a. Write the price as a function of the quantities produced by KK and NN – w_L and w_N (i.e., write the inverse demand function).

(1)

Assume $MC_K = MC_N = .10$. Write KK's profits, PK, as a function of w_K and w_N.

(2)

Write the first order condition for KK's maximum profit as a function of w_N.

(3)

Symmetrically, NN's first order condition for profit maximization, given w_N, is:

(4)

The only values of w_K and w_N that maximize both firms profits are [Hint: this equation can be easily sovled if you use the fact that the maximizing values of w_K and w_N must be equal, because of symetry.]

(5)

This is a (6) _____ equilibrium. Price in this equilibrium is

(7)

The outcome (8) (is/is not) Pareto efficient.

b. In **a,** we assumed that KK and NN knew each other's marginal costs. Continue to assume that KK knows NN's marginal cost is .01, but that NN thinks that KK's MC is

either .05 or .15, with equla probability. Let w_{KH} represent
KK's output if MC is .05, and w_{KL} represent KK's output if MC
is .15. If KK's MC is .05, then KK's first-order condition for
profit maximization, given w_N, is

(1)

but if KK's MC is .15, the condition is

(2)

NN's expected profit, PN, as a function of w_{KH} and w_{KL}, is

(3)

and NN's first order condition for maximizing expected
profit, as a function of w_{KH} and w_{KL}, is

(4)

What are the *ex ante* equilibrium quantities? [Hint: solve
Equations (1), (2) and (4). A shortcut: First add half of (1)
to half of (2) and write the result as a function of $E(w_K) = .5$
$w_{KH} + .5w_{KL}$. Also write (4) as a function of $E(w_K)$. Look
familiar?]

(5)

Compare this result to your result in a.

(6)

What is likely to happen over time?

(7)

CHAPTER 21

FIRMS' DEMANDS FOR INPUTS

derived demand

marginal revenue product:

$$MRP_L = MR \cdot MP_L$$

marginal value product:

$$VMP_L = P \cdot MP_L$$

marginal input expense:

$$ME_L = \partial(wL)/\partial L = w + L \, (\partial w/\partial L)$$

first-order conditions for a profit-maximizing firm under various market conditions:

		factor market conditions	
		competition	monopsony
	competition	$VMP_K = v$	$VMP_K = ME_K$
output		$VMP_L = w$	$VMP_L = ME_L$
market			
conditions	monopoly	$MRP_K = v$	$MRP_K = ME_K$
		$MRP_L = w$	$MRP_L = ME_L$

output constant factor demand (Shepard's Lemma):

$$L'(q, w, v) = \partial TC(q, w, v)/\partial w$$

effects of an increase in a factor's price (competitive factor market):

substitution effect:

$$\frac{\partial L}{\partial w} \text{ (q constant)} = \frac{\partial L'(q, w, v)}{\partial w}$$

output effect:

$$\frac{\partial L}{\partial w} \text{ (from changes in q)} = \frac{\partial L}{\partial q} \frac{\partial q}{\partial P} \frac{\partial P}{\partial MC} \frac{\partial MC}{\partial w}$$

cross-price effects

Harcourt Brace & Company

factors determining the size of own-price effects:

elasticity of substitution

share of the factor in total cost

price-elasticity of demand for output

factor shares under competition:

$$\text{labor's share} = \frac{wL}{PQ} = \frac{MP_L L}{Q} \quad \text{capital's share} = \frac{vK}{PQ} = \frac{MP_K K}{Q}$$

adding-up controversy

elasticity of substitution:

$$\sigma = \frac{\% \text{ change in } (K/L)}{\% \text{ change in } (w/v)}$$

$$= (\% \text{ change in capital's share}) - (\% \text{ change in labor's share})$$

wage discrimination

monopoly input supply

bilateral monopoly

PROBLEMS

(Numbers in brackets at the beginning of problems below refer to related examples and problems in the text.)

21.1. [Related to text example 21.1 and problems 21.1 and 21.2.] "Putt" Putnam is a cucumber farmer. Putt hires local teenagers in the late summer to harvest his crop of pickling cucumbers. The more teens he hires the more cukes he gets, but the marginal productivity of teens declines with the number employed—they talk to each other and sometimes step on cucumbers while they are distracted. Let q be pecks of cukes picked, and let L be number of teens employed. The production function is

$$q = 12L^{.5}$$

Putt sells his cucumbers to Peter Piper's Pickle Co., which will buy as many pecks as Putt wants to sell for P dollars each. Assume there are no transportation costs [Peter Piper's purchaser picks up pickles at Putt Putnam's place] and that, at the time of harvest, all other inputs into cucumber production are fixed.

a. Find the marginal product of labor and the value of the marginal product of labor.

$$MP_L =$$

$$VMP_L =$$

Plot VMP_L on the diagram below for P = $5.00.

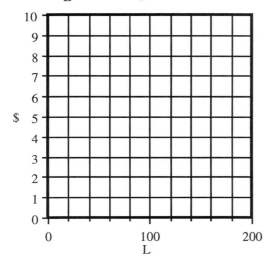

b. Putt can hire as many teens as he wants at a wage rate of w. Explain why he should hire L up to the point where w = VMP_L in order to maximize his profits. (1)_____

_____

_____

_____

_____

Now, use w = VMP_L to find Putt's demand for teenagers as a function of w and P.

L = (2)_____ Suppose P

= $5.00 and w = $3.00. How many teens will Putt hire? L =

(3)_____ Indicate this point on the graph. What

is Putt's total wage bill? wL = (4)_____ How

many pecks will be picked? q = (5)_____

What is Putt's total revenue? Pq = (6)_____

Putt's profits (ignoring fixed costs)? Π = (7)_____

c. Find Putt's (short-run) supply curve of cukes, as a function of w. [Hint: you already have found L as a function of w and P. Just plug this into Putt's production function.]

q =

Graph his supply curve on the diagram below for w = $3.00.

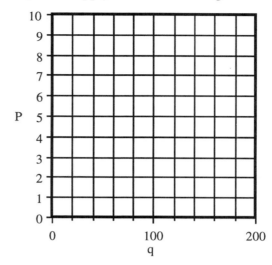

Indicate on the graph the quantity that Putnam produces when P = $5.00.

d. Suppose that P increases to $6.00. What will Putt's production be now? q = (1)_____ Indicate this point on the graph in **c**. What will happen to Putt's demand curve for labor?(2)_____

_____

Draw his new labor demand curve on the graph in **a** and determine how many teens he will hire now. L = (3)_____ Indicate this quantity on the graph.

e. The analysis in **d** implicitly assumed that Putt could continue to hire teens at a wage rate of $3.00. However, if Putt was just one of 100 cucumber growers in his state and the growers as a group were the major employer of teenagers, this might not be the case. Suppose that all one hundred growers have labor demand functions identical to Putt's. Multiply Putt's labor demand function by 100 to get total demand for teens as a function of w and P. T = 100L = (1)_____Graph total demand for teenagers on the following diagram for P = $5.00 and P =$6.00. [Note that the curves you get will look identical to Putt's VMP_L curves.]

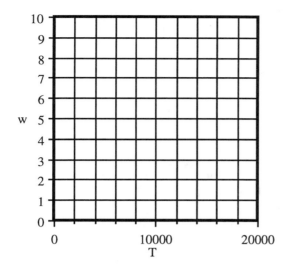

Suppose further that the supply of labor is given by:

T = 10000w/3

Add the labor supply curve to the diagram and confirm that at w = $3.00 the amount of labor supplied is just equal to the amount demanded by all producers when P = $5.00. Now, determine what the equilibrium wage rate will be when P increases to $6.00.

w = (2)_____

Indicate this value and the new level of employment on the graph. How many teens will Putt hire now? (3)_____
Indicate this value and the new wage rate on the graph in **a**. How will this affect Putt's supply curve? Show his new supply curve on the graph in **c**. How many pecks will Putt produce? (4)_____

f. It is sometimes said that demand for factors of production is "derived demand." How does this problem illustrate the meaning of this term? _____

_____

_____

_____

21.2. [Related to text example 21.2 and problems 21.1 and 21.2.] This question continues Problem 21.1. The equations that are relevant to this problem are:

Putt's cucumber supply: $q = 72P/w$

Demand for teens: $T = 3600P^2/w^2$

Supply of teens: $T = 10000w/3$

In this question we will also consider the market for Putt's cukes. Assuming again that there are 100 identical farmers, the total supply of cukes to the market is

$$Q = 100q = 7200P/w$$

Peter Piper's is just one of many pickle companies operating in Putt's state. Each has a downward sloping demand function for cukes. Their combined demand for cukes is

$$Q = 60000/P$$

Note that the equilibrium price in the cuke market will depend on the equilibrium wage rate in the teen market since cuke supply depends on w. The reverse is also true, as you discovered in the previous problem. The teen demand function is drawn in the first diagram below for $P = 5$, along with the teen supply function. The cuke supply function is drawn in the second diagram below for $w = 3$, along with the cuke demand function. Note that the equilibrium price in the cuke market is 5 and the equilibrium wage in the labor market is 3. That is, the equilibria in the two markets are mutually consistent.

Teen Labor Market

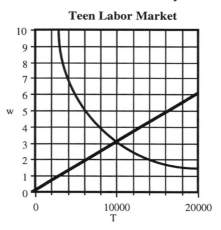

Cuke Market

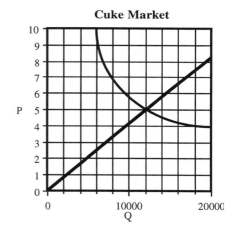

a. The demand for teens function graphed above does not take into account the fact that a change in the wage rate affects the price of cukes. The purpose of this part is to find a teen demand function that incorporates this price effect. The first step is to determine a relationship between P and w that must always hold if both markets are to be in equilibrium.

Equilibrium in the cuke market implies that Q supplied equals

Q demanded. Use this and the equations for supply and demand to determine the relationship between P and w that must hold.

Confirm that this relationship can be written as $P^2 = 25w/3$. Substitute the right-hand side of this equation for P^2 in the teen demand function to get the demand function that incorporates the effect of a wage rate change on P:

T =

Graph this new demand curve on the Teen Labor Market graph and give an intuitive explanation of why it is steeper than the "P constant" demand curve. _____

_____

_____

_____

_____

In the remaining parts of this problem, "demand for teens" refers to this new curve.

b. Suppose that the state government imposes a minimum wage of $4.00. Draw a horizontal line on the Teen Labor Market graph at this wage rate. How many teens will the pickle farmers want to employ? (1)_____ How many teens will want to work? (2)_____ What does the difference between the number of teens supplied at w = $4.00 and the quantity employed represent? (3)_____

_____ How does the minimum wage affect the cucumber supply curve? (4)_____

_____ Draw the new supply curve on the Cuke Market graph. What will equilibrium output and price be now?

P = (5)_____ Q = (6)_____

Harcourt Brace & Company

What are the profits of the typical cucumber producer now?

Π = (7)_____

How would your answers change if teen labor supply was more elastic? (8)_____

_____

_____

_____

_____

If demand for cukes was more elastic? (9)_____

_____

_____

_____

_____

c. An alternative way to raise wage rates is an employment subsidy. A subsidy of s dollars is paid to the farmer for each hour that a teen is employed, so the net cost for an hour of labor to the employer is w* = w – s. Explain why the effect of the subsidy on the demand for teens is to shift the teen demand curve up by amount s. (1)_____

_____

_____

_____

_____

Draw the shifted teen demand curve on the Teen Labor Market graph below, being careful that it passes through the supply curve at the desired wage rate of $4.00. [Note: the demand curve that already appears in this graph is the answer to part **a** of this problem.]

Teen Labor Market

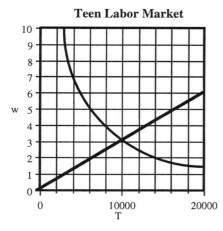

Cuke Market

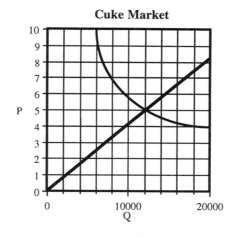

s = (2)_____ Give an intuitive

explanation of why this value is not equal to $1.00 (the

difference between $4.00 and the old equilibrium wage rate).

(3)_____

_____

_____

_____

_____

How many teens will be hired? T = (4)_____ What is

the new wage paid by employers? w* =

(5)_____ How does the

introduction of the subsidy affect the general equation for the

supply of cukes? [Hint: is the location of the supply curve

determined by w or w*?] Q = (6)_____

_____ Graph the new supply curve on the Cuke

Market graph and determine the new equilibrium price and

quantity.

P = (7)_____ Q = (8)_____

Profits of the typical cucumber farmer under the subsidy are

Π = (9)_____ How would your answers

change if teen labor supply was more elastic?

(10)_____

_____

If demand for cukes was more elastic?

(11)_____

_____

_____

_____

_____

d. Suppose you were the governor of this state. Which of the following list of constituents might you please by increasing teen wages to $4.00 by each of the two methods: teens, their parents (who are worried about keeping them out of trouble), cucumber farmers, pickle companies, the farm workers' union (members used to pick pickles, but aren't willing to for a wage rate of $3.00), and wealthy voters (who think that no one should have to work at such a low wage rate, but don't want to pay any more taxes).

_____

_____

_____

_____

_____

21.3. [Related to text problem 21.6.] This question continues Problems 21.1 and 21.2. In those questions it was assumed that L was the only input. This is fine for short-run analysis, when it might be reasonably assumed that other inputs (land, fertilizer, seed, etc.) are fixed, but in the long run these can be adjusted. Our objective is to determine whether the long-run demand curve for labor, which takes into account adjustment of other inputs, is more or less elastic than the short-run demand curve. Before beginning, what does your intuition suggest? You may be surprised by the result!

Let K represent the other inputs and assume that Putt's production function is:

$$q = 2(KL)^{.5}$$

Note that this function is consistent with Putt's original production function if K = 36. Let v represent the cost of a unit of K.

a. Show that Putt's output constant factor demand functions are:

$$L = (v/w)^{.5}q/2 \qquad K = (w/v)^{.5}q/2$$

Suppose that $v = 25/3$, $w = 3$ and that Putt produces $q = 120$. To minimize long run cost for this output level, how many units of L and K should he use?

L = (1)_____   K = (2)_____

Recall from Problem 21.1, where it was implicitly assumed that $K = 36$, that Putt chooses $q = 120$ and $L = 100$ if $w = 3$ and $P = 5$. You have just verified that, if $v = 25/3$, he has minimized costs for his chosen output level. Hence, this initial equilibrium is a long-run equilibrium, as well as a short-run equilibrium.

Now, find Putt's long-run cost and marginal cost functions. They will be functions of v and w.

Cost = (3)_____

MC = (4)_____

Verify that $MC = 5$ when $w = 3$ and $v = 25/3$. This also demonstrates that the initial equilibrium is a long-run equilibrium, since $P = MC$.

One point worth noting before proceeding is that Putt and the other cuke farmers all have constant returns to scale production functions. With free entry and exit, it would not be possible to determine how many farmers there would be and how much each would produce. For purposes of this problem, simply assume that the number of farmers is fixed at 100 and each farmer produces one one-hundredth of all cukes sold ($q = Q/100$) and hires one one-hundredth of all teens employed ($L = T/100$) and capital.

b. Recall that the demand curve for cukes is $Q = 60000/P$. Hence, each farmer's output will be $q = 600/P$. In the long run, each farmer's profit must be zero. For this problem, what does this statement imply for the relationship between P and MC? (1)_____ Use this fact and the demand curve to write long-run equilibrium q as a function of v and w.

q = (2)_____

This equation tells us how long-run q adjusts to changes in v and w. The output constant factor demand functions in **a** tell us how factor demands adjust to v and w, holding q constant. Use these and the equation you just found to find long-run demand functions for both factors, allowing q to adjust to maximize profit.

L = (3)_____

K = (4)_____

Multiply the demand curve for L by 100 to get demand for teens: T = (5)_____. Compare your result to the short run demand curve you found in Problem 2 (taking into account short run variation in P): T = 30000/w. What do you find? (6)_____

_____

To understand why this result occurs, it is helpful to examine the effect of an increase in the wage rate on long run demand for other factors, K. Does an increase in w increase or reduce the long run choice of K? (7)_____ This may seem surprising since we would expect each farmer to substitute K, which is now relatively less expensive, for L. In the short run this can't happen because K is fixed. In fact there is such a substitution effect here. To illustrate, suppose that w increased to $4.32. If q remained at 120, by how much would long run demand for K increase? (8)_____ This is the substitution effect. But q does not stay at 120; instead it falls to q = (9)_____. Hence, K will now be (10)_____, which is (11)_____ units less than what would have been used if q had remained at 120. This is the output effect.

For two inputs, the output and substitution effect of an increase in one factor's price on demand for the other factor have opposite signs. Whether long-run demand for the other factor increases or falls depends on which dominates. Under what conditions will the output effect dominate? Consider the effects of the elasticity of demand for output and the elasticity of substitution between inputs. (In the example, the first is −1 and the second is 1.)

Harcourt Brace & Company

(12)_____

_____ .

_____

The substitution effect? (13)_____

_____

_____

_____

Under what conditions will the long-run demand for the

variable factor be less elastic than in the short run?

(14)_____

_____

_____

_____

21.4. [Related to text problems 21.8–21.10.] Beaut Copper Mines, Inc. is the major employer in a mining town. The value of the marginal product of labor, L, to BCM is:

$$VMP = (400 - L)/15$$

The labor supply function it faces is:

$$L = 10 \ w$$

a. Plot the VMP and labor supply functions below.

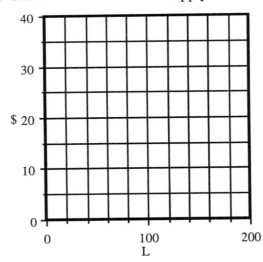

b. Total labor cost to BCM is wL. Use the supply equation to write this cost as a function of L.

wL = (1)_____

Harcourt Brace & Company

Now, find the cost of hiring an additional worker as a function of L (i.e., marginal factor cost).

MFC = (2)_____

Add MFC to the graph and determine how many workers BCM should employ to maximize profits.

L = (3)_____ What will the wage rate be?

w = (4)_____

What will the value of the marginal worker to BCM be?

VMP = (5)_____. Indicate L, w, and VMP for this solution on the graph.

c. The mineworkers form a union. The leaders of the union decide to maximize the revenue from union dues, which the union uses to support its strike fund, its pension fund, and other activities. BCM is a closed shop—everyone hired must join the union first. Let w_n be the net wage of a union member, obtained by subtracting dues, d, from the gross wage paid by BCM, w_g. The union informs BCM that it can hire as many workers as it wants at a gross wage rate that the union will determine. You are called in by the union's leaders as a consultant. Determine what gross wage the union should choose and how much the dues should be. You begin by noting that dues revenue is the difference between the firm's total wage bill, $w_g L$, and the total net wages paid to union members, $w_n L$. Think of the former as revenue to the union and the latter as cost to the union. Think of the difference, dues revenue, as the union's profit. You also know BMC's VMP curve, so you can tell how many workers the union will hire at wage rate w_g. In fact, you are implicitly choosing L when you choose w_g, so you might as well choose L directly and then find the value of w_g that BCM will be willing to pay. Use VMP to write the firm's wage bill (union's revenue) as a function of L alone:

Harcourt Brace & Company

$w_gL = (1)$_____. Find the marginal wage
bill (union's marginal revenue) as a function of L. MR =
(2)_____. As a function of L, the
total net wages (union's cost) are $w_nL =$
(3)_____. Find marginal net wages
(union's marginal cost). $MC = (4)$_____.
Add MR to the graph. You should find that MC is already
there! What value of L will maximize union dues (profit)?

$L = (5)$_____ At what wage rate will BCM be willing
to hire this many workers? $w_g = (6)$_____.
What will the net wage have to be in order to get this many
workers to join the union? $w_n = (7)$_____.
What will union dues be? Union dues are $d = (8)$_____

d. The theory of countervailing market power says that the
economic costs of market power in a particular market may
be reduced by introducing market power on the other side of
the market. Economic costs arise in a factor market when the
VMP of a factor exceeds the minimum price necessary to
induce suppliers to provide the quantity of the factor that is
demanded. Is the theory of countervailing market power
borne out it in this problem? Explain. _____

_____

_____

_____

e. How would your answer to **d** change if unions maximize
employment rather than dues revenue? _____

_____

_____

21.5. [Related to text problem 21.9.] The manager of
Megalopolis General Hospital figures that the value to the

hospital of adding another nurse to the staff is thirty thousand dollars per year, no matter how many nurses it hires. [Note: this number plays the role of "value of marginal product" in this question, although for a hospital it is not clear how such a figure would be determined for several reasons: What is the marginal product of a nurse? The price of output? Does the hospital profit maximize? Is the industry competitive?] This value is the same regardless of a nurse's sex. MGH is the only employer of nurses in Megalopolis and faces upward sloping supply curves for female (N_f) and male (N_m) nurses, given by:

$$N_f = 9\,S_f^2 \qquad N_m = 4\,S_m$$

where S_f and S_m are annual salaries of female and male nurses, respectively, in thousands of dollars. The hospital must pay all female nurses the same salary, since it can't distinguish between them. The same is true for male nurses. However, it does not need to pay the same salary to males and females.

a. What are the supply elasticities for female and male nurses?

elasticity for males: (1)_____ elasticity for

females: (2)_____ Which elasticity is larger?

(3)_____ Draw the supply curves on the

two graphs below.

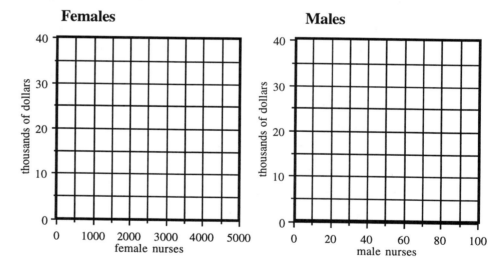

Females   **Males**

b. Find the cost of hiring another male nurse (i.e., marginal factor cost for male nurses).

MFC_m = (1)_____

Add this function to the male graph. Then find MFC$_f$ and add it to the female graph.

MFC$_f$ = (2)_____

Add a horizontal line at thirty thousand dollars on both graphs, to represent the value to the hospital of each nurse.

c. If the hospital hires female nurses up to the point where the value of the marginal female nurse just equals the cost of the marginal female nurse, how many female nurses should it employ and what will their salary be?

N$_f$ = (1)_____
S$_f$ = (2)_____

Indicate this point on the female graph. Then, answer the same question for males.

N$_m$ = (3)_____
S$_m$ = (4)_____

Indicate this point on the male graph.

d. Speculate about what would happen to N$_f$, N$_m$, S$_f$, and S$_m$ if MGH were forced to pay the same salary to male and female nurses.(1)_____

_____

_____

Which of the following groups would oppose salary discrimination: male nurses, female nurses, the MGH Nurses Union (in which each employed member gets one vote), or the MGH Board of Directors? Explain. (2)_____

_____

_____

Harcourt Brace & Company

e. What general conclusions can you draw about salary discrimination by monopsonists? _____

_____

_____

_____

_____

_____

CHAPTER 22

LABOR SUPPLY

time-allocation model:

    utility function: utility $= U(C, H)$

    combined income-time constraint: $C + wH = 24w + N$

    opportunity cost of leisure (w)

    full income $(24w + N)$

    first order condition:

        $MRS_{HC} = w$

    effects of a change in w on leisure, labor, and consumption:

        income effects

        substitution effects

individual labor supply:

    ordinary (uncompensated):

        $L_S = L(w, N)$

    compensated labor supply:

        $L_S = L'(w, N)$

    Slutsky equation:

$$\frac{\partial L}{\partial w} = \frac{\partial L'}{\partial w} + L \frac{\partial L}{\partial N}$$

    backward bending

market labor supply:

    labor force participation

job search theory

economics of childbearing

transportation choice

compensating wage differentials

KEY CONCEPTS

Harcourt Brace & Company

labor unions:

> closed shop

> wage bill maximization

> economic rent maximization

> employment maximization

> job security

> fringe benefits

PROBLEMS

(Numbers in brackets at the beginning of problems below refer to related examples and problems in the text.)

22.1. [Related to text example 22.1 and problems 22.1 and 22.2.] Mr. L. Z. Bones has the following utility function for consumption, C, and leisure, H:

$$U = C^{3/4}H^{1/4}$$

He can work up to 24 hours per day at wage rate w. Let L be hours worked per day. His time constraint is

$$H + L = 24 ,$$

and his budget constraint is

$$C = wL + N ,$$

where N is daily income from sources other than working (unearned income).

a. Find his combined income-time constraint. [Hint: solve his time constraint for L as a function of H, then substitute the result into his budget constraint and simplify.]

b. Suppose that w = \$10.00 and N = \$5.00. What is his full income? (1)_____ His opportunity cost of leisure? (2)_____

c. Recall that if a person has the utility function $U = X^{a}Y^{1-a}$, with $0 < a < 1$, and maximizes utility subject to the standard budget constraint $P_X X + P_Y Y = I$, she will choose

$$X = aI/P_X \qquad Y = (1-a)I/P_Y$$

Also, recall that "a" can be interpreted as the share of income spent on X and "$1 - a$" is the share spent on Y. Note that

Bones has a utility function of this type and that the budget constraint you found in **a** is also of the standard variety once appropriate interpretations are attached to P_X, P_Y, and I. If X is C, what is P_X? (1)_____ If Y is H, what is P_Y? (2)_____ What is I? (3)_____.

Now, use the standard result for the choices of X and Y to find Mr. Bones' choices of C and H as functions of w and N.

C = (4)_____

H = (5)_____

To get Mr. Bones' labor supply function, all you need to do is subtract the solution for H from 22.

L = (6)_____

If N = 0, what share of his time does Mr. Bones spend working? (7)_____ How many hours is this? (8)_____

d. Suppose that N = 0 and w = 10. How much could Bones consume if he never worked? (1)_____ If he worked 24 hours a day? (2)_____ Plot these points on the diagram below and draw in his budget constraint. What is the slope of the constraint? (3)_____

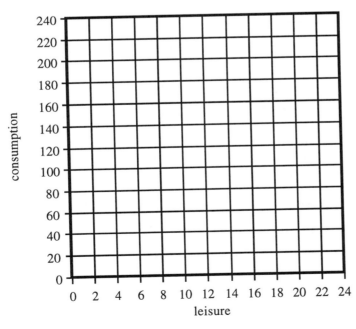

Now, draw a second budget line for N = 0 and w = 7. For

both budget lines find the points that represent his optimal choices of consumption and leisure and sketch the indifference curves that pass through them.

e. Mr. Uppin Adams has utility function

$$U = C^{1/2}H^{1/2}.$$

Find Adams' labor supply function.

$$L =$$

On the diagram in **d** sketch the indifference curves passing through the points that Adams would choose under the two budget constraints.

f. Suppose that both Adams and Bones have a wage rate of $10.00 and have no unearned income. The government introduces a proportional income tax of 30%. What is their net wage rate? (1)_____ How will the tax affect their labor supply?
(2)_____ Explain your answer in terms of the income and substitution effects of the tax.
(3)_____

_____

_____

_____

How much revenue will the government collect from Adams?
(4)_____ Bones? (5)_____

22.2. [Related to text example 22.2 and problems 22.2 and 22.6.] This problem continues Problem 22.1. Suppose that Bones has unearned income of $3 per day and a wage rate of $7.00 per hour, while Adams has unearned income of $9 and earns only $6.00 per hour.

a. How much can Bones consume if he doesn't work at all?
(1)_____ If he works 6 hours? (2)_____
12 hours? (3)_____ Draw his budget constraint on the graph following. [Be sure to notice that the scales are different from those in Problem 21.1.]

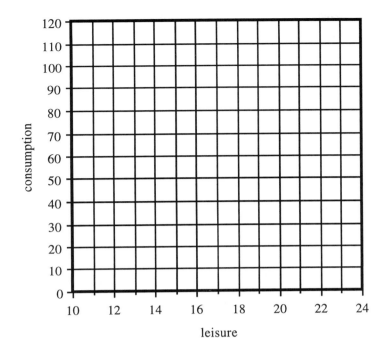

Now, draw Adams' budget constraint. Also, draw in the constraint for w = $10.00 and N = 0.

b. How many hours will Bones work? [Hint: use your labor

supply function from Problem 22.1.] (1)_____

How many hours will Adams work? (2)_____

Plot these points on their budget constraints and explain why

they work less under these constraints than under the

constraints in Problem 22.1. (3)_____

_____

_____

_____

c. Now, suppose that both Adams and Bones earn $20.00 per

hour, have no unearned income, and face the following

progressive income tax schedule (based on daily income):

total income (I)	tax (T)
$0.00 to $10.00	0
$10.00 to $60.00	.3(I − 10)
$60.00 to $200.00	15 + .4(I − 60)

You are the accountant for Adams and Bones. Figure out how much their taxes will be for each of the values of hours worked given in the following table.

Hours Worked (L)	Income (I)	Tax(T)
0	_____	_____
3	_____	_____
6	_____	_____
9	_____	_____
12	_____	_____

How much tax will Bones pay if he works 6 hours, as in Problem 22.1? (1)_____ How much tax will Adams pay if he works 12 hours, as in Problem 22.1? (2)_____ Compare these amounts to the amounts they would pay under a proportional tax of 30%. [See Problem 22.1.] (3)_____

_____ Why is this called a progressive tax? (4)_____

_____

_____ Draw the after-tax budget constraint for Adams and Bones on the diagram in **a**. [Hint: the constraint is composed of two line segments from the two constraints you have already drawn plus one additional segment.]

d. How many hours will Bones work under the tax described in **c**? [Hint: refer to **b**.] (1)_____ Adams? (2)_____ Compare these amounts to the amounts they work under a proportional tax of 40%. Why are the answers different? (3)_____

_____

_____

_____

_____

_____

_____

_____

e. Suppose that the government wants to switch from a proportional income tax to a progressive, negative income tax that collects the same amount of revenue from workers with wages equal to the average wage—which just happens to be $10.00 per hour. How will the tax affect labor supplied by workers who earn the average wage if they all have Cobb-Douglas utility functions? (1)_____ If the government assumes that labor supply will be unchanged, what will happen? (2)_____ Explain your answers. (3)_____

_____

_____

_____

_____

_____

How might your answers change if the utility functions of these workers were not Cobb-Douglas? (4)_____

_____

_____

_____

_____

_____

_____

_____

f. The 1986 Tax Reform Act made U.S. income taxes less progressive than they were previously. It was argued that this would induce the average worker to work more and allow average tax rates to be reduced without affecting tax revenue. Is this a sound argument? _____

_____

_____

_____

_____

22.3. [Related to text problem 22.6.] Joe knows that for every $10.00 he spends on consumption items he also uses an hour to actually do the consuming. The only thing he gets utility from is consumption, so all the time he doesn't spend consuming he spends working. His budget constraint is the diagonal line in the diagram below. Ignore the kinked line for now.

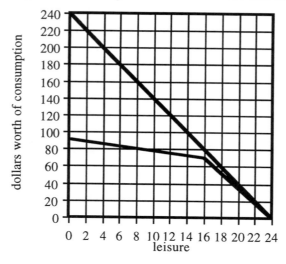

a. Draw a line that represents all the combinations of consumption and leisure that give Joe the same utility as 12 hours of leisure (consumption time) and $120 of consumption. [Hint: if he has only $120 but more than 12 hours of leisure, his utility will be the same as if he has 12 hours of leisure and more than $120 to spend.] Also, draw lines representing combinations that give him the same utility as, first, $100 and 10 hours, and second, $140 and 14 hours.

b. How many hours will Joe work if he faces the budget constraint in the diagram?

c. Suppose that Joe's wage rate changes to $5.00 per hour. Draw in his new budget constraint. How will this affect his hours worked? Explain your answer in terms of income and substitution effects. _____

_____

_____

_____

_____

_____

_____

d. Will a proportional income tax affect Joe's hours worked positively or negatively (in comparison to no tax)? Explain.

_____

_____

_____

_____

e. Now, consider the kinked line in the diagram. This is a budget constraint for a progressive income tax. If you answered **c** correctly, you should find that this constraint intersects the budget constraint for **c** at the point Joe chooses in **c**. Use this to answer the following question: If Joe works 16 hours under a proportional income tax, how many hours will he work under a progressive tax that is designed to collect the same revenue from Joe if he continues to work 16 hours?

f. Suppose that everyone in the economy has preferences like Joe's, but some have higher wages and others have lower wages. How will the change from the proportional tax to the progressive tax described in **e** affect income of higher wage persons if they continue to work the same number of hours? (1)_____ Will they continue to work the same number of hours? (2)_____ Explain. (3)_____

_____

_____

_____

_____

_____

_____ What will happen to incomes of lower wage persons if they continue to work the same number of hours? (4)_____ How will their hours worked change? (5)_____

Harcourt Brace & Company

g. Explain why the degree to which leisure and consumption are substitutable will play an important role in determining the impact of the 1986 Tax Reform Act (see Problem 22.2) on labor supply. _____

_____

_____

_____

_____

_____

22.4. [Related to text problems 22.3 and 22.5.] Inseigh Shable gets utility only from eating—the more the better—except that she can't survive on less than 8 hours of sleep. She can get consumable food in a variety of different ways. If she works long hours she can go out to restaurants and buy prepared food. She can also buy food at the store and prepare it at home, but this gives her less time to work and eat. Another alternative is to work just a little at her job, use the money to buy seeds, fertilizer, etc., and use the extra time to garden. Her choices are represented in the diagram below.

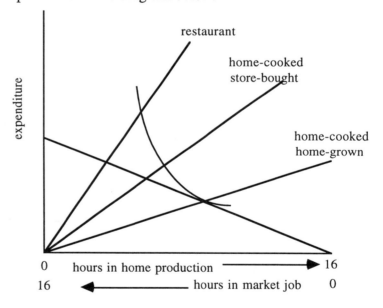

The curved line represents combinations of hours in home production (i.e., time spent eating, cooking, and gardening) and expenditures on food (including expenditures for growing and preparing) that give her the same quantity of consumed food. Think of this line as an isoquant in her "household" production function. Assume that this production function is homothetic. The slope of the steepest ray coming from the origin reflects the ratio of expenditures to home production hours for the typical restaurant meal, the slope of the middle ray reflects the ratio for home-cooked, store-bought food, and the slope of the flattest ray reflects the ratio for home-cooked, home-grown food. Her current budget constraint is represented by the straight line with the negative slope.

a. What type of meals does Inseigh consume under her current budget constraint?

b. Suppose her wage rate increases. Draw a new budget constraint representing the increase.

c. Will the hours she spends at her job increase or decrease—or can you tell? Explain. [Hint: suppose that the isoquant is actually an indifference curve from a Cobb-Douglas utility function.]_____

_____

_____

_____

Will the ratio of expenditures to household production time she uses for producing consumable food increase or decrease? Explain. [Hint: recall that for homothetic production functions, the rate of technical substitution is constant along a ray from the origin.] _____

_____

_____

_____

d. The previous two problems were concerned with the labor supply effects of proportional and progressive taxes. How does the possibility of household production—which is not taxed—affect the analysis? _____

_____

_____

_____

_____

_____

_____

_____

_____

22.5. [Related to text problem 22.5.] Once Jack and Jill finish tumbling down the hill they get married and make every effort to live happily every after. They spend 16 hours a day sleeping, climbing hills, and doing other things together, but they discover that to be really happy they have to have money, X, to buy food and other inputs into household production, and they also have to spend time preparing food and doing other types of housework. Unfortunately, Jack is so inept at housework that he can't boil water. If he spends 8 hours at housework he will get no more done than a typical person would in six. Fortunately, Jill has an aptitude for housework—she can do 9 hours worth of work in 8. Outside the home she is less fortunate. She can earn only about $6.25 per hour, whereas Jack can earn 50% more. The combinations of X and effective housework, H, they can each provide in eight hours are illustrated by the two budget constraints drawn in the graph below.

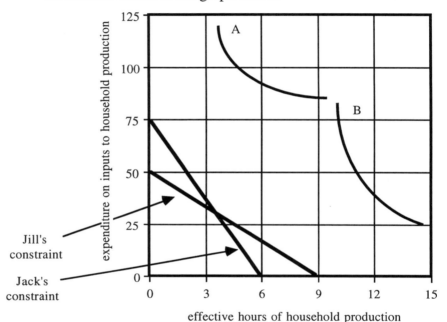

a. If they both work in the household full-time, what will total H be? (1)_____ What will X be? (2)_____ Plot this point on the graph. If Jill works full-time in the household and Jack works full-time at his job, what will H be? (3)_____ X? (4)_____ Plot this point on the graph. If they both work full-time at their jobs, what will H be? (5)_____ X? (6)_____ Plot this point. Now, draw the kinked line that represents their joint budget constraint—the maximum amount they can spend on inputs into household production for given effective hours spent in household production.

b. The curved line labelled A is an isoquant for household production. That is, it represents combinations of X and H that yield the same level of household output, Q (e.g., prepared meals). Jack and Jill wish to maximize household output. Describe how they should allocate their time. [There is no need to state exact hours in each activity.]

_____

_____

_____

_____

_____

_____

c. Answer **b** again, but using isoquant B.

_____

_____

_____

_____

_____

_____

d. If Jack and Jill each get to consume 50% of household output, Q, it seems reasonable to assume that they will both want to maximize Q. Is this assumption still reasonable if Jack gets 75% and Jill gets 25%? Explain.

_____

_____

_____

_____

_____

_____

_____

e. "In the 'traditional' family the mother is a housewife and the father is the breadwinner. The reason is that men have a comparative advantage in market work relative to housework. Even if a wife has a job outside the home, it is likely to be a part-time job for the same reason." Discuss this statement, using the above example to illustrate its meaning.

_____

_____

_____

_____

_____

_____

_____

22.6. [Related to text problem 22.4.] Charles Osgood ("The Osgood File," CBS Radio) once made the remark below about a change in the way the federal government imputes the value of a housewife's time. Prior to the change, the value of an hour of housework was set equal to the cost of hiring someone else to do the work—about $5.00. After the change, the value was set at the average wage rate a housewife could earn if she chose to get a job—about $7.00.

"It seems that it's not what you do that counts, but what you don't do!"

a. Explain to Charles why the new method is more appropriate.

_____

_____

_____

_____

_____

_____

b. What compensating differences might make a woman willingly do housework valued at only $5.00 per hour when she can earn $7.00 per hour at a job? _____

_____

_____

_____

_____

_____

_____

CHAPTER 23

CAPITAL

rate of return:

    single period:

$$r_1 = \frac{x - s}{s} = \frac{x}{s} - 1$$

    perpetual:

$$r_\infty = y/s$$

price of future goods:

$$P_1 = \frac{1}{1 + r_1}$$

    effects of a change on savings:

        income effect

        substitution effect

    determinants of the equilibrium price:

        impatience

        capital productivity

real vs. nominal interest rates:

$$1 + R = (1 + r)(1 + P_e) \quad \text{or} \quad R \approx r + P_e$$

cost of capital:

    opportunity cost

    depreciation

$$v = P(r + d)$$

    equilibrium rental rate

stocks and flows

first order condition for profit-maximizing firm facing a perfectly competitive rental market:

$$MRP_K = v = P(r+d)$$

investment:

gross

net

effect of a fall in r on investment

present discounted value of $N payable n years in the future:

$$PDV(\$N) = \frac{\$N}{(1 + r)^n}$$

present discounted value of capital:

discrete time (with no depreciation):

general case (R_i dollars worth of services i years into the future):

$$PDV = \frac{R_1}{(1 + r)^n} + \frac{R_2}{(1 + r)^n} + \cdots + \frac{R_n}{(1 + r)^n}$$

special case ($R_i = v$ every year in perpetuity):

$$PDV = v/r$$

equilibrium condition:

$$P = v/r$$

continuous time (with depreciation at rate d):

$$PDV(t) = \int_t^\infty e^{(r+d)t} v(s) e^{-(r+d)s} ds$$

equilibrium condition:

$$v(t) = (r + d)P(t) - \frac{dP(t)}{dt}$$

effect of capital gains on investment

human capital

PROBLEMS

(Numbers in brackets at the beginning of problems below refer to related examples and problems in the text.)

23.1. [Related to text example 23.1 and problem 23.1.] U. Hownley Livewonce has the following utility function for consumption in the two periods of his life:

$$\text{utility} = U(C_1) + U(C_2)/(1 + d),$$

where $d > 0$ and U is a function having the properties

$$U'(C) > 0 \quad U''(C) < 0.$$

The parameter d is known as the "subjective rate of time preference." It is the rate at which Hownley discounts second period utility from consumption before comparing it with first period utility. The larger d is, the more impatient Hownley is to consume. Preferences like Hownley's are sometimes referred to as "additively separable."

Hownley has a fixed amount of wealth, W, to spend on his consumption in the two periods. Whatever he doesn't spend in the first period can be saved for the second period and he will receive a rate of return of r on his savings. Therefore, his second period consumption will be related to his first period consumption by $C_2 = (W - C_1)(1+r)$. This relationship can be rewritten as his intertemporal budget constraint:

$$C_1 + C_2/(1+r) = W$$

a. Show that Hownley's utility-maximizing choice for C_1 and C_2 must satisfy the following condition:

$$MRS_{12} \equiv (1 + d)\frac{U'(C_1)}{U'(C_2)} = 1 + r$$

b. Consider a consumption bundle with $C_1 = C_2$. What is Hownley's MRS_{12}?

Representative indifference curves for Hownley are drawn on the diagram below. What is the slope of these curves where they cross the forty-five degree line?

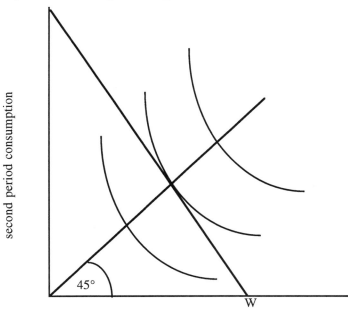

first period consumption

c. An initial budget line for Hownley appears in the diagram. How is the slope of this line related to r?

For the particular line drawn, is r greater than, less than, or equal to d?

d. Now, suppose that r increases. Draw a new budget line that is both tangent to one of the other indifference curves and reflects a larger value of r than the first budget line. Does C_1 increase or decrease? (1)_____ Would your answer be the same no matter how large the increase in r is? Explain. (2)_____

_____

_____

Does C_2 increase or decrease? (3)_____
Would your answer be the same no matter how large the increase in r is? Explain. (4)_____

_____

_____ Does first period saving, defined as $S = W - C_1$, increase or decrease? (5)_____ Would your answer be the same no matter how large the increase in r is? Explain. (6)_____

_____ Which will be larger now, consumption in period two or period one? (7)_____ Would your answer be the same no matter how large the increase in r is? Explain. (8)_____

_____

Would answers (4), (6) and (8) change if Hownley's utility function was of a more general type [i.e., utility = $U(C_1, C_2)$]? Explain. (9)_____

_____

_____

_____

_____ Does Hownley's utility increase or decrease as a result of the higher interest rate? (10)_____ Does this answer depend on the size of the rate increase or the additively separable utility function? (11)_____

e. Suppose that Hownley's wealth, W, is actually the present value of the income, I, he receives in periods one and two:

$$W = I_1 + I_2/(1+r)$$

Note that this does not change the budget line in the original diagram, just the interpretation of the horizontal intercept. The point (I_1, I_2) lies somewhere along the budget line, as depicted in the diagram below.

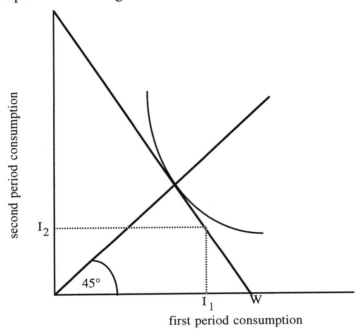

What will happen to the present value of Hownley's income if r increases? (1)_____

Draw a new budget line representing an interest rate increase. [Hint: Note that the new line will have a different horizontal intercept. At what point will it cross the old line?] Now, determine the effect of the interest rate increase on each of the following:

(2) first period consumption_____

(3) second period consumption_____

(4) first period saving $(I_1 - C_1)$_____

(5) the ratio of second period consumption to first period consumption_____

(6) utility_____

Put an asterisk (*) next to any results that depend on the size of the interest rate increase. Put a number sign (#) next to any results that depend on additive separability.

f. Repeat **e,** for the incomes depicted in the diagram below.

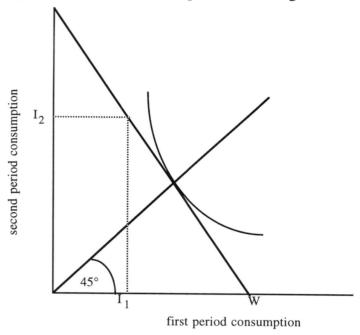

(1)_____

(2)_____

(3)_____

(4)_____

(5)_____

(6)_____

g. Based on the above, what results, if any, do not depend on whether the consumer is a saver or dissaver in period one?

What result is obtainable for additively separable utility functions that would not necessarily be true for other utility functions?

h. "Increases in interest rates always hurt people with fixed income streams (such as those on Social Security) because they reduce their wealth (i.e., the present discounted value of those streams)." Do you agree? Explain.

_____

_____

_____

_____

_____

23.2. This problem continues Problem 23.1. Many economists and policymakers are concerned about the fact that personal savings rates in the United States are much lower than in the rest of the world. The reason that low savings are a concern is that savings are required for capital accumulation unless it is financed by borrowing from abroad. Low rates of capital accumulation have been blamed for the relatively slow rate of growth of the U. S. economy. This question and the next examine two types of taxes that are thought to discourage saving. The U.S. has both types.

Suppose at first that Hownley has to pay a tax on his earned income. The tax rate is t, so his after tax income is $(1-t)I_1$ in period one and $(1-t)I_2$ in period two. Note that he does not have to pay tax on his interest income.

a. Write his post-tax budget constraint and illustrate the constraint on the diagram below, which already contains his pre-tax constraint and the indifference curve that is tangent to it.

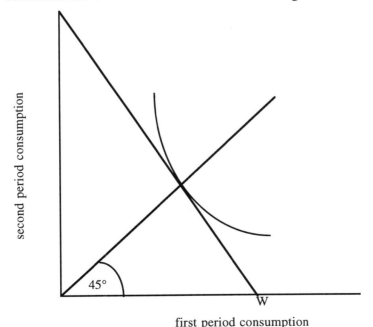

first period consumption

Compare the slopes of the pre- and post-tax constraints.

b. The government decides to change the tax system. Instead of charging a tax on just earned income, it plans to tax interest income as well. Hownley's savings from period one are:

$$S = (1 - t)I_1 - C_1$$

Assume his savings are positive. Then, in the second period he will be able to consume:

$$C_2 = (1 - t)\{I_2 + (1 + r)[(1 - t)I_1 - C_1]\}.$$

This is one form of his new post-tax budget constraint. Economists sometimes say that income taxes of this type (which the United States has) impose a "double" tax on saving. What do they mean? _____

_____

_____

_____

_____

Now, rewrite this constraint in the form $C_1 + P_2C_2 = W^*$, where P_2 is a function of r and t and W^* is a function of r, t, I_1, and I_2. Is the price of future consumption relative to present consumption higher or lower than before?

c. Since the government now taxes interest income it decides to lower the tax rate. It lowers the rate just enough so that Hownley can still choose the same consumption bundle he preferred under the old tax. Draw Hownley's new budget constraint in the diagram. What will happen to Hownley's choice of C_1? (1)_____

C_2? (2)_____ S? (3)_____

Harcourt Brace & Company

d. Now, suppose that Hownley is a borrower in the first period. Suppose also that he can deduct his interest payments from his second period income before he pays his second period tax. After deductions, his second period taxable income is $I_2 + r[(1 - t)I_1 - C_1]$. [Note that $S = (1 - t)I_1 - C_1$ is negative.] The after-tax income he now has available for consumption in the second period and for paying off his loan (both interest and principle) is $(1 - t)\{I_2 + r[(1 - t)I_1 - C_1]\}$. The amount of the loan payment is $-(1 + r)[(1 - t)I_1 - C_1]$. Hence, his budget constraint is:

$$C_2 - (1 + r)[(1 - t)I_1 - C_1] = (1 - t)\{I_2 + r[(1 - t)I_1 - C_1]\}$$

Rewrite this constraint in the form $C_1 + P_2C_2 = W^*$.

Is the price of future consumption higher or lower than under the original tax? (1)_____ If the tax rate is adjusted so that Hownley can still make the same consumption choice as under the original tax, what will happen to his choice of C_1? (2)_____ C_2? (3)_____ S (which is negative)? (4)_____

e. Prior to 1986, interest payments on most loans were deductible from income prior to computing taxes. The 1986 Tax Reform Act eliminated interest deductibility except on mortgage loans. How do you think this change will affect saving? (1)_____

_____

What do you think will happen to consumer demand for second mortgages?[1] (2)_____

_____

23.3. Continuing 23.1 and 23.2, suppose that Hownley lives for three periods instead of two. His three-period utility function is also additively separable:

$$\text{utility} = U(C_1) + U(C_2)/(1 + d) + U(C_3)/(1 + d)^2$$

Note that his utility from third period consumption is discounted by the square of $1 + d$ because it occurs two periods into the

---

[1] If the value of a home substantially exceeds the outstanding principle on the mortgage, a bank or other financial institution may be willing to make a loan to the owner, for any purpose. The owner's equity in the house (its total value minus the outstanding principle) serves as collateral. Such a loan is called a second mortgage.

future. Assume that he earns I_1 dollars in the first period, I_2 dollars in the second period, and no income in the third period. Also, assume that his second period income is greater than his first period income.

a. Find the first order conditions for Hownley's utility maximization problem. [Hint: let $W = I_1 + I_2/(1+r)$. Since I_1, I_2, and r are all fixed, treat W as fixed. Then, the budget constraint is the same as in Problem 23.1, except a third term must be added to the left-hand side for third period consumption.]

Under what condition will consumption be the same in all three periods? (1)_____ Under what condition will consumption decline over time? (2)_____ Describe Hownley's pattern of saving and dissaving over the three periods if r = d. (3)_____

_____

_____

_____

b. Assume that r = d. The government is worried about Hownley. What will he do when he's old (third period) and has no income? They decide to impose a "social security" tax on Hownley's earnings (but not on interest income) in the first two periods at rate t. Hownley's taxes will be used to make payments to people who are currently old. When Hownley is old, taxes on younger people will be used to give him a payment equal to what he would have received from investments if he had saved the money himself. Let SS represent the third period payment. Write SS as a function of I_1, I_2, and r.

SS =

Write Hownley's new budget constraint, taking into account

both the taxes he must pay in periods one and two and SS.
[Leave SS in the constraint.]

If Hownley anticipates that SS will equal the amount the
government plans to give him, how will the government
program affect his consumption in the three periods? [Hint:
Substitute the expression for SS into his budget constraint.]

(1)_____

_____ How will it affect his

savings in the first two periods? (2)_____

_____

c. What effect do you think the U.S. Social Security system,
which was implemented during the Great Depression of the
1930s in a manner similar to that described in **b**, has on both
private savings and investment? _____

_____

_____

_____

_____

23.4. [Related to text example 23.2 and problem 23.3.] As cheddar
cheese ages it becomes sharper. After six months it is sold as
"mild," after 12 months it is sold as "sharp," after 18 months it is
sold as "extra sharp," and after 24 months it is sold as "special
sharp."

Suppose that initial production costs of cheese are $2.00, that the
present discounted value of 6 months storage cost is $.50, and
that the annual rate of interest is 10% (i.e., r = .01). Assume that
the market for cheddar cheese is competitive. You are to find the
long-run equilibrium prices of the four types of cheese.

a. As a first step, it will be useful to find the 6 month rate of
interest. Let r_6 represent the value you seek. If a dollar is
deposited in the bank at this rate of interest, what will be the
value of the deposit after 6 months (as a function of r_6)?

(1)_____ After 12 months?

(2)_____ Of course, if the annual rate of
interest is 10%, the value of a dollaR deposit after a year will
be $1.10. Equate answer (2) to $1.10 and solve for the

value of r_6 that is equivalent to an annual interest rate of 10%.

b. Let P_m be the price of mild cheese. What must the present discounted value of P_m be in order for profits to be zero?

c. Now, use your answer to **b** to find P_m under long-run equilibrium.

price of mild_____

d. Let P_s be the price of sharp cheese. What relationship must hold between P_s and P_m in order that profits from keeping mild cheese for another 6 months are zero?

e. Now, use your answer to **e** to find P_s under long-run equilibrium.

price of sharp_____

f. Now, find the long-run equilibrium prices of extra sharp and special sharp.

Harcourt Brace & Company

price of extra sharp _____

price of special sharp _____

23.5. [Related to text example 23.2 and problems 23.3–23.5.] Chuck is a catfish rancher. He buys one-pound catfish from a hatchery for $1.00 each and throws them in his pond, where they stay until he catches them and sells them to a catfish wholesaler. After t years, each catfish grows to a weight of

$$W(t) = e^{4t - 2t^2}$$

Assume that Chuck has no other costs for raising catfish.

a. Suppose that the wholesale price of catfish is P dollars per pound, regardless of the weight of the fish. What is the present discounted value (PDV) of a t-year-old catfish sold to a wholesaler when Chuck first buys it from the hatchery? Your answer will be a function of P, t, and the continuous time rate of interest, r. Remember to deduct the initial cost.

b. Find the value of t that maximizes PDV if the interest rate is 10% (r = .10).

c. Under perfect competition economic profits are zero. Assuming that the $1 initial cost includes all economic costs, what must P be?

d. Let t* represent your answer to **b.** Some fish may be sold

Harcourt Brace & Company

before t* to other ranchers. These ranchers will then keep them until t*, when they are sold to a wholesaler, or until they resell them to another rancher before t*. Let V(u) represent the value of a u-year-old fish. If Chuck's profits from a fish sold at age u (< t*) are zero, what must V(u) be (a function of u and r only)? [Hint: Chuck must just recover his costs.]

What is the rate of growth of V(u)?

What is V(t*)?

What is the growth rate of a fish at time u?

Show that the rate of growth of a fish and V(u) are the same at u = t*.

Which grows faster at u < t*, the fish or V(u)?

The above results imply that V(u) exceeds the amount the rancher would receive if he sold the fish to a wholesaler at age u. Explain. [Hint: the wholesale value of the fish is P times the fish's weight, so it grows at the same rate as the animal.](1)_____

_____

_____

What would happen if V(u) was less than the wholesale value of the fish at age u? (2)_____

_____

_____

23.6. [Related to text problem 23.8] Longka Mute is trying to decide whether to travel to her job by bus or by car. She and her husband, Trav Linman, already own a car, but he takes it on business trips during the week. They have no other use for a second car. If she takes the bus, it will cost her $1.00 per day in fares for 250 days per year. She also thinks that the bus takes about half-an-hour per day longer than driving a car. She values her time at her wage rate, which is $10.00 per hour. Hence, she figures the annual cost of using the bus is $(1 + 10/2) \times 250 = \$1,500$. The car she would buy costs $10,000 dollars. She estimates that the annual costs for insurance, fuel, repairs, and parking will be about $500 per year for the first two years. At the end of two years she plans to resell the car. She estimates that its resale value will be $8,000.

    a. Find the present discounted cost of commuting by bus for two years using an interest rate of 10%. To simplify, assume that all costs are incurred on the first day of the year.

    b. Find the present discounted cost of commuting by car for two years. Be sure to subtract the PDV of the resale value of the car.

    c. On the basis of these calculations, should she buy a car?

    d. What would the PDV of the other benefits Longka expects have to be in order to make buying the second car worthwhile?

e. Would your answer to **d** be smaller or larger if the assumption that all costs are incurred on the first day of the year is dropped? Explain. _____

_____

_____

f. Would your answer to **d** be smaller or larger if the interest rate used was 5% instead of 10%. Explain. _____

_____

_____

_____

CHAPTER 24

EXTERNALITIES AND PUBLIC GOODS

types of externalities:

  interfirm:

    negative

    positive (beneficial)

  interpersonal (in utility)

  public goods

social marginal revenue product under externalities:

$$SMRP_L^X = P_Y \frac{\partial g}{\partial L_Y} + P_X \frac{\partial f}{\partial Y} \frac{\partial Y}{\partial L_Y}$$

efficiency requirement:

$$SMRP_L^X = SMRP_L^Y$$

inefficiency of competitive equilibrium:

$$MRP_L^X = MRP_L^Y$$

coping with externalities:

  Pigovian tax

  merger and internalization

  assignment of property rights:

    Coase Theorem

    distributional effects

    bargaining costs

attributes of public goods:

  nonexclusivity

  nonrival

social marginal rate of substitution:

$$SMRS_{PG} = MRS_{PG}^1 + MRS_{PG}^2 + \ldots + MRS_{PG}^n$$

Harcourt Brace & Company

efficiency requirement for public goods:

$$RPT_{PG} = SMRS_{PG}$$

inefficiency of competitive equilibrium:

$$RPT_{PG} = MRS_{PG} < SMRS_{PG}$$

Lindahl pricing

revelation of preferences for public goods:

 free rider

 voting with one's feet

PROBLEMS

(Numbers in brackets at the beginning of problems below refer to related examples and problems in the text.)

24.1. [Related to text examples 24.1 and 24.2 and problem 24.1.] When determining how much pollution we should tolerate, economists emphasize the tradeoff between pollution and production. As an example, assume that two industries produce different products but are located in the same region. The demand curves for their products are depicted below. Private marginal costs of production are zero, so the only cost of production is pollution. The cost of pollution is $.25 per unit of output for each firm.

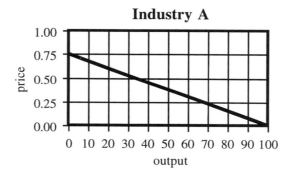

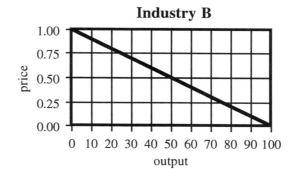

 a. What is the social marginal cost of production?

b. What will price and quantity be for each industry under perfect competition?

c. What are the efficient prices and quantities?

d. In percentage terms, how much less pollution is there at the efficient prices and quantities than at the competitive ones for both industries combined?

e. Suppose the Environmental Protection Agency directs each firm in each industry to reduce output by the same percentage that you found in **d**. What will price and quantity be in each industry?

Is this solution efficient? Explain. _____

_____

_____

_____

_____

f. Explain how an output tax could be used to obtain the efficient outcome. _____

_____

_____

_____

_____

24.2. [Related to text examples 24.1 and 24.2, and problem 24.1.] Midwestern power companies generate much of their electricity by burning coal. Tall smokestacks, required because of concerns about local pollution, carry the sulfurous smoke high into the atmosphere. Substantial evidence suggests that the sulfur is precipitated over the northeastern states and eastern Canada as sulfuric acid. "Acid rain" is believed to cause serious damage to trees and other vegetation, wildlife (especially fish), the exteriors of buildings, and so forth. Some have even suggested that it accounts for higher rates of colon cancer in these areas!

For the purposes of this problem, suppose that each megawatt of electricity produced in the midwest caused $100 worth of acid rain damage in the northeastern United States. Discuss each of the following proposed solutions to the problem. Be sure to consider all of the following questions for each proposal:

i. Is the proposal economically efficient?

ii. How will the proposal affect the welfare of people in the two regions?

iii. Is the proposal technically and politically feasible?

a. Do nothing.

_____

_____

_____

_____

_____

_____

_____

b. Impose regulations on the power companies that would force them to reduce the sulfur content of the smoke to the point where the rain returns to its natural level of acidity.

_____

_____

_____

_____

_____

_____

_____

c. Impose a tax of $100 per megawatt on electricity production in the midwest and use the revenue to give people in the northeast an income tax rebate.

_____

_____

_____

_____
_____
_____
_____

d. Impose a tax of $100 per megawatt on electricity production in the midwest and use the revenue to pay for projects designed to clean up the damage of acid rain.

_____
_____
_____
_____
_____
_____
_____

e. Give northeasterners the right to clean air.

_____
_____
_____
_____
_____
_____
_____

f. Give midwesterners the right to pollute the air.

_____
_____
_____
_____
_____
_____
_____

24.3. [Related to text problems 24.2 and 24.3.] In a certain coastal area of Maine, the total lobster catch, L, in a season is given by

$$L = 1000N - N^2$$

where N is the number of lobstermen that set their traps in the area. This area is small relative to all lobstering areas, so each lobster that is caught can be sold at the going wholesale price, $1.00. The cost of setting and tending traps in this area is $500 per lobsterman per season (including the opportunity cost of his time), regardless of how many lobsters he catches.

a. As a function of N, how many lobsters will the average lobsterman catch? $L/N =$

(1)_____

What will his profits be (another function of N)? $\Pi =$

(2)_____ How many lobstermen will set traps in this area if the market is perfectly competitive? $N = (3)$_____

b. At the competitive solution, what is the private marginal cost to a lobsterman of entering this area? $MC_P =$

(1)_____ How is the output of each existing lobsterman affected by his entry? (2)_____

How are the profits of each existing lobsterman affected by his entry? (3)_____ What is the social marginal cost of his entry? $MC_S =$

(4)_____ How much will consumers be willing to pay for the lobsters caught by the additional lobsterman? (5)_____

Explain why the competitive solution is not efficient.

(6)_____

_____

_____

_____

_____

_____

_____

c. Suppose that the State of Maine decides to take over lobster operations in this area. It pays lobstermen $500 each to set traps and then sells all the lobsters caught at the going price. To maximize its profit, how many lobstermen should the state hire?

$N = (1)$_____ What will the marginal cost to the state of hiring an additional lobsterman be at this point, taking into account the fact that this will reduce the number caught by existing lobstermen?

MC = (2)_____ How much would consumers be willing to pay for the lobsters caught by the additional lobsterman? (3)_____. Explain why your answer to (1) is the efficient number of lobstermen.
(4)_____

_____

_____

_____

_____

_____

_____ Would this "state monopoly" solution still be efficient if the state faced a downward sloping demand curve for lobster? Explain.
(5)_____

_____

_____

_____

_____

_____

_____

d. As an alternative to the state monopoly, suppose that the state decides to require each lobsterman in the area to purchase a license. Assuming that all lobster can be sold for $1.00 each, how much should the state charge each lobsterman in order to obtain the efficient level of output?

24.4. A train running through a wheat field throws sparks that sometimes set fire to the wheat. Suppose that the annual losses are valued at $50 and that the railroad company could prevent the loss by installing a spark arrestor at an annual cost of $100.

a. Is it socially efficient to install the arrestor? Explain.

_____

_____

_____

b. What will happen if the farmer is given the right to exclude the train from passing near his field if it continues to throw sparks? Is this outcome socially efficient? _____

_____

_____

_____

c. What will happen if the train has the right to throw as many sparks as it wants on the farmer's field? Is this outcome socially efficient? _____

_____

_____

_____

d. Assume that it costs the railroad $60 in legal fees to make any contract with the wheat farmer. Will this change your answer to either **b** or **c**? Explain. _____

_____

_____

_____

_____

_____

24.5. In the case of "Baby M," a New Jersey couple who could not have children of their own (the wife was infertile) hired a woman to be a surrogate mother. That is, they paid the woman to be inseminated with the husband's sperm and she agreed to give them the baby when it was born. However, the surrogate mother decided she wanted to keep the baby—a girl—when she was born. Court battles ensued. A lower court in New Jersey awarded the baby to the natural father and his wife and denied visiting rights to the surrogate mother. Eventually, the Supreme Court of New Jersey ruled that the natural father and his wife could keep the baby, but that the surrogate mother did have visitation rights. In addition, the court ruled that surrogate mothers in New Jersey could not receive remuneration in excess of medical expenses, citing state laws that prohibit payments to mothers who give their babies up for adoption. Such laws are consistent with our "right to be free." In the United States people are not allowed to own other people; hence, they can't buy and sell them. (Professional sports teams are the exception!)

Suppose that the New Jersey state legislature passes a law that assigns ownership of each surrogate baby to its surrogate mother—including the right to sell the baby to the natural father and his wife. Who would benefit from this law and who would lose? Be sure to include the following among those you consider: potential surrogate mothers, the fertile husbands of infertile women, infertile women with fertile husbands, and potential surrogate babies.

(1)_____

_____

_____

_____

_____

_____

_____

_____

_____

_____

_____

_____

_____

How would your answer change if the new law assigned ownership to the natural father?

(2)_____

_____

_____

Is the current law (as interpreted by the New Jersey Supreme Court) economically efficient? Explain, making reference to the Coase Theorem.

(3)_____

_____

_____

_____

_____

24.6. [Related to text example 24.3 and problem 24.7.] Two units in a condominium complex share a sidewalk. The Kloride family lives in one unit. During the winter they put salt on the sidewalk to melt the ice. The pounds of salt they are willing to put out in a year depends on its price, P, according to:

$$S_K = 15 - 10P$$

The other unit is occupied by the Sewdiems. They are also willing to salt the sidewalk. Their demand function for salt is:

$$S_S = 20 - 10P$$

Salt is a nonrival, nonexclusive good for both families.

a. Plot the demand functions for the two families on the diagram below.

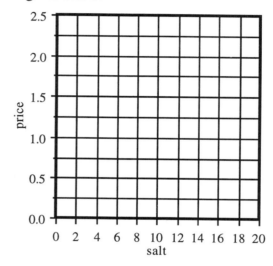

Draw a horizontal line at P = \$1.00.

b. Both families just moved in and they are not yet acquainted. Each independently buys salt and puts it out. How much does each put out? S_K = (1)_____
S_S = (2)_____ The total salt put out is S = (3)_____. Indicate answers (1) through (3) on the graph. Given the total purchased, how much would the Kloride family be willing to pay for another pound? That is, how many dollars worth of other goods are they willing to give up in order to get another pound? (4)_____
How much would the Sewdiem family be willing to pay for another pound? (5)_____ Explain why this outcome is not economically efficient.
(6)_____

_____

_____

Harcourt Brace & Company

Is S too large or too small? Explain. (7)_____

_____

_____

   c. The next year both families expect the other to put out as much salt as in the previous year. How much will the Klorides put out? S_K = (1)_____

The Sewdiems? S_S = (2)_____

   d. "Under perfect competition, the quantity of a public good that is provided and consumed is smaller than is optimal." Do you agree? Explain. _____

_____

_____

_____

   e. Another year goes by and the two families decide to cooperate. What will their joint demand function for salt be, assuming that each family pays in proportion to the marginal benefit it receives from the salt? [Hint: first find the amount that each family is willing to pay for the marginal pound of salt as a function of S. Add these together to get their total willingness to pay. This is the inverse of their joint demand function.]

S = (1)_____ Plot this function on the diagram in **a**. How much salt will they buy? S = (2)_____ Indicate this value on the diagram. What share of the price will be paid by the Kloride family? (3)_____ The Sewdiem family? (4)_____ Indicate these shares on the diagram.

24.7. [Related to text problem 24.8.] The bridge between Suburbia and Megalopolis has been washed out by a flood. The 200 residents of Suburbia who commute to Megalopolis get together to determine whether or not to replace the bridge. The alternative is to use an existing bridge that is out of their way. After some research they determine that the bridge could be paid for by selling bonds, on which they would have to pay $50,000 interest per year in perpetuity. The residents are evenly split between two groups. Group A residents reveal that they are each willing to pay up to $400 per year for a new bridge and Group B residents reveal that they are each willing to pay up to $200 per year.

a. What is the most that the bridge could cost annually and be worth building?

b. The residents vote on a proposal to build the bridge. Under the proposal, just enough tax revenue will be raised to cover the annual interest payment. Each resident will be charged in proportion to his/her willingness to pay; that is, the tax on each member of Group A will be twice as much as the tax on each member of Group B. What will the tax be on Group A members? (1)_____ On Group B members? (2)_____ Will the proposal pass? (3)_____

c. After the vote, a ferry company proposes to the town that it will establish ferry service across the river. To cover its costs, it will charge each resident that wants to use the service $280 dollars per year. Assume that, holding cost constant, all residents are indifferent between a bridge and ferry service. Will a motion to rescind the previous vote on the bridge be favored by a clear majority of the voters? Explain. _____

_____

_____

_____

_____

_____

d. Group A is not very happy with the outcome in **c**. They decide to offer all members of Group B a bribe in order to get them to switch their votes. Assuming that Group B members are susceptible to bribery, what is the smallest bribe each would be willing to switch for? (1)_____
What is the largest bribe Group A members would be willing to offer? (2)_____ What would the outcome be? (3)_____ How will Group A members travel to Megalopolis? (4)_____ Group B members? (5)_____ Is this outcome Pareto Superior to the outcome in **c**? Explain. (6)_____

_____

_____

_____

_____

_____

e. "Vote buying is inimical to the functioning of a democratic society." Do you agree? Explain. _____

_____

_____

_____

_____

_____

_____

_____

f. Is your answer (6) in **d** consistent with the fact that the cost of season ferry passes for all 200 residents is $56,000—more than the $50,000 annual cost of the bridge? Explain.

_____

_____

_____

_____

_____

_____

_____

24.8. Each of the goods and services listed below are, at least in part, provided by the government. To what extent does each conform to the economic definition of a public good? Explain, being sure to state the degree to which each good is nonrival and nonexclusive.

a. defense

_____

_____

_____

_____

_____

_____

_____

b. highways

_____

_____

_____

_____

_____

_____

_____

c. drinking water

_____

_____

_____

_____

_____

_____

_____

d. parks

_____

_____

_____

_____

_____

_____

_____

e. education

_____

_____

_____

_____

_____

_____

_____

f. launching of satellites via Space Shuttle

_____

_____

_____

_____

_____

_____

_____

PUBLIC CHOICE THEORY

welfare criteria:

    individualistic:

        Pareto optimal

    equality

    utilitarian

    maximin (Rawlsian):

        initial position methodology

    social welfare functions

utility possibility frontier

conflicts between efficiency and equity

Arrow's impossibility theorem:

    axioms of a "reasonable social ranking":

        1. complete (ranks all social states)

        2. transitive

        3. individualistic (positively related to individual preferences)

        4. independence of irrelevant alternatives (rankings of existing states unaffected by introduction of new states)

        5. not imposed

        6. nondictatorial

direct voting:

    majority rule

    Condorcet's voting paradox (cycling)

    single-peaked preferences

    Black's median voter theorem

    logrolling

representative government:

majority principle

probabilistic voting model

the candidate game

rent seeking:

special interests

public interests

rent dissipation

PROBLEMS

(Numbers in brackets at the beginning of problems below refer to related examples and problems in the text.)

27.1. [Related to text example 27.1 and problem 27.1.] Once and Twice de'Leon were left shipwrecked on an island, back in Problem 17.4. Let's return to see how they are doing. Recall that both of them were assumed to have the same utility functions: $U = (CM)^{.5}$, where C is coconuts and M is mangos. When they landed on the island, Once had an endowment of 75 coconuts and 25 mangos, while Twice's endowment was just the reverse. Below is the Edgeworth Box that you drew to represent their predicament.

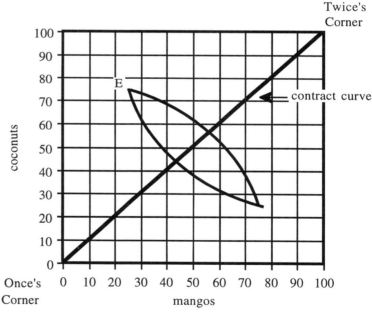

a. Explain why the contract curve in this box would be exactly the same if Once's utility function was $U_O = (CM)^{.25}$.

(1)_____

_____

_____

_____

Assume henceforth that Once has this utility function. Note that along the contract curve his allocation of C, C_O, is identical to his allocation of M, M_O. Therefore, at points on the contract curve his utility is given by $U_T = (M_O M_O)^{.25} = M_O^{.5}$. Find Twice's utility along the contract curve as a function of his allocation of M, M_T. $U_T = $

(2)_____. Use these functions and the fact that $M_O + M_T = 100$ to obtain an equation for the utility possibility frontier (UPF) of Once and Twice.

UPF: (3)_____

Plot this equation on the graph below.

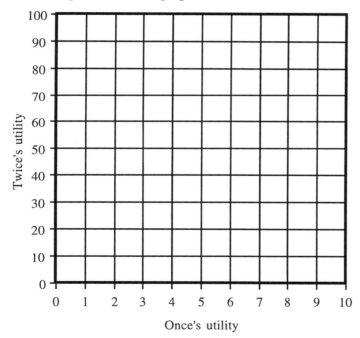

Once's utility

Compute U_O and U_T at the endowment point (point **E** in the Edgeworth Box). $U_O = $ (4)_____

$U_T = $ (5)_____ Plot this pair of values on the UPF diagram. Label the point **E** and explain why it is inside the UPF. (6)_____

_____

_____

_____

b. If M and C are allocated equally between Once and Twice, what utility will each receive? U_O = (1)_____

U_T = (2)_____

Plot this point on the UPF diagram. Label it **EQ**, for "equal quantities."

c. Once and Twice are at an impasse in their trade negotiations. They appeal to the god of the Island to mediate. It happens that he is a Rawlsian; that is, his social welfare function is:

$$W = \min(U_O, U_T)$$

What levels of utility would he choose for Once and Twice?

U_O = (1)_____ U_T = (2)_____

Plot this point on the PPF and label it **R**. How much of each good do they each get? $M_O = C_O$ = (3)_____

$M_T = C_T$ = (4)_____ Explain why Once and Twice would not both willingly accept this mediated allocation. (5)_____

_____

_____

If the god is constrained to choose an allocation that both Once and Twice will willingly accept, what allocation of utility will he choose? U_O = (6)_____

U_T = (7)_____

d. Suppose that the god of the Island has the following Cobb-Douglas welfare function instead of the one in **c**:

$$W = (U_O U_T)^{.5}$$

What is the god's marginal rate of substitution between U_O and U_T?

MRS_{OT} = (1)_____

Harcourt Brace & Company

What is the rate at which the god can transform U_O into U_T (i.e., the negative of the slope of the UPF)?

RUT_{OT} = (2)_____

Use MRS_{OT} and RUT_{OT} along with the equation for the PPF to find the utility allocation that will maximize welfare now.

U_O = (3)_____ U_T = (4)_____

Plot this point on the PPF and label it **CD**, for Cobb-Douglas. How much of each good do they each get? $M_O = C_O =$ (5)_____ $M_T = C_T =$ (6)_____

Explain why Once and Twice would not both willingly accept this mediated allocation. (7)_____

_____

_____

If the god is constrained to choose an allocation that both Once and Twice will willingly accept, what allocation of utility will he choose now?

U_O = (8)_____ U_T = (9)_____

e. "An equitable distribution of consumption in a society is not necessarily an equal distribution. Unfortunately, there is no general agreement as to what an equitable distribution is. Further, attainment of an equitable distribution might require coercion." How is this statement illustrated by the above example?_____

_____

_____

_____

_____

_____

Harcourt Brace & Company

f. "Parents who love their children equally will give their relatively 'disadvantaged' children more than their relatively advantaged siblings, but not enough to fully offset their differences in advantages." Do you agree? [Think of the god of the Island as the parent of Once and Twice. Once is disadvantaged relative to Twice; it is harder for him to convert M and C into utility.]

(1)_____

_____

_____

_____

_____

_____

_____

Consider parents of two children, a son and a daughter. They love them equally and believe that both are equally capable of doing well in college. However, they also believe that the value of education to boys exceeds the value of education to girls. In what way(s) are they likely to treat the two children differently? (2)_____

_____

_____

_____

_____

_____

g. Suppose that the god of the Island has the same utility function as in **d**, but that his power to choose an allocation is limited. Specifically, he may choose relative prices. Once may or may not choose to trade at these prices. As you found in **d**, if unconstrained the god would choose to reduce Once's utility below his utility at **E**. The constraint means that he can only choose points that are on Once's offer curve (see Problem 8.3, **d**).

A section of the UPF you found in **a** is drawn in the next graph. The points **E** and **EQ** correspond to the same points in your graph. The **OOC** is the relationship between the utility of Once and Twice along Once's offer curve. Note that this line passes through both **E**, since Once's offer curve passes through the endowment point, and **EQ**, since the latter is the point that Once (as well as Twice) would choose when the terms of trade are one M per C.

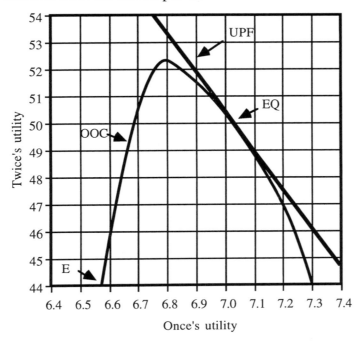

If the god of the Island maximizes his welfare function subject to the constraint of choosing a point on Once's offer curve, will he choose a point that is on the PPF? [Hint: how does MRS_{OT} compare to RUT_{OT} at EQ? How does MRS_{OT} compare to minus the slope of OOC at the same point?] Explain. (1)_____

_____

_____

Will the god's choice give Twice as much utility as Twice would get if Twice could set prices himself? [Hint: what point on OOC would Twice choose and how does minus the slope of OOC compare to MRS_{OT} at this point?] Explain. (2)_____

_____

_____

Darken the section of OOC on which the god's choice would lie. Do you agree with the following statement? "Governments generally—nondictatorial governments in particular—are limited in their ability to transfer consumption across individuals. These limitations lead to trade-offs between equity and economic efficiency." Explain. (3)_____

_____

_____

_____

_____

_____

h. "A major obstacle in the construction of Social Welfare Functions is that they require intrapersonal comparisons of utility. This cannot be done unless we are willing to accept cardinal measures of utility." Illustrate the meaning of this quotation by considering how your answers to **a** through **d** would change if Once's utility is rescaled so that his new utils are the square of his old utils and Twice's utility is rescaled so that his new utils are the square root of his old utils._____

_____

_____

_____

_____

_____

_____

_____

27.2. [Related to text problem 27.3.] Tom and Elinor have the same tastes in vegetables—they only like cauliflower (C) and lima beans (B). Their utility functions are:

$$U_T = (B_T C_T)^{.5} \qquad U_E = (B_E C_E)^{.5}$$

They decide to marry since they realize it will be convenient to do their shopping together. Nevertheless, they don't really care about each other—each would keep all the veggies if possible! Our first objective is to find their utility possibility frontier as a function of the quantities of B and C they buy. Then, we will see that they will agree to buy the same quantities, regardless of who gets to eat them. The only assumption we will make about how veggies are allocated between the two is that the allocation is Pareto optimal.

a. Let $k_T = B_T/C_T$ and $k_E = B_E/C_E$ be the ratios of Beans to Cauliflower that Tom and Elinor consume under the allocation that they eventually agree to. Show that k_T must equal k_E if the allocation is Pareto optimal. [Hint: recall the requirement for Pareto optimality in exchange.]

b. Since $k_T = k_E$ for Pareto optimal allocations, they must both equal $k = B/C$, whatever the value of k is. Show that Tom's utility for any Pareto optimal allocation can be written as $U_T = k^{.5}C_T$.

Find a similar expression for Elinor's utility, U_E.

Now, show that $U_T + U_E = (BC)^{.5}$.

c. As you have shown in **b**, their utilities must add up to a function of B and C. For given B and C, this equation is their utility possibility frontier. Describe this frontier and how it changes when $(BC)^{.5}$ increases. _____

_____

_____

_____

d. Suppose they have agreed to spend a total of 10 dollars on vegetables. The price of B is $.50 per pound and the price of

C is \$1.00 per pound. How many pounds of each will they buy? [Hint: the problem you need to solve should look like the problem of maximizing a Cobb-Douglas utility function subject to a budget constraint.]

e. Do you think that two selfish people with identical tastes can always agree on what to buy regardless of how the goods are allocated between them—provided that the allocation is Pareto optimal? Explain. _____

_____

_____

_____

_____

_____

27.3. Continuing 27.2, suppose that Tom and Elinor do care about each other after all. Since they agree on the ratio of cauliflower to beans they will buy and consume, we can treat the two vegetables as one good, V.   Let V_T and V_E represent the quantities that Tom and Elinor consume, respectively, and let V represent the quantity they buy. Tom cares about how many veggies he eats, but he also cares about how many veggies Elinor eats. Specifically:

$$U_T = V_T^{2/3}V_E^{1/3}$$

His love is requited:

$$U_E = V_E^{2/3}V_T^{1/3}$$

Of course, they can't consume more than they buy:

$$V_E + V_T = V$$

a. If Tom gets to allocate the veggies, what share will he take for himself?

Harcourt Brace & Company

b. If Elinor gets to allocate the veggies, what share will she take for herself?

c. You are familiar with an Edgeworth Box. Since there is only one good here we need an Edgeworth line. The length of the line is one unit. The distance from the left end of the line to a point on the line is the share going to Tom. The distance from the right end to the same point is the share going to Elinor.

Tom's share 0 ——>   1/3   2/3   1

1   2/3   1/3   <—— 0 Elinor's share

What points on this line are on the contract curve? Explain.

_____

_____

_____

_____

_____

_____

_____

d. Now, suppose that their utility functions are:

$$U_E = V_T^{2/3}V_E^{1/3} \qquad U_T = V_E^{2/3}V_T^{1/3}$$

What points on the Edgeworth line are now Pareto optimal? Explain._____

_____

_____

_____

_____

_____

_____

Have you ever observed your parents having the type of argument that Tom and Elinor might have about any Pareto optimal allocation?

Harcourt Brace & Company

27.4. [Related to text problems 27.4 and 27.6.] The Associated Press and United Press International publish weekly rankings of the top 20 college football teams during the season. These rankings are established by votes of sports writers. Each writer lists his/her top 20 teams in rank order. Points are allocated to each team based on the writers' votes. A team receives 20 points if it is ranked first by a writer, 19 points if it is ranked second, 18 if it is ranked third, etc. Teams are then ranked according to their vote totals.

A ranking of this sort is sometimes referred to as a "Borda count." Arrow's impossibility theorem says that any ranking that aggregates individual preferences must violate one of his reasonable "axioms." The objective of this problem is to determine which axiom is violated by the AP and UPI polls, as well as Borda counts in general.

a. If Oklahoma is ranked ahead of Pittsburgh and Pittsburgh is ranked ahead of Miami, is Oklahoma ranked ahead of Miami? (1)_____ This illustrates that the (2)_____ axiom is satisfied. Is this axiom satisfied for all Borda counts? (3)_____

b. What axiom would be violated if UCLA was ranked number one, no matter how the writers voted? (1)_____ Is this axiom satisfied for all Borda counts? (2)_____

c. The teams that are eligible for ranking are all those from NCAA Division I schools that are not on probation. Only teams that receive enough votes to be in the top twenty are ranked. Which axiom is violated? (1)_____ Is this axiom violated by all Borda counts? (2)_____

d. If the writer from the *Podunk Daily News* puts Ohio State ahead of Michigan one week and Michigan ahead of Ohio State the next week, and if all other writers don't change their rankings of these two, then the total for Michigan will increase by (1)_____ and the total for Ohio State will decline by (2)_____. This demonstrates that the (3)_____ axiom is satisfied. Is this axiom satisfied by all Borda counts? (4)_____

e. Suppose that half the writers in one poll have ranked Nebraska just ahead of Alabama and the other half rank

Alabama just ahead of Nebraska. How are these two teams ranked? (1)_____ Virtuous University is on probation for recruiting violations. Nevertheless, they play a full schedule of games and do very well. In fact all of the writers, whether they favor Alabama over Nebraska or not, think that Virtuous should be ranked just behind Nebraska if included in the poll. If Virtuous were included, which team would be ranked higher, Alabama or Nebraska? (2)_____ Which axiom is violated? (3)_____

Is this axiom violated for all Borda counts? (4)_____

f. What axiom would be violated if Texas was ranked number one whenever the writer from the *Dallas Sun Times* ranked Texas number one, no matter how other writers ranked Texas? (1)_____ Is this axiom violated for Borda counts? (2)_____ Is this axiom satisfied for all Borda counts? (3)_____

27.5. (Related to text problems 27.4 and 27.6.) The town of Indacishion is having a referendum on building a new school. There are three organized groups of voters, each of the same size. The Tightwads don't see any need for a new school, but if there is to be one they want the least expensive school the other groups will agree to. The Moderates' first choice is an "economy" school, but they prefer a "deluxe" model over no new school. The Parents and Teachers Association (PTA) want the "deluxe" model, but if they can't get that they would prefer to make do with the old school rather than suffer the disruption of building. The referendum asks each voter to vote for one of three choices: no school, economy school, or deluxe school.

a. What will the outcome of the vote be?

b. In order to resolve the matter, the school board decides to hold a series of referendums. In the first referendum voters are asked to choose between an economy school and no school. In the second referendum the winner of the first referendum will be pitted against a deluxe school. What will the outcome be?

c. A petition is circulated asking the school board to conduct another referendum, on which the voters will choose between the loser of the first referendum in **b** and the winner of the second. If the board agrees, what will be the outcome of this referendum?

d. If the board is required to hold a referendum every time a petition signed by at least half of all voters is presented to it, what will happen? (1)_____

_____

_____   _____

_____

Which of Arrow's axioms is violated by this decision process? (2)_____

e. This type of situation can arise when preferences of one group of voters are not single-peaked. Which group has "double-peaked" preferences?

f. Suppose that the preferences of the group you identified in **e** are changed so that they now prefer deluxe to economy and economy to no school. What will the outcome be? (1)_____ Is the axiom identified in **d** still violated? (2)_____

g. Continuing **f**, which group is the median group? Explain. (1)_____

_____

_____

Do they get their top choice? (2)_____

27.6. [Related to text problem 27.7.] Different public goods are provided by different levels of government (local, state, and federal). Some factors in determining the appropriate level of government are:

    i. Returns to scale. (Are they increasing, decreasing, or constant?)

ii. Degree of spillover effects. (Do goods provided by one lacality benefit or harm other localities?)

iii. Ability to reveal the willingness of beneficiaries to pay.

What level of government—or mixture of levels—do you think is the most appropriate provider of each of the following public goods? Explain your choice and comment on whether your choice is consistent with what you observe in the United States.

a. defense

_____

_____

_____

_____

_____

_____

_____

b. highways

_____

_____

_____

_____

_____

_____

_____

c. education

_____

_____

_____

_____

_____

_____

d. law enforcement

_____

_____

_____

_____

_____

_____

_____

ANSWER KEY

ANSWERS

1.1. a. (1) 15; (2) - 1/20 = -.05; (3) it is the inverse of the coefficient; (4) $5 + .05Q_D$; (5) the lowest price that producers are willing to supply Q for; (6) 5; (7) 05; (8) its inverse.

b. (i) see graph; **(ii)** $300 - 20P^* = -100 + 20P^* => 400 = 40P^*$ $=> P^* = 10 => Q^* = 300 - 20(10) = 100$ or, to check, $Q^* = -100 + 20(10) = 100$; **(iii)** $15 - Q^*/20 = 5 + Q^*/20 =>10 = Q^*/10 => Q^* = 100 => P^* = 15 - 100/20 = 10$ or, to check, $P^* = 5 + 100/20 = 10$.

c. (1) 80; (2) 140; (3) 12. **d.** (1) 80; (2) 60; (3) 12. **e.** If it is a demand shift, Q^* increases. If it is a supply shift, Q^* declines.

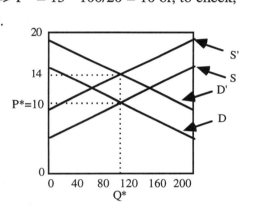

1.2. a. (1) 8; (2) 3/4 (the slope of the tangent line). **b.** (1) 6; (2) 4/3.

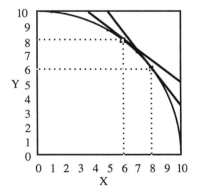

2.1. a. $f'(x) = 12x^2$. **b.** $f'(x) = -1.5x^{-3/2}$. **c.** Let $z = 4x^3$ and let $y = \ln(z)$. Then $dy/dz = 1/z = 1/(4x^3)$, $dz/dx = 12x^2$, and $f'(x) =$

CHAPTER 2

Harcourt Brace & Company

$(dy/dz)(dz/dx) = 12x^2/(4x^3) = 3/x$. **d.** $f'(x) = e^x\ln(e) = e^x$ since $\ln(e) = 1$. **e.** $z = 5x$, $dz/dx = 5$, $y = 2e^z$, $dy/dz = 2e^z = 2e^{5x}$, and $f'(x) = (dy/dz)((dz/dx) = 2e^{5x}(5) = 10e^{5x}$. **f.** $f'(x) = -b + 2cx - 3dx^2$. **g.** $f'(x) = [d(e^x)/dx]x^2 + e^x[d(x^2)/dx] = e^xx^2 + e^x(2x) = e^xx(x+2)$. **h.** $f'(x) = \{[d(x^2)/dx]e^x - [d(e^x)/dx]x^2\}/(e^x)^2 = (2xe^x - e^xx^2)/e^{2x} = (2x - x^2)/e^x$. **i.** $f'(x) = \{\ln(x)[2e^{2x}(x^3-3x+1)+e^{2x}(3x^2-3)] - e^{2x}(x^3-3x+1)/x\}/[\ln(x)]^2 = e2x\{(2x^3+3x^2 - 6x - 1)/\ln(x) - (x^2 - 3+1/x)/\ln(x)^2\}$.

2.2. a. $f_x = .7x^{-.3}y^{.3} = .7(y/x)^{.3}$, $f_y = .3(x/y)^{.7}$. **b.** $f_x = ax^{a-1}y^b$, $f_y = bx^ay^{b-1}$. **c.** Define $g(x, y) = x^2+y^2+2xy$. Then $f_x = e^{g(x, y)}g_x = 2(x+y)e^{g(x,y)}$, $f_y = e^{g(x, y)}g_y = 2(x+y)e^{g(x,y)}$. **d.** $f_x = 2bx+dy$, $f_y = 2cy+dx$ **e.** $f_x = .5(ax^2 + by^2)^{-.5}(2a) = a(ax^2 + by^2)^{-.5}$, $f_y = b(ax^2 + by^2)^{-.5}$. **f.** Note that $f(x, y) = 2\ln(x)+3\ln(y)$, so $f_x = 2/x$ and $f_y = 3/y$. **g.** Since $f(x, y) = [a\ln(x)+b\ln(y)]^{-1}$, $f_x = -a[a\ln(x)+b\ln(y)]^{-2}/x$ and $f_y = -b[a\ln(x)+b\ln(y)]^{-2}/y$.

2.3. a. (Illustration). **b.** $f'(x^*) = -4x^*+3 = 0 \Rightarrow x^* = 3/4$ and $f''(x^*) = -4 < 0 \Rightarrow$ maximum. **c.** $f'(x^*) = 2ax^*+b = 0 \Rightarrow x^* = -b/2a$ and $f''(x^*) = 2a \Rightarrow$ minimum if $a > 0$, maximum if $a < 0$. If $a = 0$ the calculus method for finding a maximum/minimum doesn't work because the maximum and minimum are $\pm\infty$, with the sign depending on whether b is positive or negative.

2.4. a. $y^* = b^2/4a - b^2/2a + c = -b^2/4a + c$. **b.** $dy^*/da = b^2/4a^2$. **c.** dy/da(evaluated at x^*) $= x^{*2} = (-b/2a)^2 = -b^2/4a^2$ — the same answer as in **b**. **d.** $dy^*/db = -b/2a$ and dy/db(evaluated at x^*) $= x^* = -b/2a$.

2.5. a. See graph. **b.** **(i)** (1) $N = 6+E$; (2) $(-3, 3)$; (3) Note that the contour line for $H = 84$ does not quite touch $(-3, 3)$. $H = 100 - 3^2 - 3^2 = 82$; (4) $H = 64$; (5) yes; **(ii)** (6) $-2E$; (7) $-2N$; (8) $6+E$; (9) $-E/N$; (10) 1; (11) 3; (12) -3; **(iii)** (13) $100 -N^2 - E^2 +1 (N - 6 - E)$; (14) $-2E - 1 = 0$; (15) $-2N+1 = 0$; (16) $N - 6 - E = 0$; (17) $-2E$; (18) $2N$; (19) $N = -E$.

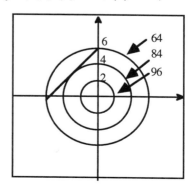

Harcourt Brace & Company

2.6. a. $£ = LW + \lambda(100 - L - 2W)$; first order conditions (a) $W - \lambda = 0$, (b) $L - 2\lambda = 0$, and (c) $100 - L - 2W = 0$; (a) and (b) => $W = L/2$; substitute for W in (c) to get $100 - L - 2(L/2) = 0$ or $L = 50$; $W = 50/2 = 25$; $A = (50)(25) = 1250$ sq. ft. **b.** $£ = (L+X)W + \lambda[100 - 2(X^2+W^2)^{-.5} - L]$; the first order conditions are (a) $W - \lambda = 0$, (b) $L+X - \lambda(X^2+W^2)^{-.5}(2W) = 0$, (c) $W - \lambda(X^2+W^2)^{-.5}(2X) = 0$, (d) $100 - 2(X^2+W^2)^{.5} - L = 0$; (a) and (b) => (e) $L+X = 2W^2(X^2+W^2)^{-.5}$, (a) and (c) imply (f) $W = 3^{.5}X$; substitute (f) into (e) and simplify to get (g) $L = 2X$; substitute (f) and (g) into (d) and simplify to get $X = 50/3$; then (f) => $W = 3^{-.5}(50)$ and (g) => $L = 100/3$; $A = (L+X)W = 1443.4$ sq. ft., which is larger than the area of the rectangle. **c.** $£ = 2W + L - \lambda(1250 - WL)$; first order conditions: (a) $2 + \lambda L = 0$, (b) $1 + \lambda W = 0$, (c) $1250 - WL = 0$; (a) and (b) => $L = 2W$; substitute for L in (c) to get $1250 - 2W^2 = 0$ => $W = 25 = L = 50$. Same answers as in **a**.

3.1. a. (Illustration) $U = X^{.5}Y^{.5}$. **b.** (i) see graph; (ii) $MU_X = 1 = MU_Y$ and they are both positive for all X and Y; (iii) $MRS_{XY} = MU_X/MU_Y = 1$ which is constant (does not diminish with X).

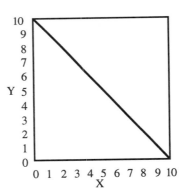

c. (i) see graph; (ii) $MU_X = 2\ MU_Y = 1$ and they are both positive for all X and Y; (iii) $MRS_{XY} = MU_X/MU_Y = 2$ which is constant (does not diminish with X).

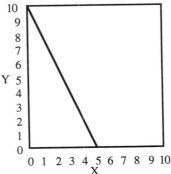

d. (i) The indifference curves will be straight lines. For $U = 10$, $Y = (10 - \alpha X)/\beta$. The slope of the line is $-a/b$; (ii) $MU_X = a$, $MU_Y = b$ and they are both positive for all X and Y;

(iii) $MRS_{XY} = MU_X/MU_Y = a/b$ which is constant (does not diminish with X). Note that this is minus the slope of the indifference curve. **e. (i)** see graph;

(ii) $MU_X = .75(Y/X)^{.25}$, $MU_Y = .25(Y/X)^{-.75}$ and they are both positive for all X and Y; **(iii)** $MRS_{XY} = MU_X/MU_Y = 3Y/X$, which diminishes as X increases and Y falls (holding utility constant)

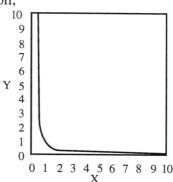

f. **(i)** For U = 1, $X^2 + Y^2 = 1$. This is the equation for a circle, centered at (0, 0) with radius 1. See graph; **(ii)** $MU_X = X(X^2+Y^2)^{-.5}$; $MU_Y = Y(X^2+Y^2)^{-.5}$; Both are positive for all X and Y; **(iii)** $MRS_{XY} = MU_X/MU_Y = X/Y$. As X increases and Y falls (holding U constant) MRS_{XY} *increases*. Hence, the indifference curve is *not* convex to the origin, as seen in the graph.

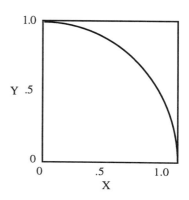

g. **(i)** For U = 1, $Y^2 = X^2 - 1$. Note that $Y^2 = 0$ when X = 1 and Y asymptotically approaches X as X goes to infinity; **(ii)** $MU_X = X(X^2 - Y^2)^{-.5}$ and is positive for all X > 0 and Y > 0 (note that X > Y when X > 0), but $MU_Y = -Y(X^2 - Y^2)^{-.5}$ is negative for all X > 0 and Y > 0. Y is a "bad." **(iii)** $MRS_{XY} = MU_X/MU_Y = -X/Y$ which is negative. As X increases, Y increases For finite X, $MRS_{XY} > -1$. MRS_{XY} approaches -1 as X goes to infinity, so it does diminish (become more negative) as X increases. It is convex to the origin.

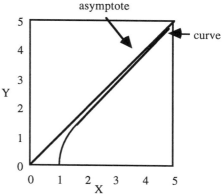

Harcourt Brace & Company

3.2. a. $MU_X = a(Y/X)^{1-a}$, $MU_Y = (1-a)(Y/X)^{-a}$, $MRS_{XY} = aY/[(1-a)X]$.
  b. $MU_X = 2(X^aY^{1-a})a(Y/X)^{1-a}$, $MU_Y = 2(X^aY^{1-a})(1-a)(Y/X)^{-a}$,
  $MRS_{XY} = aY/[(1-a)X]$. **c.** $MU_X = .5(X^aY^{1-a})^{-.5}a(Y/X)^{1-a}$, MU_Y
  $= .5(X^aY^{1-a})^{-.5}(1-a)(Y/X)^{-a}$, $MRS_{XY} = aY/[(1-a)X]$. **d.** $MU_X =$
  a/X, $MU_Y = (1-a)/Y$, $MRS_{XY} = aY/[(1-a)X]$. **e.** $MU_X = .5a/X$,
  $MU_Y = .5(1-a)/Y$, $MRS_{XY} = aY/[(1-a)X]$. **f.** $MU_X = 2a/X$,
  $MU_Y = 2(1-a)/Y$, $MRS_{XY} = aY/[(1-a)X]$. (1) the same; (2) $U_L^{.5}$;
  (3) $\ln(U_L)$; (4) $.5\ln(U_L)$; (5) $2\ln(U_L)$; (6) ordinal; (7) $\beta/(\beta+\gamma)$;
  (8) $U_L^{(\beta+\gamma)}$;

  (9) $\dfrac{\alpha Y}{(1-\alpha)X} = \dfrac{\beta Y/(\beta+\gamma)}{[1-\beta/(\beta+\gamma)]X} = \dfrac{\beta Y}{\gamma X}$.

3.3.

a. King Kole   **b**. Miss Muffet   **c**. Jack Horner   **d**. Jack Sprat

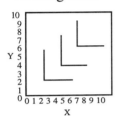 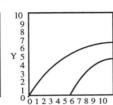 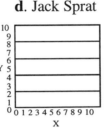

  (I have assumed that Jack Horner does not have free
  disposal! What would his curves look like if he did?)

3.4. (1) $.4/(B - 1)$; (2) $.6/(M - 2)$; (3) $[2(B - 1)]/[3(M - 2)]$; (4)
  1 unit; (5) 2 units; (6) $MRS_{BM} = [2(2 - 1)]/[3(3 - 2)] =$
  $2/3$; $MRS_{MB} = 1/ MRS_{BM} = 1.5$.

3.5 a. $MU_X = \dfrac{\partial U}{\partial X} = \alpha\delta\left(\dfrac{1}{\delta}\right)X^{\delta-1} = \alpha X^{\delta-1}$; $MU_Y = \dfrac{\partial U}{\partial Y} = \beta Y^{\delta-1}$.

b. $MRS_{XY} = MU_X/MU_Y = \dfrac{\alpha}{\beta}\left(\dfrac{X}{Y}\right)^{\delta-1}$.

c. Yes. A function is homothetic if its slope depends on the ratio
  of X to Y, irrespective of the absolute amounts of X and Y, as
  in this case.

d. $MRS_{XY} = \dfrac{\alpha}{\beta}\left(\dfrac{X}{Y}\right)$, which is the same as for the Cobb-
  Douglas function.

e. $MRS_{XY}=\frac{\alpha}{\beta}$. The indifference curve is a straight line (constant slope), the case of perfect substitution.

f. $MRS_{XY}=\frac{\alpha}{\beta}\left(\frac{X}{Y}\right)^{\delta-1}=\frac{\alpha}{\beta}(Z)^{\delta-1}\geq\frac{d(MRS_{XY})}{d(X/Y)}=\frac{d(MRS_{XY})}{dZ}$

$=\frac{\alpha}{\beta}\left(\frac{1}{\delta-1}\right)Z^{\delta-2}=\frac{\alpha}{\beta}\left(\frac{1}{\delta-1}\right)\left(\frac{X}{Y}\right)$. **g.**(1) When $\delta=1$, the derivative is not defined. This occurs because the indifference curve has a constant slope, or no curvature; (2) As δ becomes smaller than 1, the derivative becomes negative and the indifference curve becomes convex (diminishing MRS_{XY}); (3) As δ approaches $-\infty$, the curvature approaches zero, the case of complements; (4) As δ becomes greater than 1, the curvature becomes positive, creating a concave indifference curve; (5) This violates the property of convexity (diminishing MRS.)

CHAPTER 4

4.1. a. C/3P. **b.** (1) .5P+C = 4; (2) -.5; (3) 4; (4) 8. **c.** MRS_{CP} = C/3P = .5 => C = 1.5P ; .5P+C = 4 => .5P+1.5P = 4 => P = 2; C = 1.5P => C =3; (1) 3; (2) 2; (3) \$3; (4) 75%. **d.** C/3P = 2 => C = 6P; P + .5C = 4 => P + 3P = 4 => P = 1; C = 6P => C = 6; (1) 6; (2) 1; (3) \$3; (4) 75%.**e.** (1) 7.5; (2) 1.25; (3) \$3.75; (4) 75%. **f.** All the percentages are the .same. The exponent of C is 3/4, or 75. Note that for any utility function of the form X^aY^{1-a}, a is theshare spent on X and 1-a is the share spent on Y.

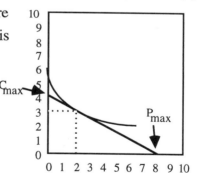

4.2. a. (1) 40%; (2) 60%; (3) \$8; (4) \$12; (5) 4 pounds; (6) 24 pounds; (7) 4 pounds; (8) 24 pounds; (9) no; (10) The budget constraint is not shifted when I, P_s, and P_p increase proportionately. **b.** (1) The share of income he spends on steak; (2) .4; (3) $.4I/P_s$; (4) $.6I/P_p$. **c.** U = $S^{.4}P^{.6}$ = $(.4I/P_s)^{.4}(.6I/Pp)^{.6}$ = $(.4^{.4}.6^{.6}I)/(P_s^{.4}P_p^{.6})$ = $.51I/(P_s^{.4}P_p^{.6})$. **d.** E = $P_s^{.4}P_p^{.6}U/.51$.

4.3. a. See diagram. **b.** Constraint: $2C + P = 10$; "medical income" $= 10$; "medical price of C" $= 2$; "medical price of P" $= 1$; spend 25% or 2.5 units of medical income on P (2.5 pounds of peas) and 75% on carrots ($7.5/2 = 3.75$ pounds of carrots); see point 'b' in the diagram. **c.** Point 'c' in the diagram is the point he chooses if he ignores the doctor's orders. Point 'd' will be chosen if he doesn't. It is the intersection of the two constraints: $C = 4$ and $P = 2$. To see why, note that utility increases along the budget constraint when moving toward 'c' and along the doctor's constraint when moving toward 'b'. Further, he would never choose an interior point of the shaded area because he gets positive marginal utility from both P and C.

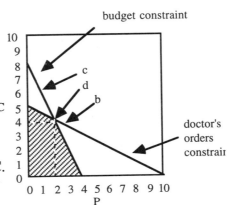

4.4. a. $MU_W = 2W$; $MU_C = 2C$; $MRS_{CW} = C/W$; as C increases, W falls to hold U constant, so MRS_{CW} increases in C. Hence, the indifference curves are not convex (see diagram). **b.** For both constraints drawn, the highest indifference curve attainable is the same. Al drinks wine and eats no chocolate; Chuck does the opposite. Concave indifference curves lead to extreme behavior.

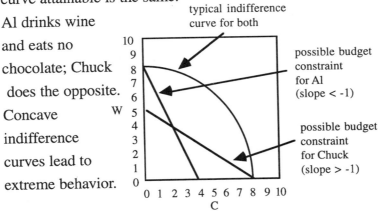

4.5. If G and M were divisible, she would spend $6 (60% of $10) on movies and go to 1.5 movies. She would also play 16 video games. If she chooses 2 movies and 8 games her utility will be $.4\ln(8)+.6\ln(2) = .832$. If she chooses 1 movie and 24 games her utility will be $.4\ln(24)+.6\ln(1) = 1.271$. Hence, the latter will be preferred.

4.6. a. 100% on curds, 0% on whey. **b.** 0% on curds, 100% on whey. **c.** No. She is indifferent to all points on her budget constraint since her budget constraint has the same slope as her indifference curve.

4.7. a. $X+Y = 1$; for each ounce of X he will buy 10 ounces of Y; $Y = 10X \Rightarrow X+10X =1 \Rightarrow X = 1/11$ ounces and $Y = 10/11$ ounces. **b.** $16X+Y = 1$; $Y = 10X \Rightarrow 16X+10X = 1 \Rightarrow X = 1/26 \Rightarrow Y = 10/26$. **c.** $X/Y = .1$ in both cases. Since X and Y are perfect complements, no matter what their prices are he will not substitute one for the other.

4.8. a. (1) 50; (2) 50 (point 'a' on graph). **b.** (1) .50; (2) 100; (3) 50; (4) $(50)(100) = 5000$; (5) $(100)(.50) = \$50$ (point 'b' on graph). **c.** $U = CY = (.5I/1)(.5I/1) = .25I^2$ or $I = 2U^{.5} = 2(5000)^{.5} = \$141.42$; (1) $141.42 - 100 = \$41.42$; (2) less; (3) Because the mother is not discouraged from matching her "willingness to trade" to the market's "terms of trade"; (4) $141.4/2 = 70.7$ units; (5) less; (6) Under the subsidy she chooses to substitute C for Y because of its relatively lower price; (7) $C = .5I \Rightarrow I = 2C = 2(100) = 200 \Rightarrow$ lump sum = 100. **d.** (1) The lump sum increases her utility more because the mother matches her willingness to trade to the market's terms of trade. This makes the cost of obtaining a given increase in her utility

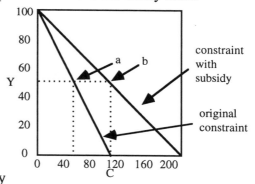

less than with the subsidy; (2) The answer changes. The cost of obtaining a given increase in C is less with the subsidy because it encourages her to substitute C for Y. This would be the preferred policy if the objective is to improve the welfare of children rather than the welfare of their mothers.

Harcourt Brace & Company

4.9. a. (1) $.01B+.01M = I$; (2) $U = .4\ln(B^*)+.6\ln(M^*)$; (3) $.01(B^*+1)+.01(M^*+2) =I^*+.03$ or $.01B^*+.01M^* = I^*$; (4) $.4$; (5) $.4I^*/.01$; (6) $1+.4(I - .03)/.01$; $2+.6(I - .03)/.01$. **b.** The utility function is $U = a \ln(B^*)+(1-a)\ln(M^*)$. The budget constraint is $P_BB^*+P_MM^* = I^*$ where $I^* = I - P_Bb - P_Mm$. The standard Cobb-Douglas result applied to this problem yields $B^* = aI^*/P_B$ => $B - b = a(I - P_Bb - P_Mm)/P_B$ => $P_BB = P_Bb + a(I - P_Bb - P_Mm)$. Analogously, $P_MM = P_Mm + (1-a)(I - P_Bb - P_Mm)$. For three goods the linear expenditure utility function would be $U = a_1\ln(B-b) + a_2\ln(M-m) + (1-a_1-a_2)\ln(C-c)$.

4.10. Suzy has incorrectly compared her marginal willingness to trade (MRS) to the *average* terms of trade. She should have compared MRS to the *marginal* terms of trade: Once she has decided to buy one orange, the cost of the second is only $.20. Since MRS = .25 between 0 and 1, it exceeds her marginal terms of trade and she can increase utility by buying the second orange. On the other hand, MRS = .10 from 2 to 3 and is less than the marginal terms of trade, which have increased to $.35. Thus. 2 oranges will give her more utility than either 1 or 3. This is clear in the diagram, where the highest indifference curve that touches her budget constraint passes through the point (2, $9.45).

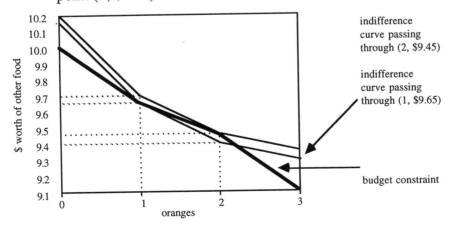

4.11 **a.** $\mathrm{MRS_{XY}} = P_X/P_Y \geq \dfrac{\alpha}{\beta}\left(\dfrac{X}{Y}\right)^{\delta-1} = P_X/P_Y \geq X/Y = \left[\dfrac{\beta}{\alpha}\cdot\dfrac{P_X}{P_Y}\right]^{1/(\delta-1)}$

b. $S_X/S_Y = P_X X/P_Y Y = P_X/P_Y \left[\dfrac{\beta}{\alpha} \cdot \dfrac{P_X}{P_Y}\right]^{1/(\delta-1)} = \left(\dfrac{\beta}{\alpha}\right)^{1/(\delta-1)} \left(\dfrac{P_X}{P_Y}\right)^{1/(\delta-1)}$

c. $S_X/S_Y = \left(\dfrac{\beta}{\delta-1}\right)^{1/(\delta-1)} (Z)^{\delta/(\delta-1)} \geq d(S_X/S_Y)/dZ = \left(\dfrac{\delta}{\delta-1}\right)\left(\dfrac{\beta}{\alpha}\right)^{1/(\delta-1)} (Z)^{\frac{\delta}{(\delta-1)} - \frac{\delta-1}{(\delta-1)}}$

d. For $1>\delta>0$, an increase in P_X/P_Y would reduce the relative share S_X/S_Y. For $\delta=0$ (the Cobb-Douglas case), a change in the relative price will not affect the relative share. For $\delta<0$, an increase in the relative price would increase the relative share S_X/S_Y. **e.** When the curvature of the indifference curve is not very great ($1>\delta>0$), a small increase in the relative price of X results in a decrease in the quantity of X relative to the quantity of Y that is large enough to offset the positive effect of the increase in the relative price on the relative share spent on X, holding quantities constant. When the indifference curve has substantial curvature ($\delta<0$), an increase in the relative price of X has an effect on the relative quantity purchased that is not large enough to offset the positive effect of the price increase on the relative share spent on X, holding quantities constant.

CHAPTER 5

5.1. a. (1) 4 lbs. (point 'a' on left-hand diagram); (2) 24 lbs.; (3) 2.67 lbs. (point 'b' on graph); (4) 24 lbs. **b.** (1) $4^{.4}24^{.6} = 11.72$; (2) $(8/3)^{.4}24^{.6} = 9.97$; (3) $3^{.4}.5^{.6}(11.72)/.51 = \$23.53$; (4) \$3.53; (5) 3.14 (point 'c' in graph); (6) 28.24; (7) $3.14 - 4 = -.86$; (8) $2.66 - 3.14 = -.48$; (9) -1.34. **c.** (1) $-.4I/P_S^2$; (2) $.4/P_S$; (3) $-.4I/P_S^2 + S(.4/P_S) = -.4I/P_S^2 + (.4I/P_S)(.4/P_S) = -.24I/P_S^2$; (4) -.77; (5) -.53; (6) -1.30; Results are close, but not identical. The Slutsky equation is exact only for infinitesimally small changes. The reason is that derivative values change as P_S, I, and S change. **d.** Engel curve for S when $P_S = \$2.00$ and $P_P = \$.50$ is labelled 'a' in middle diagram. Engel curve with $P_S = \$3.00$ is labelled 'c'. Engel curve when the price of potatoes increases to \$1.00 is labelled 'b'. Note that the

Engel curve for S does not depend on P_P. This is an unusual case; Engel curves usually are shifted by changes in the prices of other goods. **e.** Demand functions for two values of I are drawn on the right-hand diagram. The demand function is unchanged by a change in P_P — again an unusual case. **f.** (1) $.78P_P^{.6}P_S^{-.6}U$; (2) $1.18P_S^{.4}P_P^{-.4}U$; (3) $6P_S^{-.6}$; (4) compensated — Since S is normal for Mead, he would use some of his hypothetical compensation to buy more steak; (5) uncompensated; (6) compensated;(7) $\partial S^*/\partial P_S = -(.6)(.78)P_P^{.6}P_S^{-1.6}U = -(.6)(.78)P_P^{.6}P_S^{-1.6}(.51I)/(P_S^{.4}P_P^{.6}) = -.24I/P_S^2$, which is the same as found in **c**. The "substitution effect" is the slope of the compensated demand function by definition of the latter. The compensated demand function is the dashed line in the right-hand diagram.

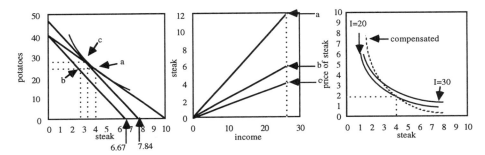

5.2. a. See diagram. **b.** (1) $.5(P - 3)+(1.0)(C - 2)$; (2) He could get $3.50 by selling everything. He would then spend 25% on peas and 75% on carrots, so $P = .25(3.5)/.5 = 1.75$; (3) $.75(3.5)/2.625$; (4) Yes — he could still have chosen to eat only what he grew, but he maximized utility by selling 1.25 lbs. of P and buying .625 pounds of C. **c.** (1) positive (the distance from A to B in the diagram); (2) negative (the distance from C to A in the diagram); (3) better off, because he could still attain his previous choice, but he chooses not to; (4) negative, because Fussy is a net buyer of C; (5) worse off because he can no longer attain his previous choice. Now the income effect is negative; (6) If Fussy took cash to the market he would be worse off in both cases because the income effect would be negative in both cases. **d.** (1) $P_XX^*+P_YY^*$; (2) P_XX+P_YY; (3) $(\partial X/\partial P_X)|_{u \text{ constant}} - X(\partial X/\partial I^*)$; (4) X^*; (5) $(\partial X/\partial P_X)|_{u \text{ constant}}$; (6) $X - X^*$; (7) If X is normal $(\partial X/\partial I^* > 0)$, the new income effect is positive if the consumer is a net seller $(X - X^* > 0)$ and negative if he is a net buyer. (8) Fussy is a net buyer of C and a net seller of P. When the price of P increases the income effect is positive. The opposite is true when the price of C increases. This is consistent with the new Slutsky equation; (9) The new Slutsky equation is unaffected by fixed income. To see why, let $I^* = P_X X^* + P_Y Y^* + I$, where I is fixed income. Since $\partial I^*/\partial I = 1$, $\partial X/\partial I = \partial X/\partial I^*$.

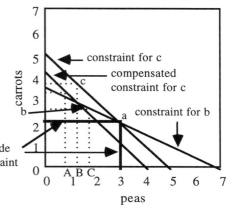

5.3. (1) They are equal since they are tangencies between indifference curves and parallel budget constraints; (2) below; (3) diminishing MRS => they can't cross; (4) no; (5) constant; (6) yes — MRS =$[a/(1-a)](Y/X)$ and depends only on the ratio Y/X.

5.4. a. and **b.** See diagrams below. The two demand curves jump to zero at $P_M = \$2.00$. **c.** The compensation would have to be enough to allow her to continue buying 10 gallons of Mobil. **d.** She wouldn't need any compensation for a price increase above $2.00 since she could switch to Gulf and maintain the same utility level as before. Hence, the compensated demand curve is vertical at 5 gallons for prices below $2.00, then jumps to zero at higher prices

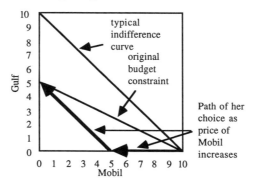

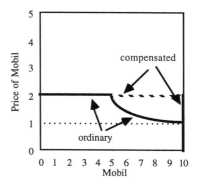

5.5. a, b, and **c.** In the left-hand diagram the X's represent uncompensated choices. In the right-hand diagram they represent

the only points on the ordinary demand curve. She will continue to purchase 2 pairs of shoes if their price increases to $40 and she receives compensation. The compensated demand curve is vertical

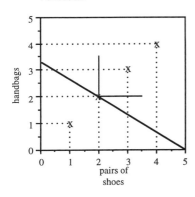 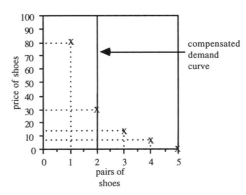

5.6. a. $MRS_{BS} = 1/B$ **b**. $MRS_{BS} = P_B/P_S \Rightarrow B = P_S/P_B$, which doesn't depend on I! **c**. (1) 2; (2) 2; graph on left depicts utility maximization. **d**. (1) 2; (2) 3. **e**. See graph on right. **f**. Demand curve is unaffected by a change in I. **g**. Since the income effect is zero, the ordinary and compensated demand curves are identical.

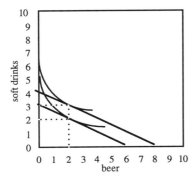 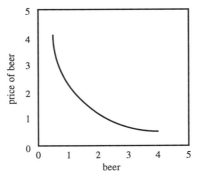

5.7. (1) yes; (2) no; (3) decrease; (4) increase; (5) better off. Her new choice will be somewhere between points 'a' and 'b' on the graph.

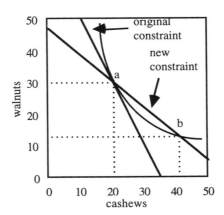

5.8. a. (1) $E = 1^{.4}.5^{.6}(11.72)/.51 = 15.16$, so the answer is no; (2) 20 - 15.16 = \$4.84. **b.** (1) 39; (2) \$1.00; (3) 39/8 = \$4.88; (4) Almost identical. They should be identical since consumer surplus is the most income that the consumer would give up to get the lower price; (5) No. There are about 2.5 more squares, or \$.31 more, so his total would have been over \$5.00. **c.** (1) $U = 8^{.4}24^{.6} = 15.47$ and $E = 2^{.4}5^{.6}(15.47)/.51 = 26.41$, so his tax would have to fall by \$6.41; (2) larger; (3) Still larger. The ordinary demand curve yields an area between that obtained with the old and new compensated demand curves.

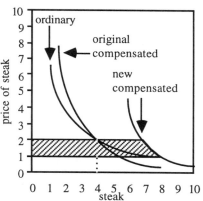

CHAPTER 6

6.1. a. (1) neutral; (2) neutral; (3) substitutes—since $\partial S/\partial P_P = 0$ and $\partial S/\partial I > 0$, $(\partial S/\partial P_P)|_{u\ constant} = P\partial S/\partial I > 0$. **b.** (1) aI/P_X; (2) $(1-a)I/P_Y$; (3) yes. **c.** (1) No—the income effect doesn't always just offset the substitution effect; (2) No, for the same reason as in (1); (3) Yes, because indifference curves are convex to the origin; (4) Now the substitution effect could be negative (net complements). **d.** (1) $[(.6)(.4)/.51]P_S^{-.6}P_P^{-.4}U$; (2) $[(.6)(.4)/.51]P_S^{-.6}P_P^{-.4}U$; (3) They are identical. **e.** This is a general result. These derivatives are "second cross-partial" derivatives of $E(P_1, P_2, U)$. Cross-partial derivatives are not affected by the order in which the derivatives are taken.

6.2. (1) complement; (2) substitute; (3) This can happen if beer is inferior and wine is normal. The price increase for beer has a positive substitution effect and a negative income effect on demand for wine and the latter may be sufficiently large to make wine consumption fall (gross complement), but a price increase for wine has both positive substitution and income effects on demand for beer — beer consumption goes up and beer is a gross substitute for wine. Note that this could happen even if

Harcourt Brace & Company

beer is normal as long as the negative income effect of an
increase in the price of wine is not large enough to offset the
positive substitution effect.

6.3. a. (1) declines; (2) no change. **b.** (1) They will always be
identical: H = S; (2) U = C[min(H, H)] = CH; (3)
$(P_H+P_S)H+P_CC \leq I$; The demand functions are readily
confirmed by recognizing that this is a standard Cobb-
Douglas problem if the sum of the prices of H and S is
treated as a single price; (4) $S = H = .5I/(P_H+P_S)$. **c.** (1)
$.5/(P_H+P_S)$; (2) $-.5I/(P_H+P_S)^2$; (3) $-.5I/(P_H+P_S)^2 +$
$[.5I/(P_H+P_S)][.5/(P_H+P_S)] = -.25I/(P_H+P_S)^2$; (4) 0; (5) 0 +
$(.5I/P_C)[.5/(P_H+P_S)] = .25I/[PC(P_H+P_S)]$; (6) gross
complements; (7) net complements; (8) gross neutral; (9) net
substitutes; (10) If they were the only goods, the
compensated effect would be zero, instead of negative.

6.4. $\partial X/\partial P_Y = (\partial X/\partial P_Y)|_{u \text{ constant}} - (Y - Y^*)(\partial X/\partial I^*)$.

6.5. In the diagram the segment
of the curve from 'a' to 'b' is
added to the old demand
curve. Demand now jumps
to zero at $3.00.

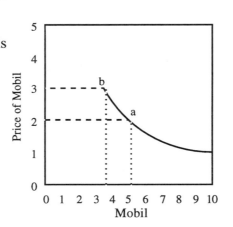

6.6. (1) The price of the composite commodity is higher in Florida
since it includes transportation costs. Hence, if syrup is not a
Giffen good, Florida consumers use less syrup (holding tastes
and income constant). (2) The relative price of Grade A syrup is
$(P_A + T)/ (P_B +T)$. Since Grade A syrup is more expensive, this
ratio exceeds one. As T increases the ratio approaches one, so
transportation reduces the relative price of Grade A syrup.
Florida consumers are expected to consume relatively more
Grade A. (3) The quantity will decline, but the average quality
will increase. The reason is that for any given quality

transportation increases the price, but the relative price of high quality goods declines.

6.7. a. See graph. $P_V/P_C = -(200-160)/(100-160) = 2/3$.

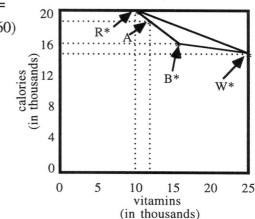

b. $160P_C + 160P_V = 1.00$ and $P_V/P_C = 2/3$ => $160P_C + 160(2/3)P_C = 1.00$ => $60(5/3)P_C = 1.00$ => $P_C = .00375$ => $P_V = (2/3).00375 = .0025$. **c.** $.00375P_C + .0025P_V = 100$; $C^* = (.7)(100)/.00375 = 18667$; $V^* = (.3)(100)/.0025 = 12000$. **d.** The two equations are **(i)** $200R^* + 160B^* = 18667$; **(ii)** $100R^* + 160B^* = 12000$. The solution is $B^* = 33.33$ and $R^* = 66.67$. **e.** See graph. Holding expenditure constant, for any combination of either wheat and barley or rice and barley, there is some combination of wheat and rice that will yield more of both calories and vitamins.

CHAPTER 7

7.1. a. (1) $.5P_C I_O/P_M + .5P_C I_T/P_M = P_C(I_O+I_T)/P_M$; (2) $(\partial M/\partial P_M)(P_M/M) = -(.5P_C I/P_M^2)(P_M/M) = -(.5P_C M/P_M)$ $(1/M) = -M/M = -1$; (3) $(\partial M/\partial P_C)(P_C/M) = (.5I/P_M)(P_C/M) = M/M = 1$; (4) $(\partial M/\partial I)(I/M) = (.5P_C/P_M)(I/M) = M/M = 1$; (5) no; (6) 50%; (7) 7.5; (8) 5%; (9) 33.3%; (10) no change.

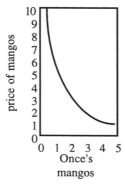

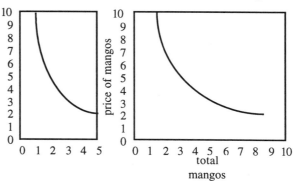

Harcourt Brace & Company

b. (1) $(.5P_C/P_M)(I_O+I_T/2)$; (2) -1; (3) 1; (4) not defined; (5) $I = I_T + I_M$ does not appear in the function; (6) Yes; With $P_C = 1$, Once's demand curve shifts right by $.5\Delta I_O/P_M = 2.5/P_M$ and Twice's shifts left by $.25\Delta I_O/P_M = 1.25/P_M$. [Note that $\Delta I_O = -\Delta I_T$.] Hence, market demand shifts right by $1.25/P_M$.

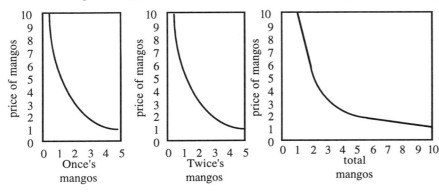

7.2. a. (1) 80; (2) 80; (3) Yes, since $100 - 1000P_C/(2I+5P_S) = 100 - 1000kP_C/(2kI+5kP_S)$ for any k. **b.** (1) $-1000P_C/([(2I+5P_S)C]$; (2) $5000P_C/(2I+5P_S)^2$; (3) $2000I/(2I+5P_S)^2$; (4) 2; (5) 4; (6) 64. **c.** (1) $e_{C,Pc} = -40P_C/C = -40P_C/(100 - 40P_C) = -1 => 40P_C = 100 - 40P_C => P_C = 100/80 = 1.25$; (2) .5a/b.

7.3. (1) $-\partial Q/\partial P$; (2) P/Q; (3) $-(\partial Q/\partial P)(P/Q) = e_{Q,P}$; (4) inelastic since AO/AB < 1; (5) elastic since EO/EF > 1; point X is between points C and D; (6) At D the curve is elastic and the slope is steeper than at C, where the curve is inelastic. This contradicts the claim! Elasticity depends on the ratio P/Q as well as the slope of the demand curve.

7.4. a **(i)** $y^* = (2x^*+5)^2 => dy^*/dx^* = d\ln(y)/d\ln(x) = (2)(2x^*+5)(2) = 8\ln(x)+20$; **(ii)** $\ln(y) = \ln(5)+.5\ln(x) => d\ln(y)/d\ln(x) = .5$; **(iii)** $\ln(y) = 3+2\ln(x)+4[\ln(x)]^2 => d\ln(y)/d\ln(x) = 2+8\ln(x)$; **(iv)** $\partial\ln(y)/\partial\ln(x) = b+d\ln(z)$; $\partial\ln(y)/\partial\ln(z) = c + d\ln(x)$; **(v)** $\ln(y) = \ln(3)+2\ln(x)+5\ln(z) => \partial\ln(y)/\partial\ln(x) = 2$; $\partial\ln(y)/\partial\ln(z) = 5$; **(vi)** $\ln(y) = \ln(3)+4\ln(x)+1+\ln(x)+2\ln(z) - 5\ln(x)\ln(z) => \partial\ln(y)/\partial\ln(x) = 5[1 - \ln(z)]$; $\partial\ln(y)/\partial\ln(z) = 2 - 5\ln(x)$; **(vii)** $\ln(y) = \ln(3)+2\ln(x) - 5\ln(z) => \partial\ln(y)/\partial\ln(x) = 2$; $\partial\ln(y)/\partial\ln(z) = -5$. **b.** (1) $(dy/dx)(x/y)$; (2) 1/y; (3) 1/x; (4) $[(1/y)dy]/[(1/x)dx] = (dy/dx)(x/y)$. **c.** **(i)** (Illustration); **(ii)** $\ln(x) = \ln(a) + \ln(I) - \ln(P_X) => e_{X,I} = \partial\ln(X)/\partial\ln(I) = 1$; $e_{X,Px} = \partial\ln(X)/\partial\ln(P_X) = -1$; $e_{X,Py} = 0$; **(iii)** $\ln(X) =$

$\ln(a)+b\ln(P_X)+c\ln(P_Y)+d\ln(I) \Rightarrow e_{X,I} = \partial\ln(X)/\partial\ln(I) = d$; $e_{X,Px}$
$= \partial\ln(X)/\partial\ln(P_X) = b$; $e_{X,Py} = c$; **(iv)** $\ln(X) = \ln(10) + \ln(P_Y) +$
$\ln(I) - \ln(5+P_X) \Rightarrow e_{X,I} = 1$; $e_{X,Py} = 1$; $e_{X,Px} = -P_X/(5+P_X)$ and
is not constant; **(v)** $e_{X,Px} = -.5$; $e_{X,I}$ and $e_{X,Py}$ are not constant. **d.**
(i) $e_{Q,P} < -1$ (elastic demand) $<=> e_{E,P} < 0$; $e_{Q,P} > -1$ (inelastic
demand) $<=> e_{E,P} > 0$; $e_{Q,P} = -1$ (unit elastic demand) $<=> e_{E,P}$
$= 0$; **(ii)** $e_{E,P'} = \partial\ln(E)/\partial\ln(P') = 0 + \partial\ln(Q)/\partial\ln(P') = e_{Q,P'}$; $e_{E,I} =$
$\partial\ln(E)/\partial\ln(I) = 0 + \partial\ln(Q)/\partial\ln(I) = e_{Q,I}$.

7.5. a. $4.605 = \ln(a)+b(0)$

$\Rightarrow \ln(a) = 4.605$

$\Rightarrow a = 100$; 4.554

$= \ln(a)+b(.0953)$

$= 4.605+b(.0953)$

$\Rightarrow b = -.55 = e_{Q,P}$.

	$\ln(Q)$	$\ln(P)$	$\ln(I)$
year 1	4.605	0	2.303
year 2	4.554	.0953	2.346
year 3	4.561	.1398	2.398

b. $4.605 = \ln(a)+b(0) + c(2.303) = 2.303 + 0 + 2.303 = 4.606$
$4.554 = \ln(a)+b(.0953)+c(2.346) = 2.303 - .0953+2.346 = 4.554$.
$.561 = \ln(a)+b(.1398)+c(2.398) = 2.303 - .1398+2.398 = 4.561$
$e_{Q,P} = b = -1$; Demand appears to be more elastic. In **a** we
ignored the increase in I. Since this increase had a positive
effect on quantity demanded, ignoring it made the negative
effect of the price increase seem smaller than it really was.

7.6. a. (1) -.68; (2) .35; (3) .49; (4) inelastic; (5) increase; (6)
substitute; (7) substitute; (8) yes—in fact it is superior (increases
by more than the percentage increase in income). **b.** (1) -.68 +
(.01)(1.21) = -.67; (2) .35+(.005)(1.21) = .36; (3) .49 + (.005)
(1.21) = .50; (4) Differences are small because the income shares
spent on the three products are small. **c.** $-8.3 - .68\ln(kP_{beef})$
$+.35\ln(kP_{poultry}) + .49\ln(kP_{pork})+1.21\ln(kI) = -8.3 - .68\ln(P_{beef})$
$+ .35\ln(P_{poultry}) + .49\ln(P_{pork})+1.21\ln(I) + (-.68 + .35 + .49 +$
$1.21)\ln(k) = Q + 1.37\ln(k) \neq Q$ unless $k = 1$. Since Q changes,
the function is not homogeneous of degree zero. **d.** If the prices
and income given in the equation are "real" — nominal values
divided by the CPI—the function would be homogeneous of
degree zero in prices and income. If all nominal prices and
nominal income increase by a factor of k, the CPI also increases
by a factor of k and real prices and income are unchanged.
Hence, the right-hand side of the equation is unchanged.

7.7 a. Variable one is the relative quantity Y/X; variable two is MRS_{XY}. **b.**The curvature of the indifference curve is inversely related to σ—the larger σ, the less curved. Thus the larger is σ, the larger is the substitution effect of a change in price.

c.
$$MRS_{XY}=\frac{\alpha}{\beta}\left(\frac{X}{Y}\right)^{\delta-1}=\frac{\alpha}{\beta}\left(\frac{1}{Z}\right)^{\delta-1}=\frac{\alpha}{\beta}(Z)^{\delta-1}\ge\frac{d(MRS_{XY})}{d(Y/X)}=\frac{d(MRS_{XY})}{d(Z)}$$

$$=\frac{\alpha}{\beta}(1-\delta)(Z)^{1-\delta-1}=\frac{\alpha}{\beta}(1-\delta)(Z)^{-\delta}=\frac{\alpha}{\beta}(1-\delta)\left(\frac{X}{Y}\right)^{-\delta}\ge\sigma$$

$$=\left[\frac{d(MRS_{XY})}{d(Y/X)}\cdot\frac{(Y/X)}{MRS_{XY}}\right]^{-1}=\left[\frac{\alpha}{\beta}(1-\delta)\left(\frac{Y}{X}\right)^{-\delta}\cdot\left(\frac{Y/X}{\alpha/\beta(X/Y)^{\delta-1}}\right)\right]^{-1}$$

$$=\left[(1-\delta)\left(\frac{Y}{X}\right)^{1-\delta}\cdot\left(\frac{X}{Y}\right)^{1-\delta}\right]^{-1}=(1-\delta)^{-1}=1/(1-\delta).$$

d. σ is independent of the quantities of X and Y; it is a constant. **e.** In the Cobb-Douglas case, δ = 0; therefore, σ = 1/(1–0) = 1. **f.** As δ approaches one, σ approaches ∞; this is the case of perfect substitution. **g.** As δ approaches –∞, σ approaches 0; this is the case of perfect complements.

8.1. a. Expected net winnings are zero for all games. To illustrate, consider Game B: expected winnings = .75(100) + .25(-300) = 0. **b.** Any answer is fine. **c.** (1) about 550; (2) about 580; (3) about 590; (4) Game A; (5) Yes. Her marginal utility of wealth declines with wealth (the slope of the function gets flatter moving from left to right); (6) Yes, by the usual definition, since the declining marginal utility of wealth guarantees that expected utility of Game A exceeds that of the other two. A risk lover would choose Game C. Convince yourself by drawing a utility function with an increasing slope

CHAPTER 8

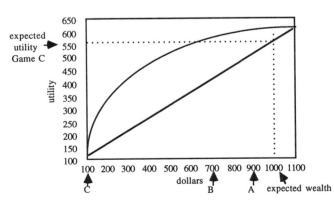

Harcourt Brace & Company

8.2. a. U= log(97.90) = 1.9908. **b.** (1) .9(100) + .1(90) = 99; (2) log(99) = 1.9956; (3) log(100) = 2; (4) log(90) = 1.9542; (5) .9(2)+.1(1.9542) = 1.9954; (6) the answer to (2) is larger; (7) Because Patty is risk averse — U"(W) < 0; (8) No. Her certain utility if she feeds the meter is less than her expected utility if she doesn't. **c.** (1) $98.00; (2) .1log(80) + .9log(100) = 1.9903; (3) Yes. Her expected utility is now less than the utility in **a**; (4) $98.00; (5) .2log(90) + .8log(100) = 1.9908; (6) She is now indifferent between feeding and not feeding; (7)The first proposal seems more likely to succeed since it reduces expected utility more, even though it increases her expected loss by the same amount as the second. (8) Since increased enforcement is costly, the answer is reinforced. **d.** (1) $90; (2) $95; (3) $50; (4) $95; (5) about 497; (6) about 488; (7) Proposition 2 since it reduces expected utility by more; (8) Yes. From the construction of the graph it can be seen that the expected utility from Proposition 2 will be lower for any shopper who is risk averse; (9) Enforcement and punishment that reduce the expected monetary gain from crime by the same amount do not reduce the willingness of criminals to commit the crimes by the same amount; punishment reduces their willingness more if they are risk averse, as defined by economists, since it increases risk more.

8.3. a. U'(I) = 1/(I-1); U"(I) = -1/(I-1)^2 < 0, so Yoshi is risk averse. Note that the utility function is only defined for I > 1. **b.** expected utility = .999ln(2) + .001ln(1.75) = .6930136. **c.** .6930136 = ln(2 - p) => 2 - p = 1.9997328 => p = .000267 million yen, or 267 yen. **d.** fair premium = .25(.001) = .00025 million yen = 250 yen. Yoshi would buy the insurance since the premium he is willing to pay exceeds the actuarially fair premium. **e.** No, since it exceeds the maximum he is willing to pay. **f.** ln(2 - p) = .999ln(2)+.001ln(1.75) => p = .000288, or 288 yen. He would buy the insurance. **g.** r = - U"(I)/U'(I) = 1/(I-1), which diminishes with I. The larger is Yoshi's income, the less he is willing to pay for insurance for a given bet.

8.4. a. (1 - .00025)bW* > (1 - .00020)b(W* - 100) => (1 - .00025 - 1 + .00020)W* > -99.98 => W* < 99.98/.00005 =

$1,999,600. **b.** $(1 - .00025)bW^* > (1 - .00020)b(W^* - 20) =>$ $W^* < \$399,920.$ **c.** If he is risk averse, the maximum value of his life is even less. He is willing to pay some premium to avoid the risk, but not as large as the cost of putting on his seatbelt. Since avoiding the risk has some value in itself, the value he implicitly attaches to his life must be even less. **d.** There are many possible criticisms of the analysis. There are other reasons that drivers don't wear seatbelts: being macho, ignorance, comfort, denial of danger, etc. It is also difficult to imagine answering the question: For what price would I sell you my life at this very moment?— especially since I won't be around to spend the money!

8.5. a.

bet	W_S	W_T
no bet	100	100
$10 on Turkeys	90	120
$20 on Turkeys	80	140
$X on Turkeys	100 - X	100+2X
$10 on Strikers	110	80
$X on Strikers	100+X	100 - 2X

b. (1) .5; (2) $1(100)+.5(100) = 150$; (3) $W_S + .5W_T \le 150$. **c.** (1) $.5\ln(W_T) + .5\ln(W_S)$; (2) $.5(150)/1 = 75$; (3) $.5(150)/.5 = 150$; (4) 25; (5) Turkeys; (6) His risk-averse utility function implies that his marginal rate of substitution between wealth in the two states of the world is diminishing. **d.** (1) $75+20 = 95$; (2) $150 - 10=140$; (3) 2; (4) 375; (5) $W_S+2W_T \le 375$; (6) $.5(375) =187.5$; (7) $.5(375)/2 = 93.75$; (8) 56.25; (9) Strikers. **e.** He should place $100 on the Turkeys in Mudville and $100 on the Strikers in Titusville. If the Turkeys win, he will receive $200 from his Mudville bets. Of this, $100 will be used to cover his Titusville losses. The remaining $100 plus his original $100 leaves him with $200. If the Strikers win he pays $100 in Mudville but receives $200 in Titusville. Either way he has $200. Ernie is an arbitragerbetween these two markets, where the prices are different. The existence of encyclopedia salesmen may guarantee that the odds will be about the same in both towns!

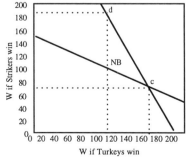

Harcourt Brace & Company

9.1. a. $.5(20) + .5(10) = 15$. **b.** $20 - 6 = 14$; the PCC members will not pay for restoration since expected profits without it exceed certain profits with it. **c.** $.5(20 - 6 - P) + .5(20 - P) = 17 - P$; $17 - P = 15 \Rightarrow P = 2$. **d.** (1) $.1(20) + .9(10) - P = 11 - P$; (2) will; (3) $.9(20) + .1(10) - P = 19 - P$; (4) will not; (5) $.5(14 - P) + .5(19 - P) = 16.5 - P$; (6) $16.5 - P = 15 \Rightarrow P = 1.5$; (7) less; (8) that the AA's information is less valuable than before because it is now less certain.

9.2. (1) $500 - 499 = 1$; (2) 6; (3) $.9(6) + .1(0) = 5.4$; (4) will; (5) $.9(55) + .1(0) = 49.5$; (6) would not; (7) moral hazard; (8) There are several possibilities. One is to base insurance premia on E as a percentage of assets. E is a signal of the riskiness of insuring an S&L since high E means the owners bear a larger share of a loan's risk. Another possibility would be to only insure a percentage of deposits so that depositors would be more reluctant to put their money in high risk S&Ls. A third possibility is to restrict the types of loans S&Ls can make to those that are low risk, or to impose strict criteria that the S&L must use in deciding whether to make a loan (e.g., the developer must have a large down payment).

9.3. a. (1) $.5(.5) + (1)(.5) = .75$; (2) $.075\%$; (3) $.00075(.250) = .0001875$ million yen, or 187.5 yen; (4) $.0005 \ln(3 - .250 - 1) + .9995 \ln(3 - 1) = .6930804$; (5) $\ln(3 - .0001875 - 1) = .6930546$; (6) will not; (7) $.001 \ln(3 - .250 - 1) + .999 \ln(3 - 1) = .6930136$; (8) $\ln(3 - .0001874 - 1) = .6930546$; (9) will; (10) good; (11) high; (12) adverse (self) selection; (13) $.001(.250) = .000250$ million yen, or 250 yen; (14) higher. **b.** (1) $\ln(3 - .000250 - 1) = .6930221$; (2) will; (3) $.6930221$; (4) will not. **c.** (1) $.0005 \ln(3 - (.250 - .025) - .0000125 - 1) + .9995 \ln(3 - .0000125 - 1) = .6930812$; (2) will; (3) $.001 \ln(3 - (.250 - .025) - .0000125 - 1) + .999 \ln(3 - .0000125 - 1) = .6930214$; (4) will not; (5) separating equilibrium. **d.** Anyone can get a high handicap and join the low risk group. Handicaps can serve as a meaningful signal only if golfers' desire for low handicaps (i.e., their desire to be good golfers) is sufficient to offset the incentive that insurance creates to be a bad golfer. If this desire is sufficient, then low risk golfers can be offered more complete insurance at a price they will find attractive, and high risk golfers will not be allowed to buy it. **e.** This creates a moral hazard. What is to prevent a group of golfers from going out and claiming that one of them who is insured got a hole-in-one, for their joint benefit? A possible solution is to only insure a fraction of the loss, so the insured golfer will have an incentive to be honest. If the fraction is too large, the playing partners might still bribe the insured golfer to cheat. The insurer might also specify that it will not pay for gifts to the partners, but this might be hard to enforce.

9.4. a. Megan. The fact that she is at SPC is an imperfect signal to the recruiter that her SAT score is higher since it is more difficult for students with low SAT scores to obtain admission at SPC. **b.** Yes. The reason is that she wants potential employers to believe that she has high SAT scores. **c.** It is not possible to tell for sure. The value of the signal will be lost, so students will not be willing to pay as much for that reason. However, there may be many students who were previously not qualified for admission but who want the country club atmosphere, so SPC may need to raise its tuition in order to clear the market.

CHAPTER 10

10.1. a.

		Driver B	
		Bull	Chicken
Driver A	Bull	A: -.5 B: -.5	A: .2 B: -.2
	Chicken	A: -.2 B: .2	A: 0 B: 0

b. No. There is no strategy for either driver which is better regardless of what the other does. **c.** No. No matter what strategy each chooses, at least one will regret not having chosen the other. **d.** $X = -.5p + .2(1-p) = .2 - .7p$; $Y = -.2p$; See graph. **e.** (1) -.15; (2) -.1; (3) .5(-.15)+.5(-.1) = -.125; (4) chicken; (5) no; (6) The probability will decline since chicken has higher expected value; (7) Yes, at $p = .4$; (8) Yes. If p moves above .4, there will be an incentive for some drivers to play bull more often, reducing p. If p moves below .4, the opposite will happen.

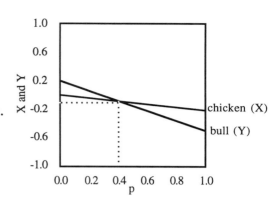

10.2. a. If you call heads all the time, expected winnings are $.5(-2)+.5(3) = 0.5$. If you call tails all the time, expected winnings are $.5(-2)+.5(1) = -0.5$. The best strategy is to always call heads if Joe calls heads 50% of the time at random. **b.** $X = p(-2) + (1-p)(3) = -5p + 3$; $Y = -2 + 3p$. **c.** (1) heads; (2) 2.5; (3) tails; (4) 0.7; (5) 5/8 - .625; (6) -2 + .625(3) = -.125; (7) no; (8) no **d.** Joe's strategy of playing heads 62.5% of the time is a mixed strategy. As long as you try to maximize your expected winnings, this is the best strategy he can choose. From your point of view there is also a strategy that will minimize Joe's maximum expected winnings no matter what he does. To figure out what it is, redo **b** and **c** after switching your role with Joe's. This is an equilibrium strategy for you. If Joe deviates from his equilibrium strategy, you can increase your expected winnings by deviating from yours, and vice-versa. Hence, you will both choose to stay at your equilbrium strategies

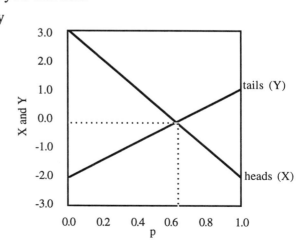

10.3. a.

	Nick	
	stonewall	confess
stonewall	Nack: 20 Nick: 20	Nack: 10 Nick: 25
Nack confess	Nack: 25 Nick: 10	Nack: 15 Nick: 15

b. They will both confess because this is the dominant strategy. This is an example of the prisoners' dilemma. **c.** No, it doesn't. Confessing is still the dominant strategy unless each twin trusts the other not to lie in order to get the payoff for confession. **d.** They might well be opposed if they think that it induces false confessions.

10.4. a. If they marry each other both could be better off. For instance, give Ralph 3 (>2) and Cindy 5 (>4.5). **b.** Dave and Joyce will not make counteroffers. They, too, can both be better off with each other. Give Dave 4.75 and Joyce 2.25. **c.** Set B is an equilibrium, at least for certain divisions of excess income. Under the divisions given above, there is no contract that Cindy and Dave can make that will leave them both at least as well off as they are in the marriages of this set. The same is true for Joyce and Ralph. **d.** Combined excess income is 13 in Set A and 15 in Set B. Hence, it is larger in B. **e.** Set B is Pareto optimal in the sense that it maximizes total excess income. No person can be made better off without making someone else worse off. **f.** Yes, it would. As long as total excess income is not maximized there will be some rearrangement of pairs that will increase total excess income. At least one man and woman will have an incentive to change partners in order to be the recipients of the incremental excess income.

CHAPTER 11

11.1. a. (i) $MP_L = 5L^{-.5}K^{.4} > 0$; $\partial MP_L/\partial L = -2.5L^{-1.5}K^{.4} < 0$; $MP_K = 4L^{.5}K^{-.6} > 0$; $\partial MP_K/\partial K = -2.4L^{.5}K^{-1.6} < 0$; **(ii)** $AP_L = 10L^{-.5}K^{.4}$; $AP_K = 10L^{.5}K^{-.6}$; **(iii)** See left-hand and middle graphs; **(iv)** $RTS_{LK} = MP_L/MP_K = 1.25K/L$; as L increases and K falls just enough to hold Q constant, K/L gets smaller so RTS_{LK} does diminish in L; **(v)** See right-hand graph.

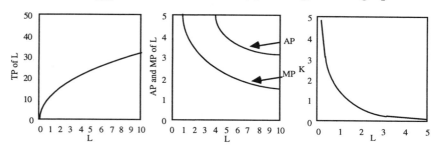

(vi) $10(mL)^{.5}(mK)^{.4} = m^{.9}[10L^{.5}K^{.4}] = m^{.9}Q =>$ homogeneous; Returns to scale are decreasing since $.9 < 1$. **b.** **(i)** $MP_L = K+1 > 0$; $\partial MP_L/\partial L = 0$, so MP_L does not diminish in L; $MP_K = L+1 > 0$; $\partial MP_K/\partial K = 0$; **(ii)** $AP_L = K + K/L + 1$; $AP_K = L + 1 + L/K$; **(iii)** See left-hand and middle graphs; **(iv)** $RTS_{LK} = MP_L/MP_K = (K+1)/(L+1)$; which does diminish in L; **(v)** See right-hand graph; **(vi)** $(mL)(mK) + mK + mL = m^2LK + mK + mL > mQ$ for $m > 1$. Returns to scale are increasing, but the function is not homogeneous.

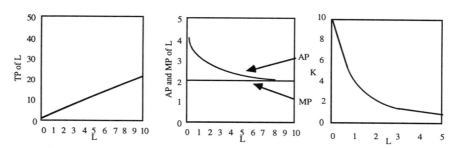

c. (i) If $L < K/2$, $MP_L = 2$, but if $L \geq K/2$, $MP_L = 0$. If $L < K/2$, $MP_K = 0$, but if $L \geq K/2$, $MP_K = 1$; **(ii)** If $L < K/2$, $AP_L = 2$, but if $L \geq K/2$, $AP_L = K/L$. If $L < K/2$, $AP_K = 2L/K$, but if $L \geq K/2$, $AP_K = 1$; **(iii)** See left-hand and middle graphs; **(iv)** If $L < K/2$, $RTS_{LK} = \infty$, if $L \geq K/2$, $RTS_{LK} = 0$. It diminishes with L only at points where $L = K/2$; **(v)** See right-hand graph; **(vi)** $\min(2mL, mK) = m[\min(2L, K)] = mQ$, so the function is homogeneous of degree one and returns to scale are constant.

Harcourt Brace & Company

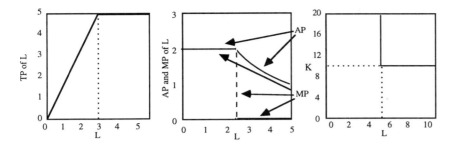

11.2. a. Let $f_1(,)$ and $f_2(,)$ represent the partial derivatives of f. Then $f_1(mx, mz)x + f_2(mx, mz)z = km^{k-1}f(x, z)$. **b.** (1) one; (2) $f_K K + f_L L$; (3) $f(K, L) = Q$; (4) The sum of the factors times their respective marginal products just equals Q. [Note: If K > 1 (increasing returns), the sum is less than Q and if k < 1 (decreasing returns), the sum exceeds Q.]

11.3. a. See graph. **b.** (1) 4; (2) 2; (3) 4.5; (4) 1.5. **c.** (1) 8.5; (2) 3.5. **d.** (1) 1; (2) same—$RTS_{LK} = MP_L/MP_K = 1$; (3) $MP_K K + MP_L L = 10000$ and $MP_K = MP_L => MP_K(K+L) = 10000$; For K + L = 12, $MP_K = 10000/12 = MP_L$ = 833.33 lbs. per worker hour.

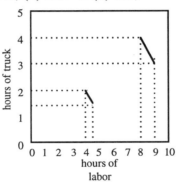

11.4. a. [Illustration]. **b.** $RTS_{LK} = 1.5(K/L) => K/L = (2/3)RTS_{LK} => \partial(K/L)/\partial RTS_{LK} = 2/3$, and $RTS_{LK}/(K/L) = 1.5$. Hence, $\sigma = (2/3)(1.5) = 1$. **c.** $RTS_{LK} = (b/a)(K/L) => K/L = (a/b)RTS_{LK} => \partial(K/L)/\partial RTS_{LK} = a/b$, and $RTS_{LK}/(K/L) = b/a$. Hence, $\sigma = (a/b)(b/a) = 1$. Note that returns to scale need not be constant. **d.** $RTS_{LK} = \{(-.5)(2)[.2K^{-2} + .8L^{-2}]^{-3/2}(-1.6)L^{-3}\}/\{(-.5)(2)[.2K^{-2} + .8L^{-2}]^{-3/2}(-.4)K^{-3}\} = 4(K/L)^3 => K/L = (.25RTS_{LK})^{1/3} => \partial(K/L)/\partial RTS_{LK} = (1/12)(.25RTS_{LK})^{-2/3} = (1/12)(K/L)^{-2}$, and $RTS_{LK}/(K/L) = 4(K/L)^2$. Hence, $\sigma = (1/12)(K/L)^{-2}(4)(K/L)^2 = 1/3$. **e.** $RTS_{LK} = \{\rho(1-\delta)\gamma[\delta K^\rho + (1-\delta)L^\rho]^{(\varepsilon/\rho)-1}(\varepsilon/\rho)L^{\rho-1}\}/\{\rho\delta\gamma[\delta K^\rho + (1-\delta)L^\rho]^{(\varepsilon/\rho)-1}(\varepsilon/\rho)K^{\rho-1}\} = [(1-\delta)/\delta](K/L)^{1-\rho} => K/L = [\delta RTS_{LK}/(1-\delta)]^{1/(1-\rho)} => \partial(K/L)/\partial RTS_{LK} = [\delta/(1-\delta)]^{1/(1-\rho)}RTS_{LK}^{[1/(1-\rho)]-1}/(1-\rho) = [\delta RTS_{LK}/(1-\delta)]^{1/(1-\rho)}/[(1-\rho)RTS_{LK}] = (K/L)/[(1-\rho)RTS_{LK}]$. Hence, $\sigma = \{(K/L)/[(1-\rho)RTS_{LK}]\}\{RTS_{LK}/(K/L)\} = 1/(1-\rho)$.

12.1. a. **(i)** $RTS_{LR} = r/L = w/r$ and **(ii)** $s = A(RL)^{.5}$. **b. (i)** $=> R = (w/r)L => s = A(w/r)^{.5}L => L = A^{-1}(r/w)^{.5}s$; $R = A^{-1}(w/r)^{.5}s$. **c.** $C = w\{A^{-1}(r/w)^{.5}s\} + r\{A^{-1}(w/r)^{.5}s\} = 2A^{-1}(wr)^{.5}s$. **d.** $\partial C/\partial w = (.5)2A^{-1}w^{-.5}r^{.5}s = A^{-1}(r/w)^{.5}s$. **e.** $AC = 2A^{-1}(wr)^{.5}$; $MC = 2A^{-1}(wr)^{.5}$. **f.** (1) constant, since $\alpha + \beta = 1$; (2) constant; (3) same; (4) increasing; (5) decreasing; (6) less than; (7) decreasing; (8) increasing; (9) greater. **g.** $e_{MC,w} = .5$, $e_{MC,r} = .5$.

12.2. a. $C = 2(200-2s+.01s^2)(5.20)^{.5}s = 20s(200-2s+.01s^2) = 4000s - 40s^2 +.2s^3$; $s = (RL)^{.5}/(200-2s+.01s^2) => .01s^3 - 2s^2 + 200s = R^{.5}L^{.5}$. **b.** $AC = 4000 - 40s +.2s^2$; $MC = 4000 - 80s +.6s^2$; first order condition for minimization of AC: $\partial AC/\partial s = -40 +.4s = C => s = 40/.4 =100$; second order condition $\partial^2 AC/\partial s^2 = .4 > 0 =>$ minimum; $AC = 2000 = MC$; AC and MC are always equal at the point where AC is minimized; first order condition for minimization of MC: $\partial MC/\partial s = -80+1.2s = 0 => s = 66.67$; $MC = 13333.33$ at the minimum. **c.** See diagram. **d.** (1) 1500; (2) 2500; (3) 12500; (4) 3125; $L = [200 - 2(50) -.01(50)^2](5/20)^{.5}(50) = 3125$; $K = 12500$. **e.** $.01s^3 - 2s^2 + 200s = R^{.5}(3125)^{.5} => R = [.01s^3 - 2s^2+200s]^2/3125 => C =(20)(3125) + 5[.01s^3 - 2s^2+200s]^2/3125 = 62500 + [.01s^3 - 2s^2+200s]^2/625$. **f.** $SAC(50) = C(50)/s$; $SMC(50) = \partial C(50)/\partial S$. **g.** 3rd row in table: 50 <u>125000 2500 125000 - 123499 = 1501</u>; 8th row in table: 85 <u>183361 2157 183361 - 181250 = 2111</u> ; (1) 50; (2) 50; (3) 85(±1); (4) 85(±1); **h.** Sedate can't adjust L to reduce costs in the short run. **i.** In the long run there are increasing returns to scale at s = 50. The reason for the scale economy, whatever it is, still exists even when L is fixed. The decline in SAC(50) to the right of s = 50 is less than that of AC because of diminishing returns to R, but it is not positive until the effect of diminishing returns becomes more severe and the effect of returns to scale diminishes. **j.** (1) 100; (2) 100; (3) 100; (4) 100. **k.** (1) 150; (2) 150; (3) MC; (4) less; (5) same.

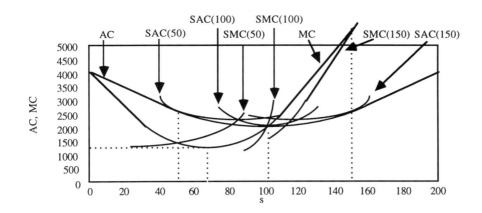

12.3. a. $SMC = t^2 + 2t + (300 - 6A)$; $SAC = t^2/3 + t + (300 - 6A) + A^2/t$. **b.** first order condition: $\partial C/\partial A = -6t + 2A = 0 \Rightarrow A = 3t$. **c.** $C(t) = t^3/3 + t^2 + [300 - 6(3t)]t + 9t^2 = t^3 - 8t^2 + 300t$. **d.** $MC = 3t^2 - 16t + 300$; $AC = t^2 - 8t + 300$.

12.4. a. See graph. **b.** ∞; No matter how much K/L changes, RTS_{LK} is constant. **c.** MC = AC = (\$90 per ton) x(tons of coal per BTU). **d.** MC = AC = (\$1.00 per gallon)x(gallons of oil per BTU).

12.5. a. $TC = (.5a + .1b)F$; $MC = .5a + .1b$; $AC = .5a + .1b$. **b.** (1) $900(.5a+.1b) + .1(100a)$; (2) $.5a+.1b+a/90$; (3) $.5a+.1b$ $-.1a = .4a+.1b$; (4) $(.5a+.1b)1000$; (5) $.5a+.1b$; (6) $.4a+.1b$; (7) ∞.

12.6. a. $L = [1+(v/w)^{.5}]Q$; $K = [1+(w/v)^{.5}]Q$. **b.** $(v/w)^{.5} = (L - Q)/Q$; $(v/w)^{.5} = Q/(K - Q)$. **c.** $(L - Q)/Q = Q/(K - Q) \Rightarrow (L - Q)(K - Q) = Q^2 \Rightarrow Q^2 = Q^2 + LK - LQ - KQ \Rightarrow Q = LK/(L+K) =$

Harcourt Brace & Company

$1/[(L+K)/LK] = (K^{-1}+L^{-1})^{-1}$. **d.** $\rho = -1$; $\gamma = 2$; $\delta = .5$; $\varepsilon = 1$; $\sigma = .5$; This is a special case of the CES. **e.** $K = .2(w/v)^{.8}Q$; $L = .8(w/v)^{-.2}Q$; $w/v = (K/.2Q)^{1.25} = (L/.8Q)^{-5} => K^{1.25}L^5 = (.2)^{1.25}(.8)^5Q^{6.25} => Q^{6.25} = (.2)^{-1.25}(.8)^{-5}K^{1.25}L^5 => Q = 1.65K^{.2}L^{.8}$.

This is a special case of the general Cobb-Douglas form.

CHAPTER 13

13.1. a. $P = 12000 - 40s$. **b.** $R(s) = Ps = (12000 - 40s)s = 12000s - 40s^2$. **c.** $MR = 12000 - 80s$. **d.** (1) twice as steep; (2) one-half. **e.** (1) $a/b - q/b$; (2) $aq/b - q^2/b$; (3) $a/b - 2q/b$; (4) $-2/b$; (5) $-1/b$; (6) 2; (7) $(a - bMR)/2$; (8) $a - bP$; (9) .5. **f.** $MC = MR => 4000 - 80s+.6s^2 = 12000 - 80s$

$=> .6s^2 = 8000$
$=> s \approx 115$;
$P = 12000 - 40(115)$
$= 7400$; $AC = 4000$
$- 40(115) + .2(115)^2$
$= 2045$; π
$=(115)(7400 - 2045)$
$= 615825$ (shaded
area on graph).

13.2. a. max $R(s) - C(s) - t$; first order condition: $R'(s) = C'(s)$ or $MR - MC$. This condition is the same as when $T = 0$, so s doesn't change — unless $T > 615,825$, in which case Sedate will lose money and go out of business. **b.** first order condition: $(1-t)MR = (1-t)MC => MR = MC$, so again no change — provided that $t < 1$. **c.** first order condition (uses the chain rule): $(\partial N/\partial\pi)(MR - MC) = 0 => MR = MC$, so again no change. **d.** first order condition: $MR = MC + t$. For $t > 0$, Sedate will produce at a point where $MR > MC$. Since MR falls with s and MC increases with s, the value of s must fall. **e.** Profits taxes don't affect output levels as long as net profits are nonnegative. Net profits are maximized at the same output level as gross profits. Output taxes discourage output. The reason is that they increase the marginal cost of output, counting the marginal tax as part of marginal cost. Profits can be increased by reducing output since the decline in revenue will not be as large as the decline in full marginal cost.

Harcourt Brace & Company

13.3. a. first order conditions: **(i)** $q = K*^{1/2}L^{1/4}M^{1/4}$ and **(ii)** $w/u = MP_L/MP_M = M/L$; **(ii)** => **(iii)** $L = Mu/w$; **(i)** and **(iii)** => $q = (K*M)^{1/2}(u/w)^{1/4}$ => $q^2 = K*M(u/w)^{1/2}$ => $M = (w/u)^{1/2}K*^{-1}q^2$ => $L = [(w/u)^{1/2}K*^{-1}q^2](u/w) = (u/w)^{1/2}K*^{-1}q^2$ => STC $= wL+uM+vK* = w[(u/w)^{1/2}K*^{-1}q^2]+u[(w/u)^{1/2}K*^{-1}q^2]+vK* = 2(uw)^{1/2}K*^{-1}q^2 + vK*$ => SMC $= 4(uw)^{1/2}K*^{-1}q = P$ => $q = .25(uw)^{-1/2}K*P$ **b.** Let $N = PK*^{1/2}/4$. First order conditions: **(i)** $NL^{-3/4}M^{1/4} = w$ and **(ii)** $NL^{1/4}M^{-3/4} = u$; **(i)** and **(ii)** => **(iii)** $L = Mu/w$; **(ii)** and **(iii)** => $N(Mu/w)^{1/4}M^{-3/4} = u$ => $NM^{-1/2}(u/w)^{1/4} = u$ => $M = u^{-3/2}w^{-1/2}N^2$ => $L = u^{-1/2}w^{-3/2}N^2$ => $q = K*^{1/2}(u^{-1/2}w^{-3/2}N^2)^{1/4}(u^{-3/2}w^{-1/2}N^2)^{1/4} = .25(uw)^{-1/2}K*P$. **c.** Increases in u and w shift supply backward. Increases in variable factor prices increase short run marginal costs, making the value of q at which SMC = MR smaller. Increases in $K*$ shift supply outward. The larger the stock of the fixed capital, the lower the short run marginal costs at any level of output since proportionally less variable factors are needed. The price of the fixed factor, v, is irrelevant because short run marginal cost is unaffected by a change in fixed cost.

13.4. a. $C(t, 45) = t^3/3 - t^2 + (300 - 270)t + 2025 = t^3/3 - t^2 + 30t + 2025$ => $P = MC = t^2 -2t+30$ => $t^2 - 2t + (30 - P) = 0$ => $t = 2 + [4 - 4(30 - P)]^{.5}/2 = (P - 29)^{.5}+1$. Note that the positive square root in the quadratic formula is the one which yields a positively sloped supply curve. **b.** SAC $= t^2/3 - t + 30 + 2025/t$; SAVC $= t^2/3 - t + 30$; first order condition for minimizing SAVC: $2t/3 - 1 = 0$ => $t = 3/2$. At the minimum, SAVC $= 29.25$ and SATC $= 1379.25$. **c.** Timothy's maximum profits at $P = 29.25$ are $(29.25 - 1379.25)(1.5) = -2025$, but he will be indifferent between staying in business and closing down since his variable costs are just covered. He would lose 2025 even if he shuts down.

Harcourt Brace & Company

13.5. a. STC = .O5q²+5q+ 125; P = SMC = .lq+5, q = 10P – 50.

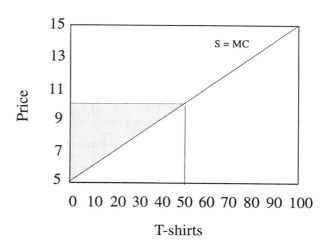

b. q* = 50. **c.** (1/2)(10 – 5)(50) = 125. This area exceeds the firm's profit because it includes fixed cost of $125; i.e., profit is zero. **d.** Area of triangle = (1/2)(P*– 5)(q*) = (1/2)(P*– 5)(10P* – 50) = 5P² – 25P* + 125 = 5P* + 125.

13.6. a (1) (200 - G)G = 200G - G²; (2) 200 - 2G; (3) 40 + G; (4) 40 + 2G; (5) 200G - G² - (40G + G²) = 160G - 2G². **b.** (1) 40; (2) 160; (3) 80; (4) 40(160 - 80) = 3200. **c.** (1) MR = 0 => G** =100; (2) greater; (3) The CEO is ignoring costs. The fact that cost increases faster than revenue for G > 40 doesn't deter her from expanding output; (4) 100; (5) 140; (6) 100(100 - 140) = -4000.   **d.** (1) Profits become zero at G = 80, where AC = P. To the left of this point MR exceeds zero, so she can always increase revenue by expanding up to this point. Beyond this point she risks the wrath of the directors. (2) 80; (3) 120; (4) 120.

13.7. a. π = P(L - .1L²) - 4L; first order condition: P(1-.2L) - 4 = 0 => L = 5 - 20/P. For P = 10, L = 3; q = 3 - .1(9) = 2.1. **b.** L = 5 - 20/8 = 2.5; q = 1.875. **c.** dA/dL = .4(L - L₋₁); d²A/dL² =

.4 > 0, so marginal adjustment cost is increasing. **d.** $\pi = P(L - .1L^2) - 4L - .2(L - L_{-1})^2$; first order condition: $P(1 - .2L) = 4 + .4(L - L_{-1}) => L = (P + .4L_{-1} - 4)/(.4 + .2P)$. **e.** L = 3; The answer is the same as in A because the previous period's value happens to equal the value that would be chosen were there no adjustment costs. **f.** L = 2.56; q = 1.90. L doesn't drop as much as in **b** because the firm is deterred by adjustment costs. **g.** See graphs.

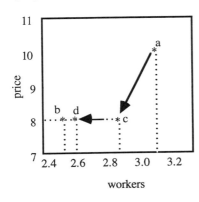

workers

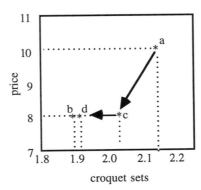

croquet sets

13.8. a. first order condition: $P(1.5 - .2L) = w => L = 7.5 - 5w/P$; For P = 10 and w = 5, L = 5 **b.** Solve the share equation for L: L = 15 - 10w/(sP); For P = 10, w = 5, and s = .5, L = 5 — the same as for the profit-maximizing firm in **a. c.** L falls to 4.375. **d.** If s = .5 is to be maintained, w must fall to .5(8)[(1.5)5 - 2.5]/5 = 4. **e.** FSLS might have a hard time getting lawyers to work for $4.00 if other firms are still paying $5.00, so L may drop despite the contract simply because not enough lawyers can be hired at this wage. In order to get the wage back up to $5.00, L must fall to 4.375 — the same as in the profit-maximizing firm.

13.9. a. first order condition for maximization of s: $PF'(L)/L - [PF(L) - R]/L^2 = 0 => P \cdot MP_L = P \cdot AP_L - R/L$; **b.** $P \cdot MP_L = w$; An increase in P increases the left-hand side of the first order condition, which is the value of the marginal worker's contribution to output. Since this now exceeds the cost of the marginal worker, the number of workers is increased until the value of the marginal worker's product declines to the marginal cost. **c.** Let ΔP represent the change in P. Holding L constant at the original value, the left-hand side of the condition increases by $\Delta P \cdot MP_L$ and the right-hand side by $\Delta P \cdot AP_L$. Since AP_L exceeds MP_L, the right-hand side increases by more! That is, the cost of the marginal worker increases by more than her marginal product. Reducing L will increase the left-hand side. It will also increase the first term on the right-hand side, but the amount it increases is likely to be less than the increase in the left-hand side.[*][PS] A reduction in L will increase R/L, and this increase reduces the right-hand side since R/L appears there with a negative sign. Hence, a reduction in L is the likely outcome. The workers want to share the higher revenue with fewer people.

13.10. a. See graph. **b.** Choose H to maximize $(24 - H)(20H - H^2) = 480H - 44H^2 + H^3$. First order condition: $480 - 88H + 3H^2 = 0$ $\Rightarrow H^* = 88 + [88^2 - 4(3)(480)]^{.5}/6 \approx 7.25$. The other root, which is 22 hours, is a minimum. His profit is about $\pi^* = 92$, which is less than the maximum profit (100). **c.** (1) π_{min}; (2) π^*; (3) No. The distance is maximized where the slopes of the two curves are the same. If you drew your indifference curves carefully, the slope of the next best indifference curve at H^* should be flatter than the slope of the profit function. (4) Yes, because then the slope of the indifference curve for the next best alternative would be the same as the slope of the profit function at H^*.

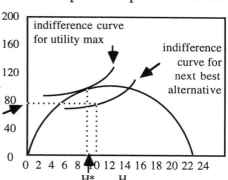

CHAPTER 14

14.1. a. Supply function: $T = 100(P - 29)^{.5} + 100$. Inverse supply function: $P = (T/100)^2 - .02T + 30$. **b.** $P_S = P_D$ $\Rightarrow (T/100)^2 - .02T + 30 = -(T/100)^2 - .02T + 480 \Rightarrow (T/100)^2 = 225 \Rightarrow T = 1500 \Rightarrow P = (1500/100)^2 - .02(1500) + 30 = 225$.

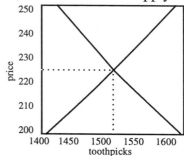

14.2. a. See diagram. **b.** (1) $e_{D,\alpha}$; (2) 5%; (3) .05/[1 - (-1)] = .25%; (4) 5(.25) = 1.25%; (5) (1.0125)(1000) = \$1012.50; (6) $1.25e_{S,P}$ = 2.5%; (7) 1.0125(10000) = 10125. **c.** (1) shifts left by 5%; (2) 5.0/[1 - (-1)] = 2%; (3) 1.025(1000) = \$1025; (4) $2.5e_{D,P}$ = -2.5%; (5) .995(1000) = 9750.

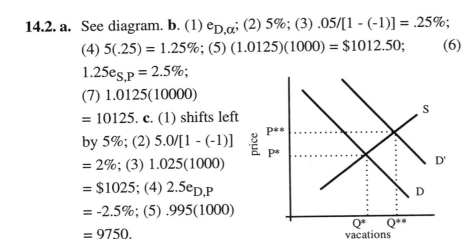

14.3. a. 100000 = 200000 - 20000P => P = 5. **b.** $(\partial Q/\partial P)(P/Q)$ = -20000(5)/100000 = -1. **c.** P = 99999/20000 = 4.9999 **d.** (1) 100(1/1000) = 0.1%; (2) 100(.00005/5) = .001%; (3) .1/.001 = 100. **e.** Supply is Q = 20000P; 20000P = 200000 - 20000P => P = 5 => Q = 100000 in equilibrium. **f.** 1 + 20000P = 200000 - 20000P => P = 199999/40000 = 4.999975. **g.** percent change in P = 100(.000025/5) = .005%; $e_{Q,P}$ = .1/.0005 = 200. **h.** ∞ **i.** The elasticity of a firm's demand curve increases with the elasticity of market demand, the number of firms in the industry, and the responsiveness of other firms to changes in price.

14.4. a. P = MC = t^2 - 20t + 30. **b.** Since 45 = 3(15), Timothy's is on its long run cost function. Hence, AC = (15)2/3 - 10(15) + 300 = 225 = P => π = 0 and there are no incentives to expand, contract, enter, or exit. **c.** The long run supply curve is horizontal at P = 225.

14.5. a (1) (P+1)/2; (2) 40(P+1)/2 = 20(P+1); To verify that P = 4.242, substitute this value into both the short run supply function and the demand function and verify that quantity demanded = quantity supplied = 104.8 at this price; (3) (4.242+1)/2 = 2.621; (4) $(2.621)^2$-2.621 = 4.249 thousand; (5) 6.869; (6) 55. **b.** (1) N/8 = .125N; (2) m^2 - m+.125N; (3) 2m - 1; (4) m - 1+.125N/m; (5) (P+1)/2; (6) An increase in P increases S, holding N constant. The increase in S will attract more pilots — but not enough to completely offset the increase in P; (7) It is at this point that AC is minimized. In the long run, P = MC. If P = MC > AC there are profits and if P = MC < AC there are losses; (8) $8m^2$ (since $2m - 1 = m - 1 + .125N/m$); (9) $8[(P+1)/2]^2$; (10) $8[(P+1)/2]^2[(P+1)/2] = (P+1)^3$. (11) The long run supply curve is flatter than the short run supply curve since new pilots enter as P rises. However it is not horizontal since salaries must increase to attract new pilots. This is an increasing cost industry. **c.** P = 4 thousand dollars per thousand miles; m = 2.5 thousand miles; N = 50 pilots; M = 125 thousand miles; S = 6.25 thousand dollars; AC = 4 thousand dollars. **d.** (1) Yes: S > AC; (2) No: P = AC.

14.6. a. (1) decline at the same rate as AC; (2) elasticity of demand. **b.** (1) AC declines less quickly; (2) output expands less quickly.

CHAPTER 15

15.1

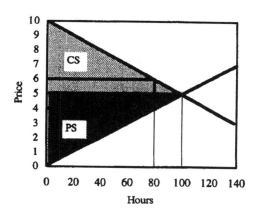

b. CS = $(1/2)(10 - 5)(100) = 250$; PS = $(1/2)(5)(100) = 250$. **c.** (1) $6.00; (2) $4.00; (3) increase; (4) $6.00; (5) $250 - (1/2)(10 - 6)(80) = 90$; (6) $(6 - 5)(80) = 80$; (7) $(1/2)(6 - 5)(10080) = 10$; (8) $(1/2)(5 - 4)(100 - 80) = 10$; (9) $80 - 10 = 70$; (10) $10 + 10 = 20$.

15.2. a. Land is scarce. Building more apartments means either using more valuable land or building taller, more expensive buildings. **b.** See graph. **c.** Excess demand: Tenants who can't find apartments. **d.** Finders fees (rental agents); illegal subletting at higher rents; waiting (lost time); more tenant responsibility for repairs; deteriorating quality; bribes to landlords; and many others. The last three in this list would benefit landlords. **e.** Without a ceiling, A would increase

Harcourt Brace & Company

to A_L and excess
demand would
be eliminated.
The ceiling will
prevent this
from happening,
causing a
housing shortage.

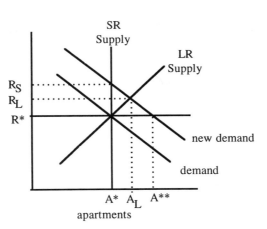

15.3 a. (1) P=215; (2) T=1460; (3) P=225; (4) T=1420; (5) P=
$-130+(T/4)$. **b.** (1)P=150+(T/4); (2) P = 205; (3) P = 215; (4)
T = 1460; (5) 10; (6) 10; (7) P = 205; (8) Q = 1500; (9) 20;
(10) 0; (11) They restored the jobs, as planned, but only by
encouraging the unhealthy habit of picking teeth and using
taxpayers' money; (12) Not really—if consumers were given a
direct subsidy equal to $20, the demand curve would shift
back to its original level and 1500 toothpicks would still be
sold. The new
equilibrium price
of $225 would be
just equal to the
sum of the $205
price under the
employer subsidy
plus the $20
employer subsidy.

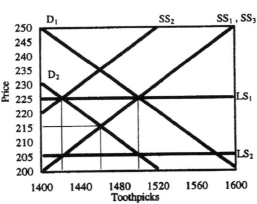

15.4. a. (1) .9B; (2) .8 + .1 + .4 + .2 + .6 + .1 + .1 = 2.3B. **b.** (1) .1 B;
(2) .6B; (3) .1B + (.2B+.4B) = .7B. **c.** First, some loss in
consumer surplus is a deadweight loss becauseconsumers
reduce their consumption and noone gains from this
reduction. Second, some of the loss is transferred to
foreigners and/or the domestic government. Third, as
production expands, marginal cost increases, so higher prices
must be used in part to cover higher costs. **d.** (1) The
purchase of foreign sugar by domestic consumers represents
a transfer of surplus from domestic consumers to foreign

producers; (2) It does not matter to consumers; (3) Political reasons — foreign aid is not popular, whereas protecting domestic jobs is. **e.** (1) Smaller—if the world market price increases then consumer surplus (the area below the demand curve and above the world price in the absence of trade restrictions) would decrease; (2) Smaller—if the world market price rises, then the producer surplus (the area below the market price and above the long-run supply curve) would decrease.

CHAPTER 16

16.1. **a.** See graph. **b.** R = B = 50. **c.** one. **d.** No change since the price ratio must still be one — but rich consumers will have twice as many as poor. **e.** Again, the price must be the same. Half the people spend 75% on R and 25% on B, while the other half do the opposite. If all income are the same, the mythical average person will choose 50% of each color. The average will be different if, say, those in the first group are richer than those in the second. Then R will exceed 50%.

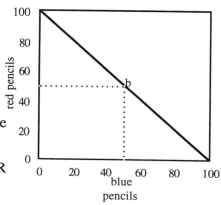

16.2. **a.** $F^2 = L_F$, $M^2 = L_M$, and $L_F + L_M = 100 => F^2 + M^2 = 100$ **b.** Differentiate the PPF to get $2MdM + 2FdF = 0 => RPT_{MF} = -\partial F/\partial M$(holding resources constant) $= M/F$ **c.** $MRS_{MF} = F/3M$ **d.** The two conditions are **(i)** $MRS_{MF} = RPT_{MF}$ and **(ii)** production must be on the PPF. Condition **(i)** $=> F/3M = M/F => 3M^2 = F^2$. Substitute for F^2 in the PPF: $M^2 + 3M^2 = 100 => M = 5 => F = 5(3)^{.5}$. **e.** $P_M/P_F = RPT_{MF} = MRS_{MF} = (3)^{-.5}$. **f.** $L_F = F^2 = 75$; $L_M = 25$.

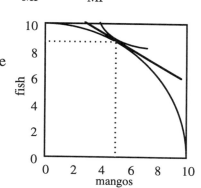

Harcourt Brace & Company

16.3. a. $RTS_{LK} = bk_X$ for X and $RTS_{LK} = dk_Y$ for Y.

Efficiency requires that both are equal: $bk_X = dk_Y$.

If $b > d$, then Y is relatively capital intensive since

$k_Y = (b/d)k_X$. **b.** $(L_X/L)(K_X/L_Y) + (1 - L_X/L)K_Y/L_Y$

$= K_X/L + (L_Y/L)K_Y/Y = (K_X + K_Y)/L = K/L$. **c.** k_X

$= (d/b)k_Y => s(d/b)k_Y + (1-s)k_Y = k => [sd+b(1-$

$s)]k_Y = bk => k_Y = bk/[b + (d-b)s]; k_X = (d/b)k_Y =$

$dk/[b + (d-b)s]$ **d.** $X = K_X{}^\alpha L_X{}^\beta = (K_X/L_X)^\alpha L_X{}^\alpha L_X{}^\beta$

$= k_X{}^\alpha(sL)^{\alpha+\beta} =$

$$\left(\frac{d}{b+(d-b)s}\right)^\alpha\left(\frac{K}{L}\right)^\alpha L^{\alpha} + \beta_s\alpha + \beta = \left(\frac{d}{b + (d-b)s}\right)^\alpha K^\alpha L \beta_s\alpha + \beta;$$

$$Y = \left(\frac{b}{b + (d-b)s}\right)^\gamma K^\gamma L^\delta_s \gamma + \delta$$

e. Third row of table: .5 82 87

last row: 1.0 141 0

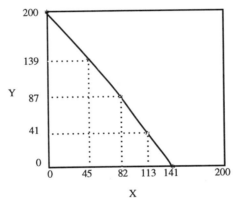

16.4. a. Recorders are more capital intensive: the slope of the line from the recorder origin to 'a' is greater than the slope of the line from the camera origin to 'a'. These slopes are the respective capital-labor ratios. **b.** (1) increases; (2) declines; (3) more capital and labor are allocated to camera production and less to recorder production; (4) increases; (5) increases; (6) increases; (7) For a Cobb-Douglas production function (as well as for any homothetic production function) RTS_{LK} is an increasing function of the capital-labor ratio. Under competition, RTS_{LK} must equal the price of labor relative to the price of capital in both industries. Since K/L has increased in both industries, the price of labor must increase relative to the price of capital. (See graphs on next page.)

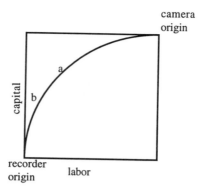
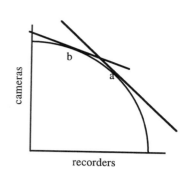

16.5. a. $T_1ED_1 + T_2ED_2 + T_3ED_3 = T_1(X_1^D - X_1^S) + T_2(X_2^D - X_2^S) + T_3(X_3^D - X_3^S) = T_1X_1^D + T_2X_2^D + T_3X_3^D - T_1X_1^S + T_2X_2^S + T_3X_3^S = 0$; Walras' law is satisfied if all tickets are sold. **b.** Yes, since multiplying all prices by the same factor does not change t_2 and t_3. **c.** $ED_1 + t_2ED_2 + t_3ED_3 = 0$ => $ED_1 = 4t_2t_3 - t_2^2 - t_2 - 3t_3^2$, which is homogeneous of degree zero in prices. **d.** $ED_3 = 0$ => $2t^2 - 3t^3 = 0$ => $t^2 = 1.5t^3$; $ED_2 = 0$ => $-1.5t_3 + 2t_3 - 1 = 0$ => $t_3 = 2$ => $t_2 = 3$. **e.** Yes - Walras' Law implies that it must be. **f.** $2000T_1 + 1000T_2 + 2000T_3 = 10000$ => $2000T_1 + 1000(2T_1) + 2000(3T_1) = 10000$ => $T_1 = 1, T_2 = 2, T_3 = 3$.

16.6. a. $1000/100 = .1w$ => $w = 100$. **b.** $(3^{.5})P_M(3^{.55}) + P_M(5) = w = 100 = P_M = 5$; $P_F/P_M = 3^{.5}$ => $P_F = 5(3^{.5})$. **c.** (1) 100; (2) 900; (3) 90/20 = 4.5; (4) 4.5($3^{.5}$); (5) 90; (6) none; (7) none; (8) reduced to 9; (9) yes; (10) no.

16.7. a. (1) open; (2) reserve; (3) reserve; (4) open. **b.** Demand for reserve seats must be continuous. That is, small changes in quantity demanded can be obtained by adjusting the price when quantity demanded is roughly equal to supply. **c.** No. Suppose that excess supply is 2. Lowering the price will increase demand, but a small reduction may cause a large group of students to switch, causing excess demand.

16.8.

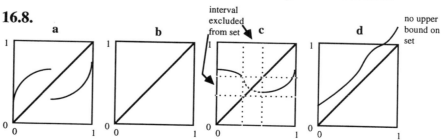

17.1. a. PPF: $F^2+M^2 = 100$; $RPT_{MF} = -\partial M/\partial F$(along PPF) $= M/F$; $MRS_{MF} = F/(3M)$ **b.** (1) 6; (2) 8; (3) $6^{.75}8^{.25} \approx 6.45$; (4) 4/3; (5) 1/4; (6) $MRS_{MF} < RPT_{MF}$ at this point. He is willing to give up M to get F at a ratio of four to one, but he only has to give up M for F at a ratio of three-fourths to one. He should spend more time fishing and less time milking goats; (7) $MRS_{MF} = RPT_{MF}$; (8) $F/(3M) = M/F => F^2 = 3M^2 => 100 = F^2+M^2 = 4M^2 => M = 5$; (9) $75^{.5} \approx 8.67$; (10) $8.67^{.75}5^{.25} \approx 7.55$. **c.** (1) 3; (2) $M+3F = 5+(3)8.66 \approx 31$; (3) $.75(31)/3 \approx 7.7$; (4) 7.7; (5) 7.7; (6) Sell $8.67 - 7.7 \approx 1$ fish and buy $7.7 - 5 = 2.7$ mangos. **d.** (1) Yes, he is on his PPF; (2) Yes, his MRS equals the world price ratio; (3) $RPT_{MF} > MRS_{MF}$. The number of fish he could get by producing one less mango exceeds the number he would need to get to compensate for the loss of a mango; (4) $RPT_{MF} = P_M/P_F$; (5) $M/F = 1/3 => 3M = F => 9M^2 = F^2 => 9M^2 + M^2 = 100 => M^2 = 10 => F^2 = 90 => F \approx 9.5$; (6) 3.16. Note that this point is a little to the left of the vertical axis; (7) $M+3F \approx 31.6$; (8) ≈ 7.9; (9) ≈ 7.9; (10) ≈ 7.9.

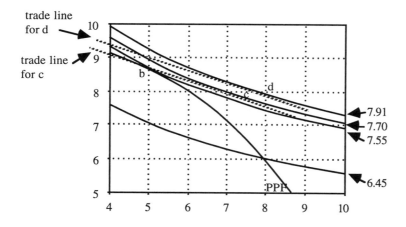

17.2. a. The vertical dimension is the sum of their sardine endowments (6) and the horizontal dimension is the sum of their reindeer endowments (12). **b.** The contract curve follows the horizontal axis from Oscar's Corner to the point (12, 0), then follows the right-hand border of the box up to Sophia's Corner (bold line). **c.** The core is the portion of the contract curve starting at point C, where Oscar's indifference curve intersects the horizontal axis, and ending at point B, where Sophia's indifference curve intersects the right-hand border (bold dashed line). **d.** (1) He will be willing to trade to any point on his indifference curve since it has a slope of -2 sardines per ounce of reindeer. (2) The choices Sophia would be offering can be represented by a line through the endowment point with a slope of -1 (dashed diagonal line). This line also passes through point A, the lower right-hand corner of the box. The highest of Oscar's indifference curves touching this line touches it at point A, so this is the point he   would want to trade to. (3) The trades offered all fall on Sophia's indifference curve. Oscar would choose point B. Oscar's offer curve runs from E to C to A to Sophia's Corner. **e.** Sophia's offer curve runs from E to B to A to Oscar's Corner. **f.** Both

offer curves pass through all points in the core and any price ratio between 2 and .5 will yield an agreement in the core.

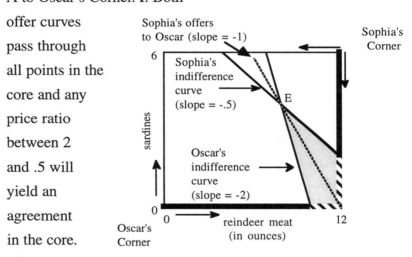

17.3. a. The endowment point is the lower right-hand corner. **b.** Note that the indifference curve for Sayma does not pass through the endowment point. Neither one of these young men can live without beer! Utility approaches $-\infty$ as B approaches 0. **c.** (1) MRS_{BS} must be the same for both; (2) $B_N = B_S$; (3) $B_N = B_S = 3$; the contract curve is the vertical line; the bold part of the line is the core. **d.** (1) The price ratio must be 1/3 (beer is one-third the price of soda) so that the slope of the trade line (see diagram) will be equal to the common value of

MRS_{BS} at $B_N = B_S = 3$. (2) Sayma will give up one soda in exchange for 3 beers and will end up with 5 sodas and 3 beers. Noah ends up with only 1 soda and 3 beers. (3) It would be the same since the common value of MRS_{BS} at all points on the contract curve is 1/3. **e.** (1) Sayma will have more utility (2) Even though Sayma is desperate for beer at the endowment point, the marginal utility of beer declines rapidly with the amount consumed. However, the marginal utility of soda is constant. Once Sayma gets his first drop of beer he is not very willing to give up much soda to get more. Noah has lots of beer and loses little utility at the margin by giving some up. **f.** (1) and (2) Identical MRS_{BS} again implies identical quantities of B, or 6 each, so now the common value of MRS_{BS} at all points in the core is 1/6, which is less than before. (3) The relative abundance of beer has increased. Since it provides very little utility at the margin (relative to soda) its price must fall to clear the market. **g.** (1) 1/3; (2) they are the same; (3) the marginal utility of soda doesn't decline.

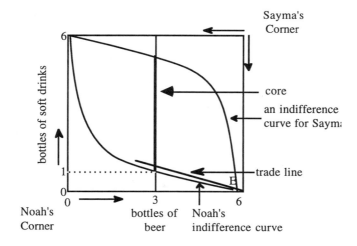

17.4. a. and **b.** See graph on page 398. **c.** MRS must be the same for both. Once's $MRS_{MC} = C_O/M_O$. Twice's $MRS_{MC} = C_T/M_T$. Equality implies $C_O/M_O = C_T/M_T$. **d.** See diagram for trade line.

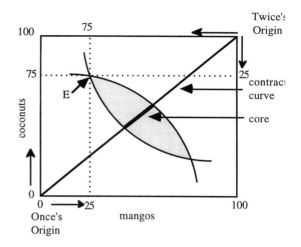

(1) The slope of the trade line is -2/3, which must equal (C - 75)/(M - 25) [point-slope formula for finding the equation of a line]. Equality implies $.67M + C = 91.67$; (2) $.5(91.67)/.67 = 68.8$; (3) $.5(91.67)/1 = 45.8$. See point 'd' in the diagram. (4) $1/X = (C - 75)/(M - 25) => C + (1/X)M = 75 + 25/X$; (5) $37.5X + 12.5$; (6) $37.5 + 12.5/X$; (7) He would stay at E; (8) The trades that Once is willing to make under various terms of trade. **e.** (1) one M per C; (2) Once would give up 25 C in exchange for 25 M; (3) yes; (4) yes; (5) Suppose the terms of trade (TOT) were .5M per C. "Once-types" would not be willing to give up (supply) as much C as "Twice-types" would demand. To induce a greater supply of C, at least some Twice-types would offer more M per C. Once won't trade with Twice under these TOT because better terms are available. The TOT will adjust until supply equals demand, which only occurs at one M per C. **f.** (1) $U_T = (87.5 - 37.5X)(62.5 - 12.5/X)$; the first order condition is $\partial U_T/\partial X = [-37.5(62.5X^2 - 12.5X)+12.5(87.5 - 37.5X)]/X^2 = 0 => -(37.5)(62.5)X^2 + (12.5)(87.5) = 0 => X = .68313$; (2) 38.12; (3) 55.8; (4) they are tangent; (5) To maximize utility Twice must choose the point on Once's offer curve where he has a tangent indifference curve. This cannot be where Once's offer curve intersects the contract curve since at that point Twice's indifference curve has the same slope as the line between E and that point (not drawn), which is steeper than the slope of Once's

Harcourt Brace & Company

offer curve. Twice can increase his utility by moving along Once's offer curve to the point labelled 'f'. Hence, the trade is not efficient. Twice is behaving as a monopolist (see Chapter 19): He chooses the price of M and Once chooses how many mangos to buy. **g.** (1) Yes. There is a new lens space which represents points that would make both of them better off. (2) Eventually, after many such trades, the lens space remaining will diminish to a point on the contract curve. No further trades could improve the utility of one without reducing the utility of the other. (3) First offer terms of trade very close to Once's MRS at E. This will induce Once to trade a tiny amount of C for M, moving the allocation along Once's indifference curve toward the contract curve. Then offer slightly better terms of trade, etc., etc. (4) Twice is now a price-discriminating monopolist. By gradually reducing the "price" of mangos, he gets Once to move to a Pareto Optimum. Twice's utility increases as much as it can, without reducing Once's utility. Once is no better off than before. Everything that can be gained from trade has been gained and Twice got all of it!

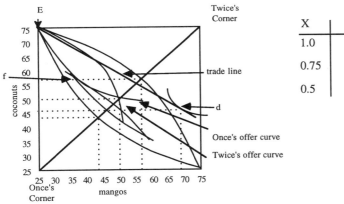

X	M_O	C_O
1.0	50.0	50.0
0.75	40.6	54.2
0.5	31.3	62.5

17.5. **a.** They will trade to point 'a'. This point is on Nick's offer curve, so his indifference curve must be tangent to the trade line at this point. Since this point is also on the contract curve, Nack's indifference curve has the same slope as Nick's and therefore is also tangent to the trade line. Note that any different trade line would yield excess demand or supply of M&Ms among the friends, so the ratio at which they would be exchanged for peanuts would eventually adjust to the one depicted. **b**. Nack will choose point 'b' by creating a trade line through the endowment point and 'b'. Given this trade line, 'b' is Nick's choice. The reason Nack chooses this point is that Nick's offer curve is tangent to one of Nack's indifference curves at this point and only this point. The utility associated with that indifference curve is Nack's maximum utility along Nick's offer curve. **c**. After many trades they will approach 'c', or at least come very close to it. Nack first offers terms of trade that will induce Nick to move just a little way along his offer curve — essentially staying on his original indifference curve. After this trade Nick has a new offer curve and Nack will improve the terms of trade just a little bit in order to get Nick to move just a little way along his new offer curve — again essentially staying on his original indifference curve. The process is repeated until a point on the contract curve is reached. If each trade is small enough, this point will be arbitrarily close to 'c'.

17.6. a. (1) 100/3; (2) 200/3; (3) 100/3; (4) 100/3; (5) 2/1; (6) 1/2; (7) the + point. **b**. (1) 100; (2) 50; (3) 2; (4) 2; (5) Production of mangos is land intensive relative to production of coconuts; the latter is relatively labor intensive. When all resources are devoted to M there is excess L. As M falls and C increases along the PPF a point is reached where L is completely used and A becomes excessive. This is because C is relatively labor intensive. Since L is now scarce, it becomes more difficult to trade M for L. **c**. (1) 1/2; (2) This is RPT_{CM} to the left of the + point. In perfect competition this will equal the price ratio since it is also the ratio of MC_M to MC_C and firms produce where $MC_M = P_M$ and $MC_C = P_C$; (3) 2; (4) M = 100/3 = C; This is the + point, where the RPT is not well defined because of the kink. Suppose $P_C = P_M = 1$, so P_C/P_M = 1. At M = 100/3 = C, $P_M M + P_C C = 200/3$. If M is reduced by 2 and C is increased by 1, this changes to 94/3 + 103/3 = 197/2 < 200/3, so the value of resources is reduced.

Harcourt Brace & Company

Someone will lose money. Hence, $M = C = 100/3$ is a more profitable point. **d.** (1) 2; (2) One, since an additional unit of and would allow production of one more coconut; (3) Zero, since there is surplus labor; (4) No one would want to work. The active labor force would be reduced until there was no longer a surplus. Then, the wage rate would become positive.

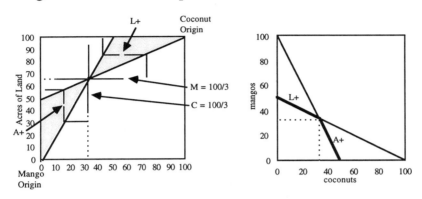

17.7. a. Region A's PPF: $X_A^2 + Y_A^2 = 100$. **b.** Region B's PPF: $X_B^2 + Y_B^2 = 25$; (1) 0; (2) $(25 - 4)^{.5} \approx 4.6$; (3) ≈ 4.6. **c.** (1) slope; (2) $-\partial Y_A/\partial X_A$ (along PPF_A) $= X_A/Y_A$; (3) X_B/Y_B. **d.** (1) RPT's for both regions must be the same; (2) 2; (3) no; (4) Less than: Reduce X_A by one unit. Y_A become $(100 - 81)^{.5} \approx 4.36$. Increase X_B by one unit (so total X is unchanged). Y_B falls to $(25 - 9)^{.5} = 4$, a loss of just .58 units. This is much less than the gain in Y_A. At the initial point RPT_{XY} is greater in region A than in region B, so more Y can be produced without producing less X by increasing X production in B and reducing X production in A by the same amount — at least up to the point where the RPT's in the two regions are identical. **e.** (1) 9; (2) 12; (3) yes; (4) $(15^2 - X^2)^{.5} => X^2+Y^2 = 225$; (5) 9; (6) The new Y. Previously, production was not allocated efficiently between regions. Now, the RPT's in the two regions are the same. **f.** (1) $.5L_{XA}^{-.5}$; (2) $.25L_{XB}^{-.5}$; (3) 1/18; (4) 1/24; (5) Move L from region B to region A since the marginal product of L is higher in A than in B. Moving one unit will increase X production by approximately $1/18 - 1/24 = 1/72$; (6) Equal MP_L's in X production for the two regions; (7) $.5L_{XA}^{-.5} = .25L_{XB}^{-.5} => L_{XA} = 4L_{XB}$. Equal MP_L's in Y production implies $.5L_{YA}^{-.5} =$

$.25L_{YB}^{-.5} => L_{YA} = 4L_{YB}.$ (8) 40; (9) 160; (10) $X_A^2 + Y_A^2 = 160$; (11) $X_B^2 + Y_B^2 = 40$; (12) $X^2 + Y^2 = (160^{.5}+40^{.5})^2 = 250$ (circle with radius of 15.8); (13) ≈ 10.3; (14) The new value is larger. Labor has been moved to the region where it is more productive at the margin — up to the point where the marginal productivities are the same.

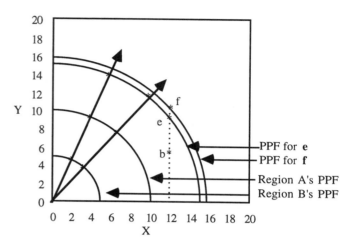

17.8. a. (1) P rises since there is excess demand; (2) Q rises since there is excess demand; (3) Under Walrasian adjustment the market is unstable since P moves away from equilibrium P, but under Marshallian adjustment the market is stable since Q adjusts toward equilibrium Q. **b.** (1) P falls since there is excess supply; (2) Q falls since there is excess supply; (3) Under Walrasian adjustment the market is stable since P moves toward equilibrium P, but under Marshallian adjustment the market is unstable since Q moves away from equilibrium Q.

17.9. a. See diagram. **b.** 75 - 14P = 80 - 20P+P2 => P2 - 6P+5 = 0 => P = -(-6) ± [6² - (4)(5)]·⁵/2 = (1, 5); P = 1 => Q = 75 - 14 = 61; P = 5 => Q = 75 - 14(5) = 5. **c.** The equilibrium at P = 5 is stable under Walrasian adjustment and the equilibrium at P = 1 is stable under Marshallian adjustment

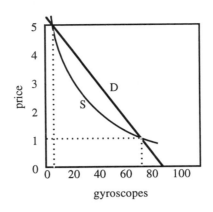

17.10. a. See graph. **b.** Here d = 2 and b = 1. Since d > b, the market is
stable. **c.** QD = 6 - 2P* = 4+P* = QS = P* = 2/3 => Q* = 4+P* =
4.67. **d.** QS = 3+2/3 = 11/3 = 6 - 2P => P = 7/6. **e.** Q = 3+7/6 =
4.17; P = 11/12 = .917 **f.** At t = 3, Q = 47/12 = 3.92 and P =
25/24 = 1.04. At t = 4, Q = 97/24 = 4.04 and P = 47/48 = .979.
g. $P_t = (2/3 - 1)(-.5)t + 1 = 1 - (-.5)t/3$. For t = 1, P_t = 7/6. For t
= 2, P_t = 11/12. For t = 3, P_t

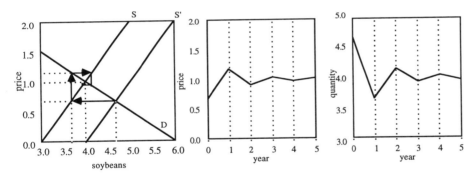

17.11. a. E(P) .5(2/3)+.5(1) = 5/6. **b.** See diagram. **c.** In a good year, Q =
29/6 = 4.83 and P = 7/12 = .583. In a bad year, Q = 23/6 = 3.83
and P = 13/12 = 1.083. **d.** Average P = .5(7/12 + 13/12) = 5/6.
Yes, on average they are right. **e.** See graph. Lines are labelled
"rational". **f.** The lines in the graph are labelled "lagged" for
lagged expectations. For good years $P_t = (P_t^{-1} - 2/2)(-.5)1 + 2/3$
$= 1 -.5P_{t-1}$. For bad years $P_t = 1.5 - .5P_{t-1}$. P_0 = .58, P_1 = 1.21,
P_2 = .40, P_3 = 1.30, P_4 = .35, P_5 = 1.33; Q_0 = 3.58, Q_1 = 5.21,
Q_2 = 3.40, Q_3 = 5.30, Q_4 = 3.35, Q_5 = 5.33. Prices are explosive
under lagged expectations, but quantity is more stable. Price is
greater than the long run "good year" price in year zero because
of the assumption made about prices in the previous year. This

encourages farmers to plant more than they otherwise would, so quantity is higher in the next year than in long run equilibrium for "bad years", and prices are lower. This discourages farmers from planting and the next year quantity is lower than long run equilibrium "good-year" quantity, etc. Of course, if this regular weather pattern persists, the rational expectations would no longer be rational! In general, we expect more stability under rational expectations than lagged expectations since farmers don't expect unusual growing conditions to persist indefinitely.

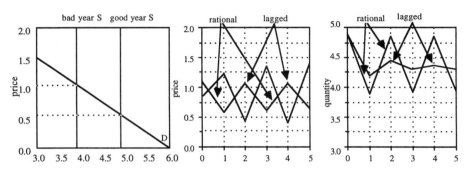

17.12. The initial effect should be to reduce demand for lawyers. Salary growth declines. Fewer people enter law school. As a result there is slower growth in the number of lawyers after a few years and lawyers' salaries start to rise faster. The pattern of salary and quantity adjustment is like that in the cobweb model.

17.13. a. $Q^S = P - 1000$. **b.** $E(V) = (1/1000)(1001 + 1002 + \ldots + 2000) \approx (1000+2000)/2 = 1500$. **c.** $1.5(1500) - P = P - 1000 \Rightarrow P = 1625$. **d.** $E(V) \approx (1625+1000)/2 \approx 1313$; $P = 1485$; The average value of machines sold $= 2485/2 = 1242.5 < E(V)$, so expectations are not realized. They should fall further. **e.** $E(V) = (1000+P)/2 \Rightarrow Q^D = 1.5(1000+P)/2 - P = 750 - .25P$; $Q^S = Q^D \Rightarrow P = 1400 \Rightarrow Q = 400$.

17.14 a. Unless he can convince customers that his car is above average in quality, he is wasting his time. **b.** The model implies improving resale value is not an incentive for maintenance. This is inefficient because people would be willing to pay more to buy a durable good which has been well taken care

Harcourt Brace & Company

of. Of course, the cost of the information is so large that it actually exceeds any benefits that would be realized from better maintenance. If we recognize that information is both valuable and costly, it may not be inefficient. **c.** Yes. The percentage of people with high-quality cars who choose to sell will be smaller than the percentage of people with low-quality cars who choose to sell. An individual may get lucky and buy a "peach", but the average buyer will be left with a lemon.

18.1. a. $P = 5 - .05Q$; $R = PQ = (5 - .05Q)Q = 5Q - .05Q^2 =>$ MR $= \partial R/\partial Q = 5 - .1Q$. **b.** See left-hand graph. **c.** If MR < MC he can increase profits by reducing output since the decline in R will be less than the decline in C. If MR > MC he should increase Q since the increase in R will exceed the increase in C. Hence, he should adjust Q until MR = MC. MR = MC => $5 - .1Q = 1$ => $Q^* = 40$ => $P^* = 5 - .05(40) = \$3.00$ => $p^* = 40(3 - 1) = \$80$; $CS^* = .5(2)(4) = \$40$; CS^* is the amount that consumers would be willing to pay to prevent a price increase from \$3.00 to \$5.00. Under a price ceiling of \$1.00 Doug will sell 80 dogs. The reason is that his MR equals the ceiling price if he sells 80 or fewer dogs, so setting MR equal to MC is the same as setting P equal to MC. He behaves like a competitor. **d.** $P_C = \$1.00$ since, under competition P = min(AC) in the long run and MC = AC = \$1.00. $Q_C = 100 - 20(1.00) = 80$; $CS_C = .5(4)(80) = \$160$; $p^* + CS^* = 80 + 40 = 120 < CS_C = 160$. The difference is deadweight loss. Consumers would lose 160 - 40 = 120 because of the price increase. The monopolist gains only $p^* = 80$ from this loss. The remainder is lost to everyone. The number of vendors can't be determined due to constant MC. There could be 80 selling one dog each or one selling 80 dogs. Even so, just the threat of entry will keep P = MC = 100. If a "monopoly" seller tried to sell at P = \$1.05, another vendor would enter and take all his business. **e.** MC is unaffected, so Q*, P*, and CS* are unaffected. However, profit drops to \$75.00. (1) \$6.00; (2) \$7.00; (3) \$1.00; (4) $1 + 5/Q$; (5) $5 - Q/20$; (6) $1 + 5/Q = 5 - Q/20 => .05Q^2 - 4Q + 5 = 0 => Q = \{4 \pm [16 - 4(.05)(5)]^{.5}/.01 \approx 40 \pm 39$. Since Q = 1 is a minimum, choose Q = 79; (7) $5 - 79/20 \approx \$1.05$; (8) He won't get any business; (9) No. If both sell at \$1.05, revenue will be 79(1.05) = \$82.95 and cost will be 2(5) + 79 = 89, so at least one will lose money; (10) No. He has the same costs as Doug. He will get all the business, but have losses since \$1.05 is the lowest price consistent with no loss; (11) Enter and sell at a price between \$1.05 and \$1.25; (12) no; (13) There will be one vendor. About 79 hot dogs will be sold at a price of about \$1.05. There will be no profits; (14) This is false unless there is some barrier to entry. As long as there is a credible threat of entry, the monopolist will be forced to sell at P = AC. Otherwise, another firm will enter and take all the business. **f.** The maximum fee is \$80 — his monopoly profit. Q will not be affected since Doug's MC and MR are unaffected. **g.** See right-hand graph. If a monopolist charged P = MC + t, the shaded area would be her profit. To maximize profits she would choose P = \$3.00. With MC = \$1.00, t = 3 - 1 = \$2.00. **h.** No. P, Q, and tax revenue will be the same in both cases.

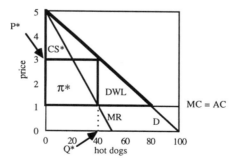 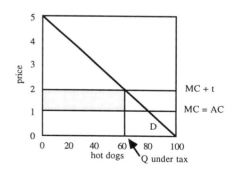

18.2. a. $MR = 5 - .1Q = MC = 1 => Q = 40 => P = 5 - .05(40) = 3$.
b. Q = 40 again; P = 5. **c.** Q = 40 again, P = 2. **d.** See graph.
e. $P \geq 1; Q \geq 0$. **f.** By definition a supply curve tells how much a firm will supply at each possible price. In this example, the quantity the monopolist will supply at any given price is not

determined by P alone. For P > 1, Q could be any positive number. The monopolist's choice depends on the slope (or elasticity) of D as well as its height at any given Q. Under perfect competition, only the height matters to each firm.

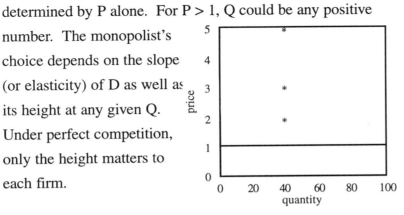

18.3. a. (1) $Q(10 - Q/10M) = 10Q - .1Q^2/M$; (2) $10 - .2Q/M$; (3) increase; (4) $MR = MC => Q = 45M$; (5) $10 - .01(45M)/M = 5.5$; (6) no; (7) $P*Q* - (Q*+1000) = 5.5(45M) - 45M - 1000 = 202.5M - 1000$. **b.** $\Pi_{net} = \Pi* - A = 202.5(20A - .01A^2) - 1000 - A$; first order condition for maximizing net profit: $\partial\Pi_{net}/\partial A = \partial\Pi*/\partial A - 1 = 0$. $\partial\Pi*/\partial A$ is marginal gross profit from A and the marginal cost of advertising is one. If $\partial\Pi*/\partial A > 1$, net profits can be increased by advertising more — marginal gross profit is greater than the marginal cost of advertising. The reverse is true if $\partial\Pi*/\partial A < 1$. $\partial\Pi_{net}/\partial A = 202.5[20 - .02A] - 1 => A \approx 1000$; $P = 4.5$; $Q = 550,000$; $\Pi_{net} \approx 2,023,000$; $\Pi* = 2,024,000$; P is not necessarily affected by A, as in this example. The benefit to the advertiser in this case comes from the increased quantity sold, not the higher price. This is not always true.

18.4. a. $P_I = 50 - .25Q_I$; $P_U = 25 - .125Q_U$; $R_I(Q_I) = (50 - .25Q_I)Q_I$; $MR_I = 50 - .5Q_I$; $R_U(Q_U) = (25 - .125Q_U)Q_U$; $MR_U = 25 - .25Q_U$. **b.** first order conditions: **(i)** $R_U'(Q_U) - C'(Q_U+Q_I) = 0 => MR_U = MC$; **(ii)** $R_I'(Q_I) - C'(Q_U+Q_I) = 0 => MR_I = MC$; **(i)** and **(ii)** $=> MR_I = MR_U$; If $MR_U > MC$, he should increase Q_U to increase profits since marginal revenue exceeds marginal cost. The reverse is true if $MR_U < MC$. The same argument applies to $MR_I = MC$. **c.** (1) $MR_I = MC$ $=> 25 - .25Q_U = .01(Q_U+Q_I) =>$

    (i) $1250 - .5Q_I - 13Q_U = 0$ $MR_I = MR_U => 50 - .5QI$ $= 25 - .25QI =>$

(ii) $\underline{-(25 - .5Q_I + .25Q_U) = 0}$

(i) + (ii) $1225 + 0Q_I - 13.25Q_U = 0 => Q_U \approx 92$; (2) $Q_I \approx 96$;

(3) \$13.50; (4) \$26.00; (5) $(.8)(96)(26) = 1996.80$. **d**. (1) $-8(13.5)/92 \approx -1.17$; (2) $-(4)(26)/96 \approx -1.08$; (3) smaller; (4) Yes. If MR is to be the same in both markets, P must be higher in the market with more inelastic demand since the more inelastic demand is, the greater is the difference between P and MR. The reason for the latter is that MR is less than P only because P must fall to induce consumers to buy more. The more inelastic demand is, the more P must fall; (5) no; (6) Demand is inelastic if and only if MR < 0. But to maximize profits, MR must equal MC. Since the latter is positive, MR must be positive and demand must be elastic. **e**. $Q = Q_I + Q_U = 400 - 12P => P = 400/12 - Q/12 => MR = 400/12 - Q/6$. MR = MC = 0.1Q => Q = 125; (1) \$22.92; (2) \$22.92; (3) 16.6; (4) 108; (5) -11.2; (6) -.84; (7) $.8(108)(22.9) \approx 1980$; (8) fell, but only by about \$17; (9) No. Insurance payments could have increased! Remember that if demand is elastic, a fall in P increases expenditures. Here expenditure fell because we moved to the inelastic part of the insured demand curve, but this does not necessarily happen; (10) Insurers might actually support discrimination if it reduced their costs, as it could. Of course, they may also have to reduce their insurance rates in order to keep their customers. Uninsured patients benefit from discrimination: They get a lower cost. Holding rates constant, insured patients lose: If they pay a percentage of the bill, as in the example, they must pay that percentage of the higher, discriminatory price. **f**. He's just trying to give a break to poor people who can't afford insurance. **g**. In general, there is no arbitrage of health services. If there was, the uninsured could buy at a low price and resell to the insured, undercutting the price discrimination.

19.1. a. See diagram on left. The monopoly point is labelled M and the competitive point is labelled "competition". **b.** (1) $P = 5 - .05Q = 5 - .05(Q_D+Q_F) => \pi_D = Q_D[5 - .05(Q_D+Q_F)] - Q_D = 4Q_D - .05Q_D^2 - .05Q_DQ_F$; (2) first order condition: $4 - .1Q_D - .05Q_F = 0 => Q_D = 40 - .5Q_F$; (3) $Q_F = 40 - .5Q_D$; (4) $40 - .5(40) = 20$; (5) Doug would respond by reducing his output to $40 - .5(20) = 30$. Frank would then respond by expanding to $40 - .5(30) = 25$. This process would continue until equilibrium is approached; (6) Equilibrium is the point where the two reaction functions intersect. $P = 7/3$; (7) 80/3; (8) 80/3; (9) 160/3; (10) $(4/3)(80/3) = 320/9$; (11) 320/9; (12) $640/9 \approx 71$. The Cournot point is labelled C in the two diagrams.

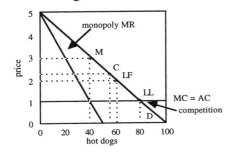

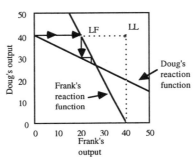

c. (1) They behave as if the other doesn't react to their own choices, whereas they can easily observe that the other does react; (2) $4Q_D - .05Q_D^2 - .05(40 - .5 Q_D) = 2Q_D - .025Q_D^2$; first order condition: $2 - .05Q_D = 0 => Q_D = 40$; (3) 20; (4) 60; (5) $5 - .05(60) = \$2.00$; (6) \$40; (7) \$20; (8) \$60; The leader-follower solution is labelled LF in the two diagrams. **d.** (1) 40; (2) 80; (3) 1; (4) 0; (5) 0; (6) 0; The leader-leader solution is labelled LL in both diagrams and coincides with the competitive solution. Now that Frank is leading, Doug would be better off following! Maybe he will switch back — but Frank may too! If they both switch, they will move back to the Cournot solution and again they will both have an incentive to lead! **e.** In the monopoly case profit is \$80. Combined profits and price fall as we move from monopoly to Cournot to leader-follower to leader-leader, while Q increases. The leader-leader outcome is identical to the competitive outcome (although this is not always so.) The more aggressive firms are in pursuing profits, the lower are industry profits. Profits are highest if they collude and control the industry as if they are a single monopolist. Markets of this sort are likely to be unstable unless firms behave cooperatively.

19.2. a. Let q and p represent the quantity and price of the typical station and let π represent its profit. $q = -.01(N-1)p + .01S + 110/N$; $\pi = pq - 1000q - 1000 = (p - 1000)q - 1000 = (p - 1000)[-.01(N-1)p + .01S + 110/N] - 1000$; first order condition: $[-.01(N-1)p + .01S + 110/N] - .01(N-1)(p - 1000) = 0 \Rightarrow p = -50[.01S + 110/N + 10(N-1)]/(N-1)$. **b**. $p^* = -50[.01(N-1)p^* + 110/N + 10(N-1)]/(N-1) \Rightarrow p^* = 1000 + 11000/[N(N-1)]$; $q^* = 110/N$; $\pi^* = (11000)(110)/[N^2(N-1)]$. **c**. (1) In the long run, entry and exit will occur until profits are zero; (2) $\pi^* = (11000)(10)/[11^2(10)] - 1000 = 0$; (3) $1100 per thousand gallons; (4) 10 thousand gallons;

(5) p^*; (6) no; (7) Under perfect competition, p^* = MC = AC and AC is minimized. This can't happen in the example since MC < AC for all values of q.

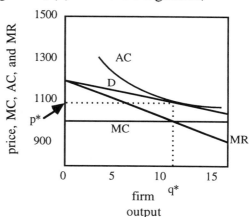

19.3. a. $P = 1 + 500 \Rightarrow q = P - 500$ for the typical fringe firm. The supply curve for all fringe firms combined is $Q_{fringe} = 10(P - 500) = 10P - 500 \Rightarrow P = 500 + .1Q_{fringe}$. **b**. (1) $m + 10q = 35000 - 10P \Rightarrow m = 35000 - 10P - 10(P - 500) = 40000 - 20P$; (2) $2000 - .05m$; (3) $2000 - .1m$; (4) MR = MC $\Rightarrow m^* = 10,000$; (5) 1500; (6) 20000; (7) 20000; The shaded area in the graph is part of the consumer surplus. Not all of the surplus appears on the graph because only a section of the demand function is plotted. **c**. (1) 1500; (2) Fringe firms would be put out of business. P would fall to 1000. Q would increase to 25000. CS would increase. **d.** P would increase to 2000 (intersection of market demand and fringe supply), Q would fall to 15000 and CS would fall. Of course, m would be zero. P* = min(AC) = 1500 in the long run. Fringe supply would shift to the right until it intersects market demand at (Q*, P*). The number of firms would double. To consumers it does not matter whether EPC is in the industry. EPC reaps all the benefits of its low costs. Consumers get no benefits, as can be seen by the fact that consumer surplus, P, and Q are unaffected by EPC's absence in the long run.

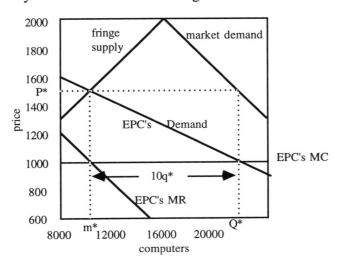

19.4. a. $P_D + .01X = P_F + .01Y = P_F + .01(120 - X) => X = 50(P_F - P_D) + 60 => Y = 50(P_D - P_F) + 60$. **b.** $\pi_D = (50 + X)(P_D - 1)$ $= [110 + 50(P_F - P_D)](P_D - 1) = 160P_D + 50P_FP_D - 50P_D^2 - 50P_F - 110$; $\pi_F = 140P_F + 50P_FP_D - 50P_F^2 - 50P_D - 90$. **c.** first order condition for maximizing Doug's profit (given P_F): $160 + 50P_F - 100P_D = 0 => P_D = 1.6 + .5P_F$; Frank chooses $P_F = 1.4 + .5P_D$. **d.** $P_D = 1.6 + .5(1.4 + .5P_D) => P_D = \$3.07$; $P_F = \$2.93$. Doug charges a higher price because he has more customers to the west than Frank has to the east. If Doug lowered his price, all west-end customers will pay less; the lost revenue from them would be greater than the revenue Frank would lose from east-end customers if he lowered his price by the same amount. **e.** Both would locate at the center. To see why, suppose first that Frank has to stay put but Doug can move. Holding his price constant, Doug can steal some of Frank's customers and increase his profits by moving closer to him—up to 14 yards away (the difference in their prices is $.14). But if Frank can move he will move closer to Doug. In fact, as long as Doug keeps his high price and Frank gets within 14 yards, Frank will get all the customers. So Doug will have to lower his price and their prices will always be the same. Whatever that price is, their objective is reduced to getting the most customers. If Doug locates at a point other than the center, Frank will locate right next to him, but towards the center, and get more than half the customers. Then Doug will want to leapfrog over Frank, towards the center, etc. Eventually, they will both end up at the center, each with half the customers. Whatever price they choose, there is some inefficiency because people are willing to pay to avoid walking. Total walking distance for all consumers combined would be minimized if Doug located 50 yards from one end and Frank located 50 yards from the other.

19.5. Monopolistically competitive. There are many texts (perhaps 15 to 20), but each is different from the rest. Since some instructors prefer one over all others and are not too concerned about prices students pay, each has a steep downward sloping demand function. However, free entry guarantees that few authors make excess profits. Some do, but others lose money (at least if their opportunity cost is taken into account). This is a risky business and it may be that expected excess profits must be positive in order to compensate for the risk taken by authors who must write their books before they know how the books will sell.

One reason books are revised frequently is to prevent resale of used books. After three or four years up to 50% of students may buy used versions of their assigned texts. This would not happen if the market was perfectly competitive since one book could not be distinguished from the next. Students would continue to buy used texts — perhaps by other authors. Almost all durable goods are "revised" frequently: automobiles, appliances, sporting equipment, electronic equipment, clothes, etc. Many revisions (e.g., styling changes) are made simply to distinguish the new from the old. Can you think of a durable good which is not frequently revised?

Harcourt Brace & Company

20.1. a. (1) Revenue - Cost = .15Q - .10Q = .5Q = .05[1000 - 100(.15)]/2 = 24.625; (2) Revenue - Cost = .14Q - .10Q = .04[1000 - 100(.14)] = 39.44; (3) 14; (4) 0; (5) 13; (6) reducing its price to 12 cents; (7) 10; (8) Bertrand; (9) 0; (10) is. **b.** (1) (.10 - .08)[1000 - 100(.10)]/2 = 9.9; (2) (.09 - .08)[1000 - 100(.09)]/2 = 9.91; (3) 9; (4) 0; (5) 0; (6) negative; (7) go out of business; (8) is not.

20.2. a. No. **b.** No. For all possible strategy pairs, one of the two will want to switch. **c.** They may not be very stable—at least if collusion is not permitted and these are the only strategies available. **d.** No, this is not an equilibrium strategy since this is not a zero-sum game. Note that minimizing the other vendor's maximum expected profits is not the same as maximizing your own minimum expected profits since the one's loss is not the other's gain. The mixed-strategy described does not yield the most profits for the two vendors together, so there will be incentives for each of them to abandon that strategy for another.

20.3. a.

	Frank's Location		
	50 yds. from west	center	50 yds. from east
50 yds. from west	D: 50 F: 50	D: <50 F: >50	D: 50 F: 50
Doug's Location center	D: >50 F: <50	D: 50 F: 50	D: >50 F: <50
50 yds. from east	D: 50 F: 50	D: <50 F: >50	D: 50 F: 50

b. Both will move to the center. This is an equilibrium since neither can get more customers by moving. All other positions are disequilibrium positions since one of them will have an incentive to move.

20.4 a. (1) $P = 10 = .01w_K - .01w_N$; (2) $p_K = (10 - .01w_K - .01w_N)w_K - .10 w_K$; (3) $10 - .02w_K - .01w_N - .10 = 0 \Rightarrow 9.9 - .02w_K -$

$.01w_N$; (4) $9.9 - .02w_N - .01w_K = 0$; (5) $9.9 - .03w_N = 0 \Rightarrow w_N = w_K = 330$; (6) Cournot; (7) $P = 10 - .02(330) = 3.4$; (8) is not. **b.** (1) $9.95 - .02 w_{KH} - .01w_N = 0$; (2) $9.85 - .02W_{KL} - .01 W_N = 0$; (3) $E(p_N) = (10 - .01(.5w_{KH} + .5 w_{KL}) - .01w_N)w_N - .10w_N$; (4) $9.9 - .01(.5w_{KH} + .5 w_{KL}) - .02 w_N = 0$; (5) $.5(9.95 - .02w_{KH} - .01w_N) + .5(9.85 - .02w_{KL} - .01 w_N) = 0 \Rightarrow$ (Equation A) $9.9 - .02 E(w_K) - .01 w_N = 0$. The equation in (4) implies (Equation B) $9.9 - .01E(w_K) - .02w_N = 0$. Equations A and B are identical to the equations you solved in **a** except that $E(w_K)$ replaces w_N. Therefore, $w_N = E(w_K) = 330$. This and your answer to (1) $\Rightarrow$ $9.95 - .02w_{KH} - .01(33) = 0 \Rightarrow w_{KH} = 335 \Rightarrow w_{KL} = 325$; (6) w_N is the same and $E(w_K)$ is the same as the certain value of w_K in **a**; (7) NN could figure out that KK's MC is .05 from KK's *ex post* choice, then adopt this value in planning output for the next month. More generally, a firm's pricing behavior can reveal information about its operating costs to it competitors.

CHAPTER 21

21.1. a. $MP_L = \partial q/\partial L = 6L^{-.5}$; $VMP_L = 6PL^{-.5}$; See left-hand diagram. **b.** (1) If $w < VMP_L$, the extra revenue he gets from hiring another teen exceeds the cost of the teen, so his profits will go up. If the reverse is true, the lost revenue from firing a teen will be less than the reduction in cost; (2) $w = 6PL^{-.5} \Rightarrow$ $L = 36(P/w)^2$; (3) $36(5/3)^2 = 100$; (4) \$300; (5) $12(100)^{.5} = 120$; (6) $5(120) = 600$; (7) $600 - 300 = 300$. **c.** $q = 12L^{.5} = 12[36(P/w)^2]^{.5} = 72P/w$; See middle diagram. **d.** (1) $24(6) = 144$; (2) shifts up; See middle diagram; (3) 144.

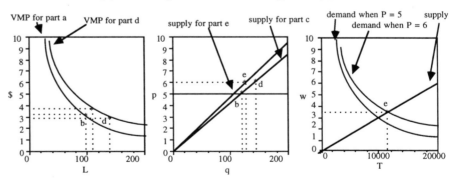

e. (1) $3600(P/w)^2$; (2) $10000w/3 = 3600(6/w)^2 \Rightarrow w = 3.39$; (3) $10000(3.39)/[3(100)] = 113$; (4) $72(6)/3.39 \approx 127$; See right-hand graph. **f.** Factor demand is derived from demand for outputs. For a competitive firm, an increase in output price shifts its factor demand functions. Here, an increase in P shifts VMP_L for Putt. If P increases for all firms together, the market demand curve for teens shifts.

21.2. a. $7200P/w = 60000/P \Rightarrow P^2 = 25w/3$; $T = 30000/w$; As w increases for all firms together, all firms' cuke supply curves shift back. If demand is not infinitely elastic, P increases. This makes it profitable for each firm to increase output by hiring more teens. Thus "teens demanded" doesn't fall as much as it would have if P had remained constant. See the left-hand diagram. **b.** (1) $30000/4 = 7500$; (2) 13,333; (3) "involuntary unemployment" or "excess supply"; (4) shifts backward to

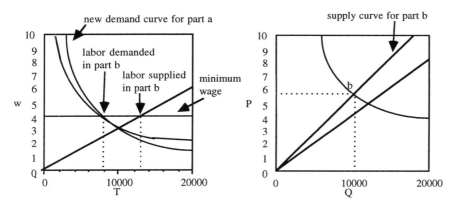

7200P/4 = 1800P; (5) $1800P = 6000/P \Rightarrow P = 5.77$; (6) $60000/5.77 = 10392$; (7) $5.77(103.92) - 4(75) \approx 300$ — almost unchanged! (8) The only change would be an increase in involuntary unemployment; (9) P would increase less, teens employed would fall more, quantity would fall more, unemployment would increase, and profit would fall. (To help understand this, consider infinitely elastic demand. Then, the old demand for labor is relevant.) **c.** (1) See left-hand diagram. The marginal cost of labor to Putt is now w*. To maximize profits he chooses L such that $w* = VMP_L$. Hence, $w - s = VMP_L$ or $w = VMP_L + s$. His old demand curve is shifted up by amount s. Since total demand is 100 times Putt's demand, it too is shifted up by s; (2) teens demanded = $30000/(4 - s) = 100000(4)/3$ = teens supplied $\Rightarrow$ s = $1.75; (3) s > $1.00. Raising w encourages more teens to work. They must be employed to keep w up, but producers won't employ them unless their net wage ($w*$) falls; (4) 13,333; (5) 4 - 1.75 = 2.25; (6) $7200P/w*$ See right-hand graph below; (7) $7200P/2.25 = 60000/P => P \approx 4.33$; (8) 13,856; (9) $4.33(138.56) - 2.25(133.33) \approx 300$; (10) The subsidy would be greater, employment would be greater, the price would be lower, and quantity sold would be higher. Profits would be unchanged. Revenue is unchanged because the cuke demand curve has unit elasticity. Wages are unchanged because the labor demand curve has unit elasticity; (11) Price would decrease less, quantity would increase more, the subsidy would be less since teen demand would be more elastic, and employment would be the same. Profit would increase, as can be seen in the extreme case of infinitely elastic demand: Both revenue and labor cost increase, but the former increases faster. **d.** Teens and parents would both favor subsidies. Cuke farmers don't care — but this depends on their production functions and the elasticity of demand. Pickle companies prefer the subsidy. The farm workers' union and wealthy voters prefer the minimum wage.

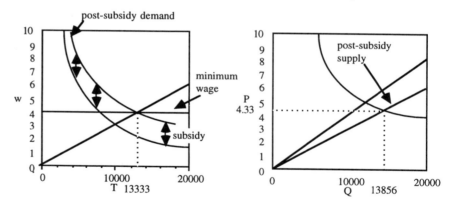

21.3. a. $RTS_{LK} = K/L = w/v => K = wL/v => q = 2(w/v)^{.5}L => L = (v/w)^{.5}q/2 => K = (w/v)^{.5}q/2$; (1) 100; (2) 36; (3) $wL + vK = w[(v/w)^{.5}q/2] + v[(w/v)^{.5}q/2] = (vw)^{.5}Q$; (4) $(vw)^{.5}$; When $w = 3$ and $v = 25/3$, $MC = (25)^{.5} = 5$. **b.** (1) $P = MC$ (= AC); (2) $q = 600/P = 600/MC = 600/(vw)^{.5}$; (3) $300/w$; (4) $300/v$; (5) $30000/w$; (6) They are identical; (7) no effect; (8) $[4.32(25/3)]^{.5}(120/2) - 36 = 7.2$; (9) 100; (10) 36; (11) 7.2; (12) The output effect dominates if demand is very elastic and the elasticity of substitution is small (substitution is difficult); (13) The substitution effect dominates if the

Harcourt Brace & Company

elasticity of substitution is large and the demand elasticity is small; (14) In this example the two effects are the same because the short run output effect on labor demand is just enough so that the desired long run ratio of capital to labor is achieved without adjustment of the capital stock. Suppose instead that the ratio achieved is actually greater than the desired long run ratio. For a given level of output the firm would hire more labor and get rid of capital. This would make labor demand less elastic in the long run. However, long run MC may exceed short run MC since the cost of capital must be taken into account, so output may be reduced, causing labor demand to be more elastic. The relative sizes of these effects will determine whether long run demand is more or less elastic than short run demand.

21.4. a. See diagram. **b.** (1) $L^2/10$; (2) $L/5$; (3) MFC = VMP => L = 100; (4) $L/10 = 10$; (5) $(400 - 100)/15 = 20$. **c.** (1) $(400-L)L/15$; (2) $(400 - 2L)/15$; (3) $L^2/10$; (4) MFC = $L/5$; (5) MR = MC => L = 80; (6) $(400-80)/15 = 21.33$; (7) 8; (8) $21.33 - 8.00 = 13.33$ **d.** No. If the union gets its way (which is unlikely) the difference between the marginal cost to the firm and the net wage paid to the marginal worker is bigger than when there is no union. L is cut back even further below the efficient level (the level where supply and VMP intersect). **e.** Then, countervailing power might work. The union would choose a wage rate equal to the wage at the intersection of VMP and supply. Given this wage the firm would buy the corresponding amount of labor since MFC would be horizontal at this wage rate up to this point. Any higher wage would reduce demand and any lower wage would reduce supply.

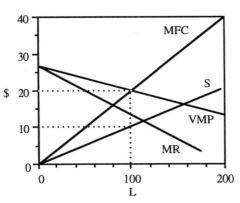

21.5. a. (1)1; (2) 2; (3) female; See diagrams below. **b.** (1) total factor cost of male nurses is $S_mN_m = N_m{}^2/4 => MFC_m = N_m/2$; (2)

$N_f\cdot 5/2$. **c.** (1) 3600; (2) 20,000; (3) 60; (4) 15,000. **d.** (1) The number of female nurses will fall, the number of male nurses will increase, the female salary will fall, and the male salary will increase. MFC for the two groups combined will be somewhere between MFC for the separate groups. Fewer nurses will be hired; (2) Male nurses oppose discrimination since there will be fewer employed and at lower salaries. Female nurses and the female-dominated labor union will favor discrimination since the effects on female employment and salaries are opposite those for males. The Board will also favor discrimination since it lowers the marginal cost of hiring nurses. **e.** They will do it if they can get away with it, since it lowers their marginal factor costs. Their union is likely to support it too, since most of the union members are better off.

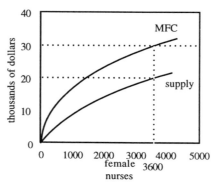
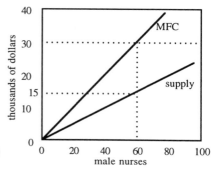

CHAPTER 22

22.1. a. L = 24 - H => wH + C = 24w + N. **b.** (1) $245; (2) $10 per hour. **c.** (1) $1.00; (2) w; (3) 24w + H; (4) 6w + .25N; (5) 18 + .75N/w; (6) 6 - .75; (7) 25%; (8) 6. **d.** (1) zero; (2) 240; (3) -10. **e.** L = 12 - .5N/w. **f.** (1) $7.00; (2) no effect; (3) the income effect of the tax is negative but the substitution is positive and exactly cancels the income effect; (4) 3(12) = 36; (5) 3 (6) = 18.

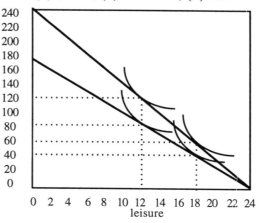

22.2. a. (1) 3; (2) 45; (3) 87. **b.** (1) 5.68; (2) 10; (3) The reason is their higher unearned incomes. Leisure is a normal good, so they both want to consume more for any given wage rate.

c.

Hours Worked (L)	Income (I)	Tax(T)
0	0	0
3	30	6
6	60	15
9	90	27
12	120	39

(1) 15; (2) 39; (3) 18 and 36, respectively. Bones pays less and Adams pays more; (4) Because taxes as a percentage of income increase with income. **d.** (1) 5.6; (2) 11.25; (3) For people in high income brackets, the effect of making the tax progressive is the same as the effect of increasing the proportional tax rate and partially compensating for the higher taxes with a lump-sum transfer. Whatever the effect of the tax rate increase alone on labor supply is (it is zero in the example), the transfer is certain to have a positive effect on demand for leisure and, equivalently, a negative effect on labor supply. **e.** (1) reduce it; (2) revenue will fall; (3) Total revenue would remain the same if labor supplied was unchanged, but since labor supplied declines revenue must decline; (4) The implicit compensation effect of a progressive tax on labor supply would still exist, but the income and substitution effects of an increase in the tax rate might not exactly offset each other. If the income effect is large enough and the substitution effect is small enough, a progressive tax could increase labor supplied by high income individuals, rather than decrease it.

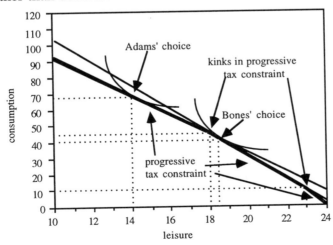

f. This is an empirical matter because of the possibility that the income effect is large enough to cause a decrease in labor supplied when an income tax becomes less progressive. Most economists believe this can be ruled out, but the evidence is less clear than we would like it to be.

22.3. a. See diagram. **b.** 12. **c.** Hours worked increases to 16. There is no substitution effect. Since the income effect of the wage decline on leisure is negative, he reduces leisure and increases labor. **d.** It will increase labor supply as illustrated by the wage drop in **c.** This is because of the negative income effect and the zero substitution effect. **e.** 16 hours **f.** (1) income will decline; (2) no; (3) They will work more since they will have excess time for consumption if they don't; (4) They will increase. (5) They will decline. **g.** This further illustrates a possibility pointed out in the previous problem. If income effects of a wage rate increase dominate substitution effects by a sufficient amount, high wage workers will increase labor supply.

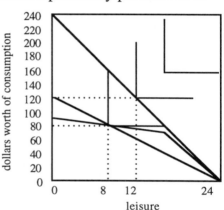

22.4. a. home-cooked, home-grown **b.** See diagram. **c.** If the income effect is large enough, she may reduce hours of work at her job. The expenditure-to-household time ratio will increase since homotheticity implies that the new choice must be above the "home-cooked, home-grown" ray. **d.** In general, wage taxes make household production relatively more attractive. When taxes increase, people may substitute household work for market work. As demonstrated in the previous two questions, progressive taxes have a greater negative impact on labor supply when "leisure" is a good substitute for consumption. If leisure is interpreted as household work, it may be a very good substitute for consumption of market goods.

Harcourt Brace & Company

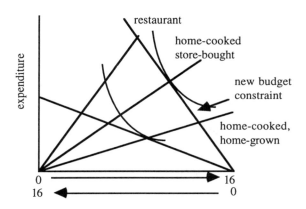

22.5. a. (1) 15; (2) 0; (3) 9; (4) 75; (5) 125; (6) 0. **b.** Jack should work at his job full time. Jill should work at her job part time and at home part time. **c.** Now, Jill should spend all of her time doing housework. Jack should do some housework and work part time at his job. **d.** As long as Jill consumes a fixed percentage of household output, an increase in total output will increase her consumption. Hence, she will want to maximize Q. **e.** Jill has a comparative advantage in housework. The opportunity cost of a unit of housework for her is less than for Jack both because of her lower wage rate and because she is more efficient at housework. Jack has a comparative advantage in market work. His opportunity cost of a unit of household expenditure is lower than Jill's both because he has a higher wage rate and because he is less efficient at housework. By specializing (at least to some degree) in the activities in which they have comparative advantages they are able to increase household output above what it would be if they each spent the same percentage of time in the market.

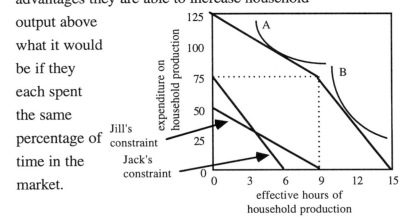

22.6. a. The opportunity cost of the housewife's time is $7.00. If she is freely choosing to be a housewife, her time is worth $7.00 an hour to her. **b.** Enjoyment of time with her children, better working environment, higher quality housework and childcare than she can purchase at $5.00 an hour, protection of family privacy, and many others. There may be negative differences too — being alone, hectic rushing around on errands, driving the family taxi, etc.

CHAPTER 23

23.1. a. maximize $U(C_1) + U(C_2)/(1+d) + \lambda[W - C_1 - C_2/(1+r)]$ first order conditions: **(i)** $U'(C_1) = \lambda$; **(ii)** $U'(C_2)/(1+d) = \lambda/(1+r)$ => $MRS_{12} = (1+d)U'(C_1)/U'(C_2) = 1+ r$. **b.** Since $C_1 = C_2$, $U'(C_1) = U'(C_2)$ and $MRS_{12} = 1+d$. The slope of the indifference curves is $1+d$ where they cross the 45 degree line since $C_1 = C_2$ on that line. **c.** The slope is $1+ r$. For the line drawn, $r = d$ since it is tangent to an indifference curve on the 45 degree line. **d.** (1) increases; (2) No. The income effect might not be large enough to offset the substitution effect if the increase in r is small; (3) increase; (4) Yes. The income and substitution effects are both positive; (5) decrease; (6) No, since C_1 could decline for small increases in r; (7) period two; (8) Yes, since $r > d$ now; (9) Only the last answer would change. There would be no guarantee that C_2/C_1 would increase; (10) increase; (11) no. **e.** (1) W falls; (2) increases*; (3) increases; (4) declines*; (5) increases#; (6) increases. **f.** (1) W falls; (2) declines; (3) increases*; (4) increases; (5) increases#; (6) falls. **g.** The result that C_2/C_1 increases does not depend on whether the consumer is a saver in the first period, but is obtainable only for additively separable utility functions. **h.** No. If the stream is constant, $I_1 = I_2$. If $d = r$, then $C_1 = C_2 = I_1 = I_2$. The higher rate rotates the budget line clockwise around (C_1, C_2), increasing utility. If $d > r$, the recipient is a dissaver. His impatience leads him to borrow against future income. Dissavers will be worse off, as in **f**, unless the interest rate increase is large enough to cause them to become savers. Savers will be better off.

Harcourt Brace & Company

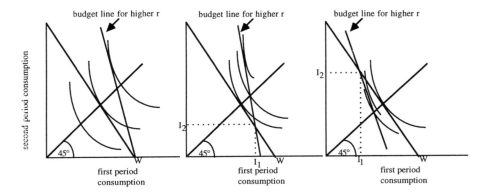

23.2. a. $C_1 + C_2/(1+r) = (1-t)I_1 + (1-t)I_2/(1+r) = W^*$; The pre- and post-tax constraints have the same slope, $-(1+r)$. See diagram.
b. Note that the constraint can be written as $C_2 = (1-t)I_2 + (1+r)(1-t)^2S$. If S is taxed, $(1-t)S$ will be left. If this amount is taxed a second time, only $(1-t)^2S$ will be left. It is this amount, plus interest on it, which appears in the budget constraint. The rewritten constraint is: $C_1 + C_2/[(1-t)(1+r)] = (1-t)I_1 + I_2/(1+r)$. P_2 is higher than before since $(1-t)(1+r) < 1+r$ for $t > 0$. **c.** See diagram. (1) increases; (2) increases; (3) falls. **d.** $C_1 + C_2/[1+r+r(1-t)] = [(1+2r)(1-t)I_1 + (1-t)I_2]/[1+r+r(1-t)]$; (1) higher; (2) increases; (3) increases; (4) decreases (he borrows more). **e.** (1) Eliminating interest deductibility should increase savings; (2) Demand for second mortgages should increase dramatically, as has already started to happen. Deductibility of second mortgages may substantially reduce the expected increase in saving.

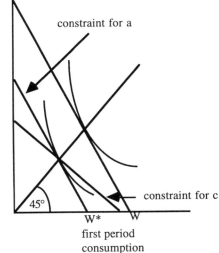

23.3. a. first order conditions: **(i)** $U'(C_1) = \lambda$; **(ii)** $U'(C_2)/(1+d) = \lambda/(1+r)$; **(iii)** $U'(C_3)/(1+d)^2 = \lambda/(1+r)^2$; (1) $d = r$; (2) $d > r$; (3) In order to achieve the same consumption each period he must save at least in period two, when his income is highest.

He may save or dissave in period one, depending on whether his income exceeds his constant consumption level. In the third period he must dissave since he has no income. This pattern seems reasonable as a description of savings for individuals over their lifetimes. **b.** SS = $(1+r)^2 tI_1 + (1+r)tI_2$; $C_1 + C_2/(1+r) + C_3/(1+r)^2 = (1-t)I_1 + (1-t)I_2/(1+r) + SS/(1+r)^2$; (1) No change since his budget constraint reduces to $C_1 + C_2/(1+r) + C_3/(1+r)^2 = I_1 + I_2/(1+r)$; (2) He will save less because he thinks the government is saving for him. **c.** It depresses savings. This hurts investment since the taxes are not used for that purpose.

23.4. a. (1) $1+r_6$; (2) $(1+r_6)2$; $r_6 = .0488$. **b.** $2.00 + .50 = P_m/1.0488$. **c.** $P_m = 2.62$. **d.** $P_m + .50 = P_s/1.0488$. **e.** $P_s = \$3.27$. **f.** $P_{xs} = \$3.96$; $P_{ss} = \$4.67$.

23.5. a. PDV = $e^{-rt}PW(t) - 1$. **b.** $\partial(PDV)/\partial t = -re^{-rt*}PW(t*) + e^{-rt*}PW'(t*) = 0 \Rightarrow W'(t*)/W(t*) = r$; Since $W'(t) = (4 - 4t)W(t)$, $W'(t*)/W(t*) = 4 - 4t*$. Hence, $t* = 1 - r/4 = 1 - .10/4 = .975$ years or about 356 days. **c.** PDV = $0 \Rightarrow P = e^{rt*}/W(t*) = e^{.0975}/e^{1.99875} \approx \$.15$ per pound. Each fish will weigh $e^{1.99875} \approx 7.38$ pounds, so the selling price per fish will be $e^{.0975} \approx \$1.10$. **d.** $e^{-ru}V(u) = 1 \Rightarrow V(u) = e^{ru}$; The rate of growth of V(u) is $V'(u)/V(u) = r$; $V(t*) = e^{.10(.975)} = \$1.10$ — the same as the wholesale price per fish. The growth rate of a fish at time u is $W'(u)/W(u) = 4 - 4u$. The fish's growth rate and the growth rate of its value in a sale to another rancher are both equal to r when $u = t*$ since $W'(t*)/W(t*) = 4 - 4t* = r = V'(u)/V(u)$. For $u < t*$, $W'(u)/W(u) = 4 - 4u > r = V'(u)/V(u)$, so the fish is growing faster than its value if sold to another rancher. (1) Since V(u) equals the wholesale value of the fish at $t*$ and the latter is growing at a faster rate, then it must be that V(u) exceeds the wholesale value of the fish at $t < t*$; (2) No rancher interested in making a profit would sell a fish of age less than $t*$ to another rancher when he can sell it to a wholesaler for more.

23.6. a. PDV(bus) = $1500 + 1500/1.1 = \$2864$. **b.** PDV(car) = $1000 + 500 + 500/1.1 - 8000/(1.1)^2 = \$4343$. **c.** no. **d.** $\$1479$. **e.** PDV(bus) would fall substantially since only the first day's fare will not be discounted. PDV(car) will also fall since fuel, repairs, parking fees and, perhaps, insurance would not all be paid on the first of the year. However, PDV(car) would not fall as much because the car would still be bought and sold on the first day of the year. Hence, the difference would be greater. **f.** The difference would be smaller, primarily because the resale value of the car would be discounted by much less. This can also be seen from the fact that the difference is zero for an interest rate of zero — the one that Longka implicitly used.

24.1. a. Social marginal cost is $.25 per unit of output in both industries. **b.** Price will be zero and quantity will be 100 in both industries. **c.** The efficient price is $.25 in both industries. At this price, quantity in A would be 66.67 and quantity in B would be 75. **d.** The total cost of pollution under competition is .25(100) + .25(100) = $50. At the efficient allocation the total cost is .25(66.67) + .25(75) = $35.42. This is 29.16% less than $50. **e.** Output in both industries will be 100 - 29.16 = 70.84. Price in industry A will be .75 - .0075(70.84) ≈ $.22. Price in industry B will be about $.29. This solution is not efficient since the price in industry A is less than social marginal cost and the price in industry B is greater than social marginal cost. **f.** An output tax of $.25 per unit in both industries would lead to the efficient allocation. The private marginal cost of production, including the tax, would just equal the social marginal cost. Since marginal cost is constant, there will be profits in each industry if the price exceeds $.25 and losses if it is less. Competition guarantees that profits will be zero in equilibrium. Therefore, the price will be $.25 and the quantities, determined by the demand curves, will be the efficient ones.

24.2. a. If the price of electricity equals the private MC of production (does it?), this is inefficient. The social MC exceeds private MC by $100 per mw. Too much electricity is produced. The marginal benefit of a megawatt is less than social MC. Northeasterners pay the price while midwesterners benefit. Viability depends on the relative political power of both regions. **b**. This may not be technically feasible and is almost certainly inefficient since the marginal cost of eradicating the last unit of pollution is likely to be much greater than the marginal social cost of that unit. The policy benefits northeasterners at the expense of midwesterners and is probably not politically feasible since it would not get support from both groups. **c**. This would be efficient since private MC will now coincide with social MC. Since the policy benefits northeasterners at the expense of midwesterners, it is probably not politically feasible. If the rebate (plus, perhaps, a little extra) went to midwesterners, both regions might benefit. Midwesterners could still buy the same amount of electricity if they wanted to, but would choose to buy less because of its relatively higher price. The northeast would benefit from reduced emissions. **d**. This would not be efficient unless the marginal cost of cleaning up just equaled the marginal benefit. In fact, this equality may already hold. If marginal cost of cleanup is increasing and/or marginal benefit of cleanup is declining, further cleanup would be inefficient. This is not feasible since northeasterners would benefit at the expense of midwesterners. **e**. This would be efficient since the northeasterners would be willing to sell their right to clean air for $100 per mw. worth of pollution. Social and private MC for producers would then coincide. This is not politically feasible since it benefits northeasterners at the expense of midwesterners. Another serious problem is the difficulty of organizing the northeasterners for the purpose of deciding how much clean air to sell and how to distribute the income. **f**. One might argue that they already have this right. However, they don't have it in the sense that they can sell it to someone else. If they did, they could sell a megawatt's worth of "clean air" to northeasterners for up to $100. The opportunity cost of selling clean air would be part of private marginal cost, so they would produce at the point where price equals social MC. This might be politically feasible since both regions would benefit. Midwesterners would produce less electricity but would receive enough compensation from selling clean air to make

Harcourt Brace & Company

them better off (otherwise they wouldn't do it) and northeasterners will be better off since they are choosing to buy clean air. However, again we encounter the problem of organizing northeasterners, this time for the purpose of buying clean air.

24.3. a. (1) 1000 - N; (2) 1000 - N - 500 = 500 - N; (3) 500 (where profit is zero). **b.** (1) 500; (2) reduced by one; (3) reduced by $1.00; (4) 500 + 500 = 1000; (5) $499; (6) SMC > 499 = benefit to consumers who buy lobsters from the marginal lobsterman. The area is "overlobstered" because each lobsterman does not take into account the full effect that his traps have on total lobsters produced. **c.** π = PL - 500N = $1.00(1000N - N^2) - 500N = 500N - N^2; first order condition for profit maximization: 500 - 2N = 0; (1) 250; (2) 500 + 250 = 750; (3) 1000 - 250 = 750; (4) Now, the social marginal cost equals the social marginal benefit; (5) No. The state would hire lobstermen until MR = SMC. Then P > SMC, or social marginal benefit exceeds social marginal cost. **d.** Charge $250. The private MC = 500 + 250 = SMC when N = 250. Profits will be zero.

24.4. a. No, since the cost of the arrestor exceeds its benefit. **b.** He would be willing to sell the right to the railroad for any price exceeding $50 and the railroad would be willing to buy the right for any price less than $100—provided that this purchase is compatible with no long run losses. The outcome is efficient because the arrestor does not get installed. **c.** The farmer would be willing to pay up to $50 to the railroad to get them to install the arrestor, but the railroad won't do it for less than $100. The arrestor doesn't get installed, so the outcome is efficient. **d.** The answer to **b** changes. Now, the railroad will install the arrestor for $100 rather than pay the farmer $50 and the lawyer $60, a total of $110. This is inefficient and illustrates why transaction costs prevent efficient outcomes when property rights have been clearly assigned.

24.5. (1) All of those listed are likely to benefit, including couples with fertility problems. Contracts for surrogate babies would be legal and might specify that surrogate mothers may renege after the baby is born. Even that would not prevent an efficient outcome. The price of surrogate babies would be lower than if reneging was not allowed since surrogate mothers might be willing to provide their services for a lower price if they have that option and infertile couples will want to pay less because of the option. Since both parties are willing to enter the contract, both presumably are better off. There are possible externalities. Many people find surrogacy morally offensive. They would be worse off. (2) This is equivalent to not allowing surrogate mothers to renege. They would still get paid for services rendered. No one would be forced to be a surrogate mother. (3) The current law is inefficient because it says that no one "owns" a surrogate baby. In fact, no one owns non-surrogate babies, either. Some economists have argued that present adoption laws, which prevent the buying and selling of infants, are extremely inefficient.

24.6. a. The inverted demand curves are $P = 1.5 - .1S_K$ and $P = 2.0 - .1S_S$. See diagram. **b.** (1) 5; (2) 10; (3) 15; (4) $1.5 - .1(15) = 0$; (5) $2.0 - .1(15) = .5$; (6) The sum of the amounts they are willing to give up (in terms of dollars worth of other goods) is less than the price of salt. That is, the sum of their marginal rates of substitution of salt for other goods exceeds their marginal cost; (7) Too large. Both families would prefer less salt. In fact, if it was costless to return their salt, each would want to return at least some of it once they knew what the other family had done. **c.** (1) Zero, since they expect the Sewdiems to put out 10 and are only willing to pay $.50 per pound when $S = 10$. (2) Five, since they expect the Klorides to put out 5 and would like a total of 10. **d.** This is true if people free ride, as in **c**, but not true if they assume others will provide none. Then too much is consumed. **e.** Think of the inverse demand curves, given in the answer to **a**, as giving the amount each family is willing to pay per unit. Remove the subscripts on S and add the inverse demand curves together to get total willingness to pay (per unit): P = 3.5 - .2S. This is vertical addition of the demand curves. This function is drawn in the diagram. The dashed part of the line represents points where the amount that the Klorides are willing to pay per unit is negative. This would be part of the demand curve if the Sewdiems were required to bribe the Klorides to accept more salt. If they don't, then the public demand curve follows the Sewdiems' demand curve for prices below the price at the intersection. (1) S = 17.5 - 5P (invert the total willingness to pay function); (2) 12.5; (3) 1.5 - .1(12.5) = .25; (4) 2.0 - .1(12.5) = .75.

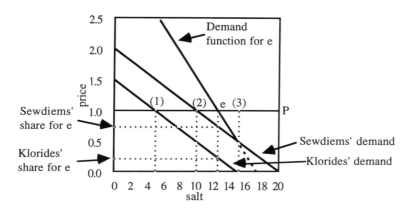

24.7. a. 400(100) + 200(100) = $60,000. **b.** (1) (5/6)400 = 333.33; (2) 166.66; (3) Yes, unanimously. **c.** No, it will be 50/50, with group B members voting against. **d.** (1) A bribe of $33.33 will make them indifferent between the bridge and no bridge; (2) A bribe of $53.33 will make them indifferent between the bridge and the ferry; (3) A bribe somewhere between these two values and a vote to rescind; (4) ferry; (5) the nearest bridge; (6) Yes. Both groups are better off. Group B willingly accepted the bribe which group A willingly offered. **e.** The example illustrates that vote buying can improve economic efficiency. Of course, this assumes that everyone fully understands the issues and the consequence of the voting. **f.** Yes. Group A would only willingly pay $28,000 for the bridge. The marginal cost of providing a bridge for Group B is then $22,000, which is greater than that group's willingness to pay of $20,000. Only 100 passes will be bought.

24.8. a. Defense is nearly 100% nonrival and nonexclusive. We are defended as much as our neighbors, whether we like it or not! **b.** Drivers can be excluded from using highways by the use of toll booths, although at some cost. Highways are nonrival as long as there is no congestion, but become rival as congestion increases. **c.** Drinking water is neither nonrival nor nonexclusive. You can't drink the water I drink and my consumption can be measured at the tap, as it is in most cities. **d.** Parks can be exclusive, although preventing unauthorized entry may be difficult. Like roads, they are nonrival up to the point where congestion becomes a problem. **e.** Exclusion from education is clearly possible. There are two senses in which it is nonrival. First, one student's presence at a lecture has little if any effect on what another student learns. Second, improvements in literacy benefit everyone in society, not just those who achieve them. **f.** Satellite launches are both exclusive and rival, although the functions of the satellites themselves may be nonrival (defense, communications, etc.). One sense in which a launch itself is nonrival is that many people enjoy the excitement of the launch.

CHAPTER 25

25.1. a. (1) Once's preference map is unchanged by rescaling his utility to be the square root of his former utility; (2) $(C_T M_T)^{.5} = (M_T M_T)^{.5} = M_T$; (3) $U_O{}^2 + U_T = 100$; (4) 6.6; (5) 43.3; (6) E is not on the contract curve. There are trades that Once and Twice could make which would make them both better off. **b.** (1) 7.1; (2) 50. **c.** He would choose the point on the UPF where $U_O = U_T$; (1) 9.5; (2) 9.5; (3) $9.5^2 \approx$ 90.5; (4) 9.5; (5) Twice is worse off than at E; (6) and (7) He will maximize Once's utility subject to the constraint that $U_T \geq 43.3$. This is point 'c' in the left-hand diagram. At this point $U_T = M_T = 43.3$ and $U_O = (100 - U_T)^{.5} = 7.53$. **d.** (1) U_T/U_O; (2) $-\partial U_T/\partial U_O$ (along UPF) $= 2U_O$; (3) $MRS_{OT} = RUT_{OT} \Rightarrow U_T = 2U_O{}^2$; substitute for U_T in the UPF to get $3U_O{}^2 = 100 \Rightarrow U_O = 33.33^{.5}$; (4) 66.67; (5) 33.33; (6) 66.67; (7) Once has higher utility at E. (8) and (9) See point 'd' in

Harcourt Brace & Company

the left-hand diagram. The God maximizes his utility function subject to the constraint that Once's utility is at least 6.6. U_O = 6.6 and U_T = 56.7. **e.** Each of the welfare functions considered treats the utility of both Once and Twice equally, but reaches different conclusions as to the allocation of consumption — none of them are the "equal consumption" solution, and only in an extreme case is the equal utility solution realized. Some might argue that the Rawlsian solution is equitable, but others might argue that it is inequitable to penalize Twice so much for Once's difficulties in converting M and C into utility. In fact, for some welfare functions that treat the utility of Once and Twice equally, Once's difficulties are so severe that Twice is actually rewarded for his good fortune! **f.** (1) If "love equally" means each child's utility appears in the parents' "child welfare" function symmetrically, parents may actually give less to the disadvantaged child, just as the God does in the Cobb-Douglas case. Only in the extreme case of a Rawlsian child welfare function will they fully offset differences. Even then, utility will only be equalized if the parents are technically capable of doing so; (2) They will probably not invest the same amount in each child's education, but which child gets more depends on their particular child welfare function. If their beliefs about the value of education are correct, the girl is likely to end up with less value than the boy — unless the parents are Rawlsians. **g.** (1) At EQ

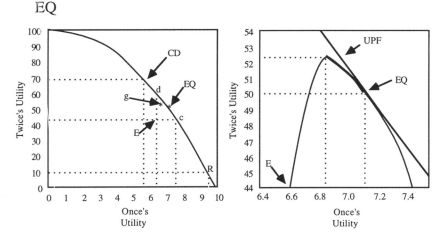

MRS_{OT} < RUT_{OT}. The UPF and OOC are tangent at EQ, so MRS_{OT} < -(slope of OOC). Hence, higher welfare can be attained along OOC to the left of EQ; (2) Twice would

Harcourt Brace & Company

choose the highest point on OOC, where the slope is zero. Since $MRS_{OC} > 0$, the God can attain higher welfare to the right of this point. Hence, the God's choice will be along the bold portion of OOC in the right-hand diagram; (3) Yes. In this example the God's power is limited. Using his concept of equity, he finds that the best he can do is to choose an inefficient allocation. Governments that try to redistribute income and consumption through altering prices (e.g., taxes on luxury goods, subsidies on necessities, progressive income taxes) cause distortions which lead to economically inefficient outcomes. These outcomes may be socially preferred, despite their inefficiency. **h.** In each case the allocations and utilities of Once and Twice would be switched. Hence, arbitrary changes in scale lead to different welfare maximum allocations. Such arbitrary changes can't be ruled out unless we are willing to use a common scale for Once and Twice—cardinal utility!

25.2. a. Tom's MRS = Elinor's MRS => $B_T/C_T = B_E/C_E$ => $k_T = k_E$. **b.** $U_T = (B_T C_T)^{.5} = (kC_T C_T)^{.5} = k^{.5}C_T$; $U_E = k^{.5}C_E$; $U_T + U_E = k^{.5}C_T + k^{.5}C_E = k^{.5}(C_E + C_T) = (B/C)^{.5}C = (BC)^{.5}$. **c.** The UPF is a line with a slope of minus one and intercepts of $(BC)^{.5}$. An increase in $(BC)^{.5}$ shifts the PPF out. **d.** The problem is to maximize $(BC)^{.5}$ subject to the constraint $.5B + C = 10$. The solution is $B = .5(10)/.5 = 10$ and $C = .5(10)/1 = 5$. **e.** Not necessarily. Tom and Elinor agree because their UPF shifts in the same direction at all points as they move along their budget constraint. They both agree that they want the UPF which is as "far out" as possible. But for other utility functions the UPF might shift out at some points and in at others. Whether Elinor prefers one UPF to another will depend on the points that she and Tom agree to. The same holds for Tom, and a UPF that looks good to him may not look good to her.

25.3. a two-thirds **b.** two-thirds **c.** The points in the range [1/3, 2/3], measuring from Tom's end. Points to the left of 1/3 and to the right of 2/3 have lower utility for both. Tom's utility increases and Elinor's utility declines to the right of 1/3, up to 2/3. **d.** The answer is unchanged. The only difference is that Tom's utility declines and Elinor's increases as we move from 1/3 to 2/3. For all points on the contract curve, each would like the other to take more!

25.4. a (1) yes; (2) transitivity; (3) yes. **b.** (1) not imposed; (2) yes. **c.** (1) completeness; (2) No, the others could be ranked. **d.** (1) 1; (2) 1; (3) individualistic; (4) yes. **e.** (1) tied; (2) Nebraska. The first group would give Nebraska two more points than Alabama, since Virtuous is in between. The second would give Alabama only one more point than Nebraska; (3) independence of irrelevant alternatives; (4) yes. **f.** (1) nondictatorial; (2) no; (3) yes.

25.5. a. Each alternative will get one third of the votes. **b.** First referendum: no school wins. Second referendum: deluxe school wins. **c.** Economy vs. deluxe; economy wins. **d.** (1) There will be another referendum: no school vs. economy. Economy will win. Then the cycle will be repeated, indefinitely; (2) independence of irrelevant alternatives. **e.** PTA. The peaks are no school and deluxe school, with a "valley" between — economy school. **f.** (1) economy school; (2) no. **g.** (1) Moderates. The peak in their preferences is between the highest peaks of the other two groups; (2) yes.

25.6. a. The most important factor is the degree of spillover effects. Returns to scale may also be important. The combination of these two factors may be important enough to make international alliances attractive (e.g., NATO), although the ability to reveal the willingness to pay off beneficiaries makes such alliances more difficult to achieve. This is consistent with the U.S. experience. **b.** Local roads have few spillover effects for nonlocal people, so local provision seems optimal. Thruways benefit people from large areas, so provision by higher levels of government is more appropriate. **c.** For elementary schools positive returns to scale exist only at very low enrollment levels. Most are provided by local governments. Returns to scale are more important for secondary education. Many small local governments join with neighboring governments to establish "union" schools, primarily for this reason. Returns are even more significant at the postsecondary level, and it is not surprising that most public colleges and universities are run by state governments. Spillover effects of education affect large areas and some would argue that higher levels of government should be more involved in the provision of education at lower levels than they are. However, a large share of the benefits accrue to students and their immediate families and friends. It is easier to reveal the willingness of family and friends to pay for these benefits at the local level. **d.** Spillover effects are essential in determining the level at which law enforcement is provided. Spillover effects for many enforcement activities (e.g., enforcing speed limits on local roads) affect only local people, and these activities are provided by local governments. However, other activities, such as enforcement of interstate commerce laws, have larger spillover effects and are provided by higher levels of government. Increasing returns to scale are also important for some activities. For example, the FBI provides crime laboratory services to local governments because it would be impractical for those governments to have their own labs.

Harcourt Brace & Company